PARIS 1900
ARCHTECTURE AND DESIGN

First published in 1978 by
Rizzoli International Publications, Inc.

Revised, enlarged edition published in
the United States of America in 1989 by
Rizzoli International Publications, Inc.
300 Park Avenue South
New York, NY 10010

ISBN 0-8478-0801-7
LC 77-77672

Printed and bound in Spain.

FRANCO BORSI   EZIO GODOLI

PARIS 1900

Architecture and Design

RIZZOLI
NEW YORK

4. L. Majorelle. Restaurant Lucas-Carton. 9 Place de la Madeleine, Paris 8ᵉ.
Detail of a screen.

CONTENTS

PREFACE

In an historical study it is the custom to start by sketching a picture of the manners and cultural, social and political background which temper in various ways every factor in the history of architecture, which itself is generally held to embody the very form and structure of history. In considering the Paris of 1900, however, this convention encounters difficulties which may in themselves constitute an introduction directly relevant to the theme of this book.

These difficulties are not entirely due to the extent and complexity of the panorama of an artistic and literary culture which dominated Europe, nor even to the contradictions of policies which were at once unscrupulous and intensely emotive, full of reverberating incidents and idealistic ferment and upheaval, characterizing the Third Republic, and culminating in the explosive climate of the Panama scandal and the Dreyfus affair, nor indeed to the international context marked at that time by the golden age of colonialism and the threat of German might. Nor do they arise from the brilliant society painted by Boldini, of which the Parisian boulevard was the most conspicuous ornament and provided an inexhaustible source of inspiration for fashionable gossip, memoirs, "romans roses", epigrams and that psychological twilight pervading the yearnings of Proust, any more than from the impenetrable atmosphere, "Boeotian", aestheticizing, steeped in convention, fascinating and at the same time slightly repellent, usually summarized as the "Belle Epoque". In fact the most comprehensive bibliography will never drain the secrets of the Parisian society which bestraddled the end of the nineteenth and the beginning of the twentieth centuries.

Behind this well-worn and well-established image, France was nonetheless at this time a great and coherent nation. Her bureaucracy, untouched despite political scandals, displayed a sense of status which in France has always been a historic prerogative and privilege and which at this period still constituted one of the foundations of French society. The latter rested upon an institutionalized culture which in its breadth embraced every aspect of knowledge and technology, from which architecture broadly profited. It is only after noting the enormous void left in architectural scholarship by the antics of the avant-gardists, by dilettantism and the myth of science surrendered to the most vulgar commercial interests, and after having propounded as a fundamental fact, as do the very young, the need for a recasting of architectural education, that one can really appreciate the grandeur, the inspiration, the integrity and the courage of the defenders of French "fin de siècle" architectural standards, too often dismissed with facile contempt as academic.

In spite of the high level of this debate, it cannot be claimed in the final analysis that architecture at this time held a central place in French culture, as it had done in the period of Louis XIV; but it played a role as a public utility and, as such, it shared in the effectiveness and dignity of public administration, and in some cases could be regarded as a kind of State ceremonial. There remained therefore little room for the avant-garde, except for the pinnacles and most resounding successes in steel and glass architecture. After that we must wait for Art Nouveau to reveal a burst of creativity, even though it was hobbled by official culture and conditioned by its ephemeral nature.

Neither France nor Paris was at home in Art Nouveau. They welcomed it with a distrust prompted by nationalism, for it came from a part of Europe to which France felt far from well disposed, either politically or culturally. England was foreign, Belgium provincial, Germany dangerous and Italy non-existent; although Austria inspired more sympathy, Russia alone enjoyed France´s favour, especially since the gesture of Czar Alexander III in baring his head to hear the Marseillaise at Kronstadt. The newspapers and reviews of the period, including those which defended Art Nouveau, always called for the pursuit of a national road as an alternative solution to the suspicion of internationalism which they saw as tainting the "Modern Style" – a suspicion similar to that engendered by socialists and anarchists in the field of politics. All attempts to marry novelty and tradition were encouraged, even when they resulted in travesty.

Therefore, not only did Art Nouveau fail to reflect the pluralism of French culture and society, not only did this movement, stemming from historicist roots, conflict with the institutional nature of French styles considered as elements of a language adapted to respond to every demand, whatever the circumstances might be: it was also, with no respect paid to its outrageousness, courteously requested to step back into line, in the manner normally reserved for visionaries and lunatics. On the other hand, the acceptance and success of Art Nouveau served as a springboard for charlatans and opportunists, all those whom Frantz Jourdain compared to thieves and pickpockets mingling with the crowd at political manifestations and popular demonstrations. By speculating in the vague optimism, ignorant character and superficial comfort of architectural constructions intended for middle-class circles of the time composed largely of upstarts, these people destroyed the tenuous aspirations towards authenticity born of the ingenuous nature and contradictory aims of Art Nouveau.

Under these conditions it is scarcely astonishing that the cultural outlook

of architects and decorative artists involved in the movement seems to some extent lacking in perception and refinement in comparison with the work of painters and writers of the same period. A kind of cultural barbarism steeped in a certain distinctive artistic spirit leads one in general to link Hector Guimard with the hedonism of Jules Lavirotte, with the historicism of Charles Plumet and even the subtle experimentation of representatives of the School of Nancy, such as Emile Gallé and Louis Majorelle, who become questionable when ambition goads them into evolving a theory of art. This faculty, which may be called in the better instances creative inspiration and in a more general sense professional realism, represented a period of decline compared with the cultural catholicity of such masters as Viollet-le-Duc (with the exception perhaps of that brilliant and contradictory character, anarchist writer and architect, who nevertheless aspired to the Legion of Honour, Frantz Jourdain). Yet this entire period offered opportunities also in the field of the decorative arts, revived by commercial demands, in which the processes of mechanical reproduction brought about a lowering in standards of quality which affected the creations of

Art Nouveau, when the latter became a force to be reckoned with. But from the tangled skein of architecture and crafts there emerged a new vision, a power of attraction which also influenced the major arts.

Maurice Denis had declared: "Art must become decorative again, in other words it must rediscover its function in our every-day life", and some sought to become expert in following out this idea to the letter, i.e. by abandoning the figurative arts to the benefit of decoration as Georges De Feure, Eugène Gaillard, Alexandre Charpentier and François-Rupert Carabin were to do, thus echoing Henry Van de Velde. And the trend was to become widely embracing, if we include graphic art, glass and jewelry. Clearly the conditions for this fluidity and exchange of experience lay in the side-tracking of institutional taste, to which poetry had delivered a fatal blow, and in the new notion of "durée" put forward by Bergsonian intuition; it was not a mere coincidence that "Matter and Memory" was published in 1896.

Today there is a general belief that the architecture of Paris in 1900 was a vital phenomenon, genuinely creative and hence worthy to take its place among the more significant phases in the history of European architecture, despite the prosaic environment in which it appeared and the limited critical success which, after a long period of silence and stagnation, has risen to paeans of praise. In order to destroy the old fallacy which temporarily paralysed the creative impulse in Art Nouveau and put it back into the ranks of a national art, we must recognize it as a community of historic values, thanks to which Paris, the Paris of 1900, is a homeland for all of us.

PREFACE TO THE 2nd EDITION

The Art Nouveau architecture of Paris has yet to be carefully analysed in its complexity. Ten years after this book was first published, the literature on the subject has not grown significantly.

We still need extensive scientific studies on such protagonists as Guimard, Lavirotte and Plumet, as well as a careful survey of buildings featuring elements of Art Nouveau. The latter need has been fulfilled only partially by the development of a literature which chose to study such specific types of architecture as the department store and working class housing. In this second edition, we chose to renew a large portion of the illustrations, as well as revise and complete the text, especially in the chapters I, IX and X.

Although these changes are limited, they reflect an evolution in the study of the Art Nouveau architecture in Paris: While it is less focused on the works of the major architects, it pays more attention to the sometimes equally influencial contributions of lesser talents, bringing to light a few significant examples in the use of this architectural idiom and hoping to suggest fruitful indications for future research.

5-6. A. de Baudot. Church of St Jean de Montmartre, Place des Abbesses, Paris 18ᵉ.
(1897-1905). General view and detail of the ceramics.

I

THREE RATIONALISMS

Art Nouveau, it is often asserted, is a reaction against eclecticism, a logical opposition with a rationalist foundation, born of a desire to replace the mixture of styles and riot of tastes by constructive argument, and deriving from nature; this interpretation, however, is in flagrant contradiction to the cultural climate of France at the end of the nineteenth century. In fact, far from exalting the imagination and "art for art's saké" or surrendering to the joys of historicist exercises, cultivated France was dominated by the quarrels of rationalists.

In this positivist atmosphere, facing an opposition swaying between the cynicism of the opportunists and an extreme radicalism, the various streams of architectural opinion converged in conflict on the field of reason. Already, in the five volumes of his work "Eléments et théories de l'architecture", Julien Guadet, the very personification of the Academy, adopted a functional, scientific and rational attitude.

A former pupil of Henri Labrouste and collaborator with Jules- Louis André and Charles Garnier, he placed his emphasis on liberty, as the great masters had taught it, while proposing to make "concessions to the living".

He preached a scientific attitude with regard to history, analysed minutely the elements of architecture, defined the role of composition and had elaborated a "corpus", as valid for academicians as for modernists. It is impossible to examine in depth the logic of this instructional and practical "corpus" of architecture, just as it is difficult to evaluate the impact made on the training of his contemporaries by the five volumes of Guadet's treatise, given the nature, the assurance and the exhaustive character of the publication.

The important thing here is to underline that Guadet represents the rational side of classicism opposed by the rationalism of the neo-Gothics. And it is to this classic image of eclecticism that the experience of another pioneer of the modern movement, Auguste Perret, can be directly linked.

From a biographical point of view, a kind of portent can be seen in the fact that Perret's father, exiled in Belgium after the events of the Commune, worked as contractor for the construction of the greenhouses at Laeken, of which the importance in the relations between Alphonse Balat and Victor Horta has been pointed out elsewhere. However, Auguste Perret was then only two years old. After the political amnesty, when their father returned to France, the Perret brothers attended the Ecole des Beaux-Arts and notably Guadet's studio, where they made friends with Paul, Julien Guadet's son, and became regular visitors to the master's home. The incompatibility, however, between the title of architect and their role as contractors in the family business prevented them from obtaining diplomas. As Peter Collins much later observed: "Auguste Perret's later skill in planning and composition, his critical awareness of the subtleties of classical scale and proportion, his method of analysing the elements of architecture, indeed his

whole cultural background, were quite manifestly formed or reformed under Guadet's influence, as he himself acknowledged, and they certainly owed little to Viollet-le-Duc or the parental milieu."[1]

Among the key buildings realized by Perret in his early days should certainly be included the garage in the Rue Ponthieu, erected in 1907, the year in which, after his father's death, he took charge of the firm of Perret Frères. In spite of the revolutionary character of the reinforced concrete building and its pre-rationalist appearance, a whole series of elements recall, in their lack of prejudice, the lessons of Guadet. The discerning variation of distance between axes, the dominant theme of the central glazed bay with its faint evocation of Gothic, the rhythmic relationship of the upper storey and the entasis of the pillars made the building as a whole "far more classical than the Grand Palais which reared its contemporary Ionic columns on the opposite side of the Champs-Elysées."[2]

It is also useful to recall certain other episodes which confirm the bond between Perret and Guadet. When the Perrets built at 119 Avenue Wagram the house which provides the main evidence of their attachment to the distinguished Art Nouveau house as a type, and which, with its floral decoration in stone, comes close to Xavier Schoellkopf without revealing any sign of a break with contemporary taste, the review "L'Architecte", which included on its editorial committee Julien Guadet, published an article attributed to one of the Perret brothers, in which the work was hailed as a very interesting venture in pointing the way to a satisfying manner of building, or rather, of formulating architecture. Later, in 1912, the Perret brothers

8. A. Perret. Garage, Rue Ponthieu, Paris 18e. (1907). Demolished. Façade.

9. P. Guadet. Town house, 95 Boulevard Murat, Paris 16e. (1912). Façade.

built at 95 Boulevard Murat a house which Paul Guadet had designed for himself, with an obvious enthusiasm for reinforced concrete, refining the dimensions of components and even introducing a few applications of reinforced concrete to the furnishing.

Earlier, Paul Guadet had built a house for Dr Carnot at 8 Avenue Elisée-Reclus. There he used a mixture of techniques: buhrstone for the piers on the façade, reinforced concrete for the interior pillars, floors and the terrace. Reviews in architectural publications commented it in particular for the varied use of glazed earthenware in the façade and the paving. [3]

The most significant work by Auguste and Gustave Perret remains the well-known apartment block (1903-04) at 25 Rue Franklin in Paris. Built as an investment, it offered the most favourable conditions for allowing the Perret brothers to express themselves freely. By the brilliancy with which the

elements of the façade are interlinked, the clever exploitation of every condition imposed by the planning regulations and the undisguised expression of the structural frame, this work is considered by historians of the modern movement to be a model of its kind. However, whether to make it more acceptable to public taste or for the technical reason of diminishing the possible speed of deterioration due to weather, the façade was entirely faced with ceramics. The elements of the cladding emphasized, by the ingenious positioning of the angles close to-

gether, the linearity of the vertical and horizontal loadbearing structures. The infill panels were composed of plaques in relief, of a different colour, adorned with stylized floral motifs, while other ceramic elements were used for the window recesses or for the smaller panels, where the vertical structures were nearer together, accentuating their slenderness.

The ceramics were designed by Alexandre Bigot, who worked also with Anatole de Baudot and Jules Lavirotte. His recourse to delicate pastel shades and cool tones originated in his experience as professor of chemistry which, for the Art Nouveau architecture of Paris, assumed an importance equal to that of certain researches into light and vision for Pointillist and Divisionist painting. If one can term pointillist and neo- Byzantine his contribution to the church of Saint-Jean de Montmartre, and neo-Renaissant his work on the Ceramic Hôtel of Lavirotte, which is expressed in almost opulent faience in which the historical grotesque contends with a taste for floral motifs, his share in the Rue Franklin house anticipates future commercial demands by showing a technique more concerned with simplicity of execution and economic needs, and therefore the promise of a richer future. The captivating floral decorations add nothing to the exposed structural design of 25 Rue Franklin, but contribute nonetheless to establishing its period, since it otherwise appears curiously "contemporary"; although it may call to mind the countless derivative and vulgar constructions in reinforced concrete it

10-12. A. Perret. Apartment block, 25 bis Rue Franklin, Paris 16e. (1903). Details of the façade.

has inspired for seventy years, it preserves a certain dignity thanks to its aesthetic character and historical standing.

The shattering encounter with Henry Van de Velde in connection with designs for the Champs-Elysées theatre was the fruit not only of the chauvinist attitude afflicting Art Nouveau in the bias of contemporary reviews and which was to be accentuated still further in subsequent historical writing. Nor was it the result of the mutual incomprehensibility of the training, aesthetic and intellectual, of

13. *Henry Van de Velde. Théâtre des Champs-Elysées. Project.*

the artist from Antwerp (it was not by chance that his candidature was put forth by the Symbolist painter, Maurice Denis) and that of the engineer, rationalist and positivist, who was the supreme specialist of his time in reinforced concrete.

Their difference was not merely the impact of two conflicting mentalities or of two characters little disposed to cooperation, but a clash of two methods, of two figurative worlds; on the one hand the classicism of Guadet, on the other the naturalism of Art Nouveau. Far beyond any technical, psychological or aesthetic argument,

this clash was the central factor in the dispute which finally ended Auguste Perret's occasional flirtation with Art Nouveau. His interest was limited to a few commissions only and was linked in any case to practical and commercial needs, also to a phase in his formative years, when the artist was trying to assert his personality. This phase was

to coincide with the end of Art Nouveau and to constitute indeed the dawn of a historic alternative.

Beside this classicist rationalism, moulded in eclecticism but with purist affinities, represented by the Guadet-Perret axis, the most significant influence was that of Eugène Viollet-le-Duc, who found his source in neo-Gothic art. He defended reason in an allegorical way: "We have a sentimental architecture, as we have had a sentimental public policy and a sentimental war.... It is time we gave thought to the application of sober reason, of practical common sense: to

consideration of the requirements of the times, of the improvements offered by manufacturing skills, of the use of economy, of questions of health and hygiene".[4]

This rationalism does not emerge in the mediaeval rigour of the diocesan works any more than in Art Nouveau. "Viollet-le-Duc", wrote Anatole de Baudot, "was the first to know how to bring out the artistic genius of the France of the Middle Ages and, above all, the lessons to be learnt, even in the practice of minor crafts, from its masterly conceptions, and methods of execution and composition". But he added: "This influence, which until now has remained more theoretical than visible, has not so far guided architecture in an openly modern direction, but the analytical knowledge of Gothic art is a sure pointer to the path to be followed".[5]

De Baudot kept his distance in his attitude to the two factions, although he was the disciple and direct heir of Viollet-le-Duc: "The classicals, accustomed, by their education, to submit to the conventional yoke of imitation, did not understand the rational training which their antagonists, whom they treated as 'diocésains'', had absorbed. Nevertheless, in spite of this fraternal hostility, good sense prevailed again in many instances, and the standard of execution in all departments of building recovered remarkably after the first period of the nineteenth century, in which it had fallen so low".[6]

14. A. de Baudot. Church of St Jean de Montmartre, Place des Abbesses, Paris 18ᵉ. (1897-1905). Inside view. (After a photograph of the time).

On the one hand, thanks to works like the church at Rambouillet, De Baudot applied the neo-Gothicism of Viollet-le-Duc, but on the other he tackled the problem of iron buildings, the merit of which he recognized (he mentions the Halles Centrales and the church of Saint-Augustin, and deplores the destruction of the Galerie des Machines), but also the limitations: "The use of iron offers irrefutable possibilities, but which are limited and seem especially applicable to open constructions".[7] He even proposed a solution of a more neo-Gothic character for the Galerie des Machines. But it was reinforced cement, or more particularly the Cottancin system, which was to offer a third way, enabling him to overcome the contradiction between the historical element in Viollet-le-Duc's manner and the "coarseness" of iron engineering. Patented in 1889, the Cottancin system represented a method of construction which differed from reinforced concrete in the utilization of materials acting in compression like stone and brick and in the intro-

duction of steel elements to ensure greater freedom with curved structures. In the vertical and horizontal components the reinforcement was composed of thin metal elements, continuous and without bracing, while the mix contained no gravel. This composite and, to a certain extent, hybrid system offered a number of possibilities and, by his contribution, De Baudot pushed it to the ultimate in expression. However, because of its cost and complexity of execution, the Cottancin system had to yield place to the one developed by François Hennebique and was to disappear after 1914.[8]

For De Baudot, reinforced cement presented the attraction of a homogeneous framework of great rigidity and extremely slender section while manifesting a level of expressiveness unattained until then. De Baudot protested against the custom of using cement in place of wood and imprisoning it in stone or brick elements and he insisted on the need to reduce if not to abandon the use of stone: "Without claiming that the use of reinforced cement applied to the general framework of any sort of building is the only proper course, I do not hesitate to assert, with entire conviction, that such a procedure will supply from now on all the ingredients for a transformation ensuring all the material order needed in modern buildings. There remains the question of appearance upon which I would not presume to pronounce, confident that the talent and ability of the contemporary architect, which are

15-16. *A. de Baudot. Church of St Jean de Montmartre. Details of the ceramics and view of the interior.*

not in dispute here, will easily solve this genuine difficulty, but the latter will not be overcome until the foreman on the job takes the trouble to study in depth the possibilities of the system, instead of relying on specialists who have no feelings about the advantages of a unified system of the type represented by this new method of building and see in it only particular applications, which do not interfere with their normal routine. If, it must be admitted, their pretensions were to go further, it would be they who would become the real architects in the task of concentrating the various elements, which is the basis of all design; do not let us allow them to take that road".[9]

De Baudot's lack of interest in everything which amounted to a thorough study of construction, the trouble caused by the unusual thinness of elements which upset his usual approach to design, had to be overcome for the sake of the unity and solidarity of all elements, the positioning of which in space had to be seen in its entirety. And in this search to express continuity, there were many meeting-points with Art Nouveau. For example, one may quote an unrealized project of 1914 for a large room lit from above, or certain parts of the

church of Saint-Jean de Montmartre. But De Baudot's attitude was precise: "I am not trying to generate an'art nouveau', but to develop a rational doctrine, the foundations of which have been established since the middle of the nineteenth century, but which has not been applied in a decisive manner'.[10]

Architects as well as their clients were slightly uneasy with this new architectural idiom. De Baudot tells a story which clearly illustrates the state of mind: "In connection with stone, let me mention a small but significant fact. When I finished, after many administrative difficulties, the church of Saint-Jean de Montmartre, I was summoned to the palace of the archbi-

shop of Paris and received by Monsignor Richard, who questioned me closely regarding the use of reinforced cement and seemed satisfied with my explanations - slyly commenting, however, that cement, even if reinforced, would never replace the stone of our cathedrals. I answered that I was absolutely of his opinion, but we were no longer in the Middle Ages, when religious faith had so lavishly supplied the material resources necessary to raise such monuments. I added that nowadays a lot had to be achieved with very little and, for the construction of the churches then proposed by the archbishopric for erection in Paris, they would find themselves obliged to relinquish stone and adopt alternatives, the best of which was cement."[11]

Begun about 1897, the church of Saint-Jean de Montmartre provided the first major practical example of De Baudot's theories on the subject of construction and followed his experiments with the De Baudot house in the Rue Pommeret and the Lycée Victor Hugo. After having demonstrated the function of the continuous columns extending through the two storeys of the church to the roof and the use of masonry simply as an in fill element, De Baudot states: "From this explicit

*18. J. Richard. Apartment block, 3-9 Rue
Général Delestraint, Paris 16ᵉ. (1911).*

fact there results (it cannot be too often repeated) a complete revolution in the conception of buildings designed in the interests of particular structural arrangements, and the basis of a new architectural expression conceived in the interests of economy, which is considerable. It is surely clearly apparent that everything is new in this solution. In particular, this novelty is proclaimed, not only by the fact that the vaults are held in position by reason of their interrelation and structure, but that they themselves constitute the roof of the building, while providing, in the upper part, the free passage sometimes so useful but so rarely feasible at the top of our buildings. The shape of these vaults, which necessarily take the form of a more or less curved ceiling, is very flexible while yet conforming entirely to the structural system, if this has been properly understood. In the present example, the form obtained is the result of fixing curved spines, intersecting and interconnected by double-curved slabs, reinforced by secondary spines, which might have been exposed, but which have been placed between the slabs and embedded in the rubble providing the insulation. As can be seen, there is no question here of applying known forms of vaulting, but of demonstrating structural and visual relationships resulting from a system absolutely unfamiliar before now".[12]

The vault of the roof is made of two layers, each 2 3/4 inches thick (7 centimetres), separated by a space 1 9/16 inch wide (4 centimetres) for insulation; the walls of the church are 75 feet high (25 meters) and 9 11/16 inches thick (25 centimetres). The structure cost at the time 400,000 francs, taking into account the considerable expenditure on the excavation and the foundations. Lighting is supplied by glazing which entails no structural interference, being composed of panes of glass in ribbed squares of reinforced concrete. Because of lack of resources, the interior decoration consists of stucco surfaces with monochrome paintings. To minimize the displeasing effect of reinforced concrete on the outside - and after 70 years there are still plenty who will sympathize with this - De Baudot appealed to Bigot to create a large number of ceramic circles and triangles: "Thanks to the metal mesh frame [De Baudot wrote] there are plenty of points of connection for fixing ceramic or metal elements, hollow or filled-out with cement; in this way the advantages of a theoretical permanence which the whole system offers extend also to the decoration. If the decorative elements are small in size, by assembling them in repeated and varied forms they can be directly fixed to the cement before it is fully cured, and much more interesting combinations will be found, especially of mosaic, which is able to contribute the precious virtue of colour".[13]

Thanks to Alexandre Bigot, Pierre Roche, the "wrought-iron worker" Emile Robert and the "carpenter" Lecoeur, all four adept in Art Nouveau, the church of Saint-Jean de Montmartre emerged as a direct response to the taste of the time - which, however, could by no means be said to be reflected in De Baudot's work. Indeed, this work was to provide De Baudot with a number of practical experiments from which a host of designs were to take shape, the increasing complexity of which, and daring in the logic of ribbed vaults, come appreciably close to the models of Guarino Guarini.

These structural experiments had their repercussions. De Baudot's influence could clearly be detected in the structural types in some of Paul Vorin 's designs, among which that of a "Poste aéronautique exhibited at the Salon de la Société Nationale des Beaux-Arts in 1912.

If the experiments "in reinforced cement" (which is not to be confused - as De Baudot insists - with "reinforced concrete") result in a kind of kaleidoscopic fantasy in which late Gothic and Baroque are mingled, De Baudot also reveals premonitions of an uncompromisingly modernist character. Evidence of this can be found in the field of "thin membranes (shells)", in his expressionism or in the ribbed constructions of floors, their geometric grid, even though it is closely associated with formulae derived from studies in organic tension, already foreshadowing Pier Luigi Nervi and Riccardo Morandi.[14]

19. *J. Richard and E. Audiger. Town house,
40 Rue Boileau, Paris 16ᵉ. (1907-08). Detail
of the façade.*

Aside from the contributions of De
Baudot and the Perret brothers to
architecture in reinforced concrete,
mention should be made of works by
Louis Süe, Paul Huillard, Joachim
Richard, Henri Deneux, André Arfvidson and Louis Bonnier as pioneering
experiments with this new building
material. In 1906, Süe and Huillard
built a house for the artist Lucien
Simon at 3 bis Rue Cassini. The house
was unusual for Paris because of its
reference to both Flemish architecture
and British Victorian houses. Its structure, however, remained adapted to
timber-framing. Like many other
contemporary works, it revealed the
architects' difficulty at conceiving of
structural types that would use the
characteristics of reinforced concrete
rather than imitate that of other materials. The same could be said of the
house built at 40 Rue Boileau (1907-
08) by Joachim Richard and E. Audiger, in an unusual style with mozarabic
overtones. The pillars featured curves
evoking metal structures, and the
string courses between floors were
marked by ceramic studs suggesting
the rivets of steel beams. Richard often
used ceramic-tile covering, made
mostly by the company Gentil et
Bourdet. Whether in the house on Rue
Boileau or the apartment block at 15
Avenue Perrichon (1907), this tile
cladding emphasized the arrangement
of structural elements on the façade.
Arfvidson's block of studios on Rue
Campagne-Première (1910-1911)
won an award at the competition for
the design of façades in 1911. It was a
significant example of the use of
glazed earthenware. The façade was
made of a grid in reinforced concrete,
with brick infills framing picture
windows; the cladding was made of
glazed earthenware executed by
Alexandre Bigot. The plan of the
building offered an interesting solution

20. *J. Richard. Apartment block, 15 Avenue Perrichont, Paris 16ᵉ. (1907).*

21. *L. Süe and P. Huillard. Town house of the painter Lucien Simon, 3 bis Rue Cassini, Paris 14ᵉ. (1906).*

22-24. H. Deneux. House, 185 Rue Belliard, Paris 18ᵉ. (1913). Overall view and façade details.

to the problem of combining an artist's studio with a duplex apartment; each apartment featured an entrance hall, diningroom and kitchen on the ground floor, and, on the upper floor, bedrooms and a living-room connected with the studio by a balcony. The lay-out and spatial arrangement of these artist's dwellings was to appear again later in several housing units designed by Le Corbusier.

From the beginning, Bonnier had established himself as one of the most interesting architects of Art Nouveau. His fame was due mostly to his school complex in the district of Grenelle (1909-10), which was acclaimed by all contemporaries as a significant step towards renewing the architecture of schools. He designed three buildings – respectively for the boys' school, the girls' school, and the kindergarten – arranged around a great courtyard in the shape of a trapezium; the classrooms faced this courtyard. It was an examplary case of honesty of purpose and construction, which De Baudot applauded when he praised the work for "its great simplicity, which did not exclude ... an aesthetic dimension perfectly adapted to the purpose and the nature of the materials used". "Everything is honest, sincere and in good taste.... The structure alone provided the decorative element". [15]

The building used a mixture of techniques: reinforced concrete for the floors, window lintels and door canopies; brick for the main piers. It combined masterfully aesthetic criteria with economy of means. It also made full use of the expressive possibilities of the materials – stone, brick, reinforced concrete and ceramic – which, left exposed, created felicitous chromatic arrangements. Finally, it did away with the schools' usual resemblance with barracks by adopting wide glazed surfaces that ran almost the full length

of the classroom and fulfilled a purpose of hygiene. Through this work, Bonnier established himself as an architect with a social outlook, which he confirmed by designing low-cost housing.

Deneux, a student of De Baudot, was appointed architect of the Monuments Historiques. After the First World War, he worked for many years on the restoration of the cathedral at Reims. His apartment building at 185 Rue Belliard (1913) was his contribution to architecture in reinforced concrete. He chose to leave the structure exposed and used an interesting technique for the ceramic cladding. De Baudot included this building in the short list of works that he regarded as examplary for their exploration of the possibilities offered by reinforced concrete – next to Bonnier's school complex, François Lecœur's telephone office on Rue Bergère (1911-1912), Paquet's Jules Ferry girls' school (1913) and Robert Danis's house at Auteuil. "This building", he wrote, "features a ground floor and three upper floors, designed for modest apartments, albeit perfectly fitted and laid-out. It is based on a general system of piers and floors in which reinforced concrete and brick play a major role. The brick is not left exposed, but covered with cement into which a very original arrangement of glazed ceramic tiles is set, creating a noteworthy decoration.... The architect himself oversaw everything. As a result, neither the details nor the whole building have this banal and industrial aspect, which can be seen in most apartment buildings for rental and which make Paris look so monotonous." [16]

More open and at the same time more deeply rooted, the third rationalist road was centred upon unexplored possibilities offered by the iron structures which had reached their apotheosis

25-27. A. Arfvidson. Apartment house, Rue Campagne-Première, Paris 14e. Overall view and details of the façade.

28-29. *L. Bonnier. School, Rue de Schutzenberger, Rue Sextus-Michel, Rue Emeriau, Rue du Dr Finlay, Paris 15ᵉ. (1908-1911). Outside and inside views.*

30. *G. Chédanne. Mercédès Hotel, Rue de Presbourg and Avenue Kléber, Paris 16ᵉ. (1902-04). Overall view.* ▷

with the Exhibition of 1889. But iron, symbol of progress and hero of Emile Zola's novels, was thrust into architectural oblivion by the mass of classicists, neo-traditionalists and symbolists. So, at the time of the Exhibition of 1900, it was to be used simply as a tool and only considered in its historical and eclectic context. It would be possible to reconcile this problem of contention between engineers and architects and thence proceed to a detailed examination going beyond the usual rhapsodies of the positivists and the historical perspective in which the works of the pioneers of the modern movement are always considered. But it is appropriate to pause here for a moment to refer to a curious contradiction. In fact it was precisely at the moment when the possibilities of iron architecture were limited from a cultural point of view that it rediscovered its true vein and essential purity, in works of a strictly functional character by virtue of which they escaped aesthetic judgment and were accepted by the authorities responsible for planning control. The latter displayed exemplary tolerance and liberality.

Leaving aside "La Samaritaine", which was associated with the incisive and contradictory personality of Frantz Jourdain, this was the case, for example, with the startling building for "Le Parisien Libéré" (1903-05), erected by Georges Chédanne.[17] Here, the unhesitating adoption of iron construction assumed the same progressive significance and revolutionary momentum as in the People's Hall built by Horta in Brussels. The means of expression became all the more vital with the total absence of masonry.

31. *G. Chédanne. Offices of the newspaper Le Parisien Libéré, 124 Rue Réaumur, Paris 3ᵉ. (1903-05). Overall view.*

Despite Chédanne's complete abandonment of all decorative elements, the principle of "branches" is manifest in the outward movement of two of the supporting members which carry the bow-windows, while the other two stanchions remain vertical. In the same way, elements which spring out to join those of the bow- window consoles also contributes to the creation of a nature- inspired continuity, which is the key to the idiom of Art Nouveau. The consoles, very slightly curved back at the ends, which while presenting a homogeneous structure, lie in two orthogonal planes, the wide inflexions described by the webbed beams serving as basements to the bow-windows, and the contrast between the riveted flanges of the stanchions and the webs of the beams in polished metal used as window-basements, enable the work to carry the theme of "continuity" to its ultimate extreme. This continuity is applied not only in the disposition of the vertical load bearing elements, but also in that of the "continuous horizontal beams". Every attempt, based on a similar functional approach, to establish a relationship between Perret's garage in the Rue Ponthieu and the "Parisien Libéré" of Chédanne can only be arbitrary and superficial. The point of departure may be the same, but such an attempt takes no account of the profound difference of idiom: the garage in the Rue Ponthieu is classical, a bridge linking the architecture of the century of enlightenment and the revival of neo-monumentalism (a view championed to-day in certain architectural quarters to-day); the building for "Le Parisien Libéré" by Georges Chédanne, winner of the Prix de Rome, is romantic, true to the spirit of Art Nouveau, which is too often betrayed by hedonism, middle-class wealth, facile allegory and vegetal inspiration.

1 Peter Collins, *Concrete:* "Vision of a new architecture", London 1959, p. 160.

2 *Ibid.*, p. 165.

3 See C. Saunier, "Nouvelles applications du grès flammé au revêtement des façades", in *L'Architecte,* November 1908, pp.80-85-87; December 1908, pp. 91-93.

4 E. Viollet-le-Duc, "Entretiens sur l'architecture", Paris 1872, vol. II, p. 296 (English translation by B. Bucknall, London 1881).

5 Anatole De Baudot, *L'Architecture. Le passé. Le présent.* Paris, Henri Laurens 1961, p. 139.

6 *Ibid.*, p. 140.

7 *Ibid.*, p. 144.

8 For a chronology of the most significant buildings in reinforced cement (Cottancin system) and concrete (Hennebique system) erected in Paris around 1900, see *Familièrement inconnues... Architectures, Paris 1848-1914*, exhibition catalogue by Bernard Marrey and Paul Chemetov, Paris 1976, p. 151.

9 A. De Baudot, *op. cit.*, p. 147.

10 *Ibid.*, p. 171.

11 *Ibid.*, p. 170.

12 A. De Baudot, *L'Architecture et le ciment armé*, Paris, 1916, pp. 30-31.

13 *Ibid.*, p. 34.

14 See F. Boudon, "Recherches sur la pensée et l'œuvre d'Anatole de Baudot, 1834-1915", in *Architecture, mouvement, continuité,* 8 (March 1973).

15 A. De Baudot, *L'Architecture. Le passé. Le présent*, pp. 148-149.

16 *Ibid.*, p. 160.

17 Some authors have questioned whether the building at 124 Rue Réaumur was by Georges Chédanne. They pointed out that it was radically different from the rest of the work by Chédanne, an architect who had been awarded the Grand Prix de Rome in 1887. Bernard Marrey and Paul Chetemov noted, for instance, that the building "is generally believed to have been designed by Chédanne on the basis of the drawings submitted with the request for a building permit dated 6 April, 1903. Chédanne's drawings, however, are very different from the actual building, and nothing in his earlier or later work allows for a comparison. The contemporary press, which paid a close attention to that which was happening in the Rue Réaumur, remained strangely silent about this building, in spite of the fact that it was rather unusual. One could think that Chédanne, who was then occupied with some important works outside of Paris and abroad, left this building to a needy colleague (*op. cit.*, p. 114). It could be answered that it happens among academically trained architects that they should use a very different idiom for utilitarian works and prestigious commissions. It is also inaccurate to say that the turn-of-the-century press remained silent on the identity of the building's architect. In a fairly well documented essay, Pascal Forthuny credited Chédanne with the design of the building (*Dix années d'architecture*, in "Gazette des Beaux-Arts", LI (1910), 635, p. 436). So di E. Delaize in his biographical dictionary, *Les Architectes Elèves de l'Ecole des Beaux-Arts, 1793-1907*, Paris, Librairie de la Construction moderne, 1907.

34

32. *International Exhibition of 1900. General view on the Palais des Nations. (After a postcard of the time).*

II

THE EXHIBITION OF
1900

33. *International Exhibition of 1900. Alexandre III bridge. (After a postcard of the time).*

The international exhibition which was inaugurated on 14 April 1900 and which was to be dubbed "exhibition of the century" was the fifth of its kind to take place in Paris. Indeed, with the four exhibitions of 1855, 1867, 1878 and 1889, Paris already gave the impression of holding some degree of monopoly, implying for France a national role which was hers by right. But this exhibition marked rather the end of the old century than the dawn of the new. Without in any way portending the agony which was to engulf the twentieth century, it was content to draw up an impressive and encouraging balance-sheet of the art and sciences of the nineteenth. It would be misleading and mistaken to try to attribute to it an exclusively Art Nouveau character and to deduce from its artistic message merely that which was relevant to an idiom regarded as original at the time. Over and above the rationalist path opened by the iron structures of 1889, the 1900 exhibition reflected the multitude of French architectural trends and more particularly those of Paris, which had marked the last decades of the past century. One could read in the very established "Gazette des Beaux-Arts": "At the outset, with the inauguration barely over, a number of reactions were harshly unfavourable, and the plaster city, four years in preparation for a life of six months, was declared inferior in workmanship compared with the achievement of 1889. The novelty and daring of the iron structures of eleven years ago were missing. It was a retreat, a deliberate renewal of composite-style architecture, a mixture of Greek, Louis XV, Louis XVI and Art Nouveau".[1]

Frantz Jourdain, to whom we owe "La Samaritaine", wrote in the "Revue des Arts Décoratifs": "I leave to others the patriotic, but painful office of strewing with flowers the heterogeneous mass of constructions in plaster, papier-maché, ticky-tacky and make-believe which form, in large part, world fair of 1900. This architecture of confectionery and icing sugar assembled to indulge a tribe of Caribs, cynically insults both good taste and good sense; it is the logical consequence of the baneful doctrines taught at the Ecole des Beaux-Arts, and it ingenuously demonstrates, under a hotchpotch of mendacity and falsehood, the impotence of academic teaching. If one compares the admirable effort of 1889, the work of youth, vitality, daring, rationalism, confidence in the future, with the pitiful plagiarism and bungling imitations of 1900, one is forced to acknowledge that a wind of reaction is searing and withering our wonderful country".[2]

The curiosity of nineteenth century society with regard to races, customs and the genius of nations was gratified by architecture with an essentially didactic aim; it can be compared with a sort of magic carpet offering visits to the four corners of the globe. Even though one may have reservations about the artistic quality, audacity and provocative lines of the modern idiom, the fact remains that the true finality of architecture is the creation of this world of enchantment.

Here, the impressions of faraway travels were assembled in a picture of which we possess ample evidence describing the great river, the electric lights, the pleasure steamers, the minarets, the varied domes, the white cubes of Africa, Tunisia, China, the Ganges and the Bosphorus.

Electricity, a recent invention, triumphed with its thousand brilliant spots, restless beams and fountains of light: "The fairyland of night begins and, as the darkness deepens, culminates in an apotheosis of unforgettable delight. If one were to ask visitors to the exhibition what gave them most pleasure, it is probable that almost all would point to the view of the Seine illuminations. For unexpectedness, for the sumptuous, mysterious charm of colour, nothing can compare with the triumphant effect of light on water".[3]

But to turn to Frantz Jourdain: "The panorama of the Palaces of the Nations reflected in the silken waters of the Seine furrowed by bateaux-mouches; the sunset behind the domes, the turrets, the pinnacles and the minarets bristling on the Trocadéro; the multi-coloured symphony of lights ablaze at nightfall in this city of dreams; yes, it is no less than the entire sweep of this unique and magnificent setting, suggesting a painting by Turner, that compels us to deplore the fairy world of 1900 which, when all is said, was to have credited France with the most extraordinary effort of brain and hand of the century".[4]

This "Turner-like picture" was started in 1893 when, following Chicago, the idea was launched for an exhibition which France was to organize with the enthusiastic agreement of the great powers. Germany requested a covered area of 360.000 square feet (40,000 meters ^{2}), and England insisted on being the best represented foreign power. The laying of the first stone of the Alexandre III Bridge by Nicholas II celebrated the Franco-Russian alliance, while the general plan was the theme of a competition with 280 entries, 28 of which were by engineers and 252 by architects. The competitors had complete liberty in deciding the fate of the monuments on the site of the exhibition, including the

35-37. *International Exhibition of 1900. The Champ de Mars and the Palais de l'Electricité (above); the Château d'eau (centre); the Petit Palais (below) after postcards of the time.*

38. *Festival hall. (After a postcard of the time).*

Eiffel Tower; they could propose their retention, transformation, or even demolition. Article 2 stated that "only Frenchmen are permitted to take part in the competion". Among the judges are found Charles Garnier, Julien Guadet, Auguste Vaudremer and Léon Ginain. "The competition maintains, Girard observed, a satisfactory average. Certainly, amid the multiplicity of ideas, there are no schemes which command attention by the loftiness of their vision and inspired conception... If one presumed to criticize, it might perhaps be said that oriental motifs have been overdone. Such is the fashion of the moment.... It is a fact that architecture is passing through a pediod of transition. Scientific progress has modified the rules of the art. Our social life has been transformed and with it the role of architecture.... One cannot say that this is a bad thing. But it is no less a fact that architecture is in search of its aesthetic philosophy".[5]

But it was the Eiffel Tower, centre of attraction of the 1889 exhibition, which opened the floodgates of polemic; some, who regarded it as a monument to iron technology, wished to destroy it but others emphasized that its demolition would be expensive and that, from a financial point of view, it was preferable to keep it since it was subject to a 20-year concession. The architects did their utmost to disguise it by enclosing its base in peculiar constructions and using its upper part as a supporting stand for gigantic statues: "Many of the competitors have embellished the tower and thus aligned themselves with the view of the judges, who until now have favoured its retention. Some, however, have not considered the wind hazard which would be created by this considerable mass and have overloaded it with ornaments which, if the occasion arose, might present a real danger. As

for those who would have it razed, they have not been able to propose any more inspired replacement".[6]

While the Eiffel Tower was destined to survive, the Galerie des Machines was to be demolished; on the Pont Alexandre III, the arches of which have a total spar of 325 feet (107 meters), the ironwork was to be completely masked by Louis XVI friezes, cartouches and festoons in cast-iron. At the Grand Palais, the imposing iron and glass structure with the dome forming the intersection of the four wings was to be integrated in an monumental classical colonnade and, inside, the great staircase was to be built in iron in a style linking Gothic with Louis XV and rejecting any conscious concession to Art Nouveau. Louis- Albert Louvet took charge of the Grand Palais, as a result of a competition the jury of which included Julien Guadet, Auguste Vaudremer and Gustave Raulin, all three professors at the Ecole des Beaux-Arts, the centre of the deliberations. As for the Petit Palais, this was entrusted to Charles-Louis Giraud, who displayed a greater facility in its typically Louis XVI refinement, even if the wrought-iron portal offers a skilful intertwining of Louis XV and Art

Nouveau elements. These three works were each built according to the principles of a masterly eclecticism and demonstrate a similar freedom, especially in the sculpture and decorative elements. The architect René Binet gave his name to a door which displays a certain audacity in its oriental exoticism. It features pseudo- Siamese obelisks; its triangular layout capped by a dome conveys an unusual perspective view which aroused much criticism; finally, the silhouette of an elegant Parisienne, the work of Jules Chéret, stands on the dome: "I support the general intention, the unexpected orginality, the pretty notion of getting rid of Venus, Mercury and Apollo and replacing the mythological rubbish with a modern woman, the modern woman; of the low-relief in the base, evoking the working man, the manual worker, who is too often forgotten in a century in which his place is none the less dominant".[7] And once again it is Jourdain who points out the accomplice that decoration has discoverd in electricity, which "has offered us the enchanting distillations of violet that in the evening delight the eyes of the passer-by."[8] The decoration, to which the ceramic artist Bigot contributed, drew its originality from "rosettes and

39. R. Dulong and G. Serrurier-Bovy.
Restaurant Le Pavillon bleu. Overall view.

40. G. Tronchet. Restaurant La Belle
Meunière. Overall view.

cabochons decking the two pylons which flank the entrance, and the voussoir of the principal arch, on which paterae stand out as if stitched on to a ground of oriental semblance executed in relief". Again, "there are truly charming ideas in this facing of iridescent glass which forms the background to the sculpture, in the arrangement of the cabochons, some shining in natural radiance, others formed of the bulbs of electric lights which at night become so many dazzling sapphires".[9]

The foreign pavilions punctiliously reflected the national formulae: the Swedish in traditional wood, the German Wagnerian, the English Tudor, the American neo-classical, the Italian Veneto-Byzantine, the Greek entirely Byzantine. Alone to distinguish itself by discreet and polished digression from tradition was the Finnish pavilion, the work of Eliel Saarinen, Azmas Lindgren and Hermann Gesellius. In fact there was very little connection with Art Nouveau: "A superficial observer, visiting the world exhibition, noticing the classical pedantry and uninspired reactionary design of the palaces erected by government architects, would conclude

that we as a people are finished, incapable, and devoid of initiative and origniality".[10]

There were only two Art Nouveau buildings in the exhibition, and these in general were of marginal significance: a restaurant near the Eiffel Tower, the Pavillon Bleu by René Dulong and Gustave Serrurier-Bovy, and the theatre of Loïe Fuller by Henri Sauvage and the sculptor Pierre Roche. Dulong designed a structural frame jutting out according to a formula dear to Hector Guimard, adopting a fluid construction which balanced the rigidity of the masses and softened the outlines, so that the rooms appeared to be suspended inside a cage of plants.

The Loïe Fuller theatre, named after the little American dancer who conquered Paris, appeared as if enveloped in a tangle of materials which covered the façade and were gathered about the single central door, a theme to be taken up by Josef M. Olbrich at Darmstadt: "These walls, stated Frantz Jourdain, which seem to shimmer like the gossamer draperies of the divine ballerina, to whom we owe never-to-be-forgotten moments of artistry; these ventilators, latticed in

copper cut in serpentine sprials; these figures of women, laughing, bathed in light; these windows of exquisite radiance, representing the many-faceted polychromatic dance of the wonderful artist, whose vivacious statue, carved by that outstanding sculptor, Pierre Roche, crowns and dominates the little building".[11]

But despite of his always very eulogistic comments on Art Nouveau, Jourdain turned to a style for his Moët et Chandon design which was both Louis XVI and rustic, which placed him in an equivocal situation: "Our friend is a valiant champion of artistic causes, more often than not engaged in cutting classical solutions to ribbons, and generous, prodigal even with his favours for minor flirtations with Art Nouveau. I do not find here any longer his pugnacious advocacy of the 'young' enamoured of ' modern style.'"[12] And so it was with the installations for the Perfume section, in which Jourdain proposed a winter garden where perfumes mingled with natural flowers, a fountain in the Gustave Moreau manner and a pergola of artificial flowers. "Frantz Jourdain, as you know, Louis-Charles Boileau wrote in L'Architecte, is one of the most eloquent apostles of the new artistic revelation, devoted defender and panegyrist of the faithful practitioners of the cult, but he is still an architect like you and me, doing his best to satisfy his clients' whishes."[13]
Other features are even less familiar, such as the monumental banquette of Paul Hankar, which was both an advertisement for Soignies stone (quarried in Hainault) and an exercise in the continuing popularity of late Gothic, closer to Victor Horta's style than to his owm. This historicist triviality, even if concealed by the blandishments of Art Nouveau in the lower part of the building, was apparent in the Restaurant de la Belle Meunière by Guillaume Tronchet, which suffered in

comparison with the Pavillon Bleu. It was, in fact, in the interior decoration of the various national restaurants that wider experiments with Art Nouveau appeared. The German restaurant, for instance, was entrusted to the Berliner Bruno Moehring, while the Viennese was the work of Hermann Neukomm. The popularity of Art Nouveau was always much greater in the field of interior decoration.

Significant examples of Art Nouveau interiors can mostly be found in such installations executed under Louis Bonnier's direction as the one for Pharmacie et Cuirs designed by Léon Benouville, or exploitations et Industries Forestières by Gabriel Guillemonat, Instruments de Musique by Jacques Hermant, Décoration Fixe by Charles Plumet, and Papeterie by Louis Sorel. Felicitous examples of "street decorations" should not be overlooked either, such as André Jules Collins's door on the Quai d'Orsay, "a door made of elegant wood arabesques that are garlanded with a flowering of electric bulbs, as if decorated by gigantic peacock feathers of light". [14]

Contemporary critical judgment conformed to a pattern. According to the prevailing contention, modern architecture was divisible into two kinds: the monumental and the intimate. The latter accepted coexistence between rationalism marked by an extreme sobriety and the fantasies of an architecture drawing its inspiration from symbolist poetry. Even Boileau mentions in L'Architecte the contribution of Charles Plumet, Tony Selmersheim, Louis Majorelle, Jules Lavirotte and Hector Guimard. And it was the same with Charles Genuys: "In these sumptuous palaces, the outward extravagance of which seems, for the most part, to have been borrowed

41. F. Jourdain. International Exhibition of 1900. Installation of the Perfume Section, on the Champ de Mars.

from a Louis XV returned from South America, and which in themselves express little more than the state of decadence of our official modern architecture, who would not be surprised to note the existence, in every country which has an artistic entity, of the same tendencies to shake off the old exhausted styles in order to create works that are young, virile and modern?" [15]

This time, in the international panora-

ma of interior decoration, the English had to yield first place. The tapestries of Edward Burne Jones, with their priggish pedanticism, were boring. Jourdain, inevitably, described the cavaliers of uncertain sex as "a sort of narcoticized Lohengrin with a vague resemblance to the curly-haired first comunicants seen on prints in the Rue St Sulpice". [16] The Belgians were absent; Horta, Serrurier-Bovy and Van de Velde did not come "for regrettable reasons of siting". [17] Germany was the

42. *Ch. Plumet. International Exhibition of 1900. Installation of the Classe de Décoration fixe.*

43. *L. Benouville. International Exhibition of 1900. Installation of the Classe des cuirs et des peaux.*

revelation: Bruno Paul, Bernhard Pankok and the Darmstadt artists were determined to be in the vanguard of the modern movement: "It was agreed, the catalogue reads, to banish... the superfluity of architectural forms, and it was required that every part should correspond to its utilitarian function without concern for history".[18]

Austria, too, occupied an important place. Gentler, far removed from the imperialist heavy-handednes of her German neighbours, she put her faith in the sensibility, linearity and dominant violet tones of Hoffmann. Hungary and the whole Slavic world had nothing to contribute but their traditions; the same applied to Italy and Spain, despite the reputation of Catalua and Lombardy, which were not represented. On the French side, beside the great tradition of excellent craftsmanship in carved woods and marquetry and the feeling for fine materials, chiefly were to be noted the rare woods (sycamore and pear), the silvered and gilded bronzes, the enamels and a certain artistic aptitude for combining style and realism.

The floral motif avoided any suggestion of the abstract and the theory of the "stem" dear to Horta: it was introduced in the form of a plant luxuriant and pliant in the typological

44. *Ch. Plumet and T. Selmersheim. Dining-room shown at the International Exhibition of 1900.*

45. *L. Bigaux. Living-room shown at the International Exhibition of 1900.*

convention of eighteenth-century furniture. "Yet some artists, following in the train of the Belgian architect Horta, have sought to find in nature, and even apart from it, an uniform adaptation of short, spiral, or 'whi-plash' lines to the decoration of all materials. Disdaining the leaves and flowers of plants, their enthusiasm has been directed to the roots, and in their eagerness to be original at any price they have thought it novel to disfigure the usual decorative idiom. Thus have been born these curious zigzag patterns, incoherent reliefs. .. which have quite rightly provoked the critics and have driven ill-informed observers to believe in the abortion of contemporary artistic.evolution".[19]

Emile Gallé, who presented a significant collection of sample models

entitled "Adaptation de la flore au petit meuble contemporain", was to write, without Jourdain's vivid and polemical pen, a eulogy of the "Pavillon de l'union Centrale des Arts Décoratifs", which returned to the formula of elegant historicism on the outside and exposed T-form iron structures inside, and of the panelling by Georges

Hoentschel in which "a single chosen flower, the wild rose, modestly sings the poetry of youth and spring. The dark pampres and corymbs of age-old ivy, somewhat stylized, provide a melodic accompaniment to the flower of love. On all sides the rose of Provins, the Rosa gallica, entwines or is entwined, turn by turn".[20]

Let us also mention the colours: the subtle tones, the tenuous blends, call to mind Gallé's text, and his visual memory is more eloquent than names and facts: "cinder grey", "steel blue with silver-grey foliage", "dawn pink with silver flecks", "silver- grey flowers on silver suède", "enamelled gold goblet", "greys subtle and calm", "reticulated platanus", "copper rose", "pale rose", "intense and delectable green", "water green".[21]

NOTES

1. G. Geoffroy, "Promenade à l'Exposition", in *Gazette des Beaux-Arts,* série 3ᵉ, XXIV (1900), p. 24.
2. F. Jourdain, "L'Architecture à l'Exposition universelle. Promenade à bâtons rompus" First article, in *Revue des Arts Décoratifs,* XX (1900), p. 245.
3. G. Geoffroy, "Promenade à l'Exposition", *op. cit.,* p. 342.
4. F. Jourdain, "L'Architecture à l'Exposition. Promenade à bâtons rompus", continuation, *op cit.,* p. 342
5. G. Cordier, "A propos des expositions universelles. Essai d'intégralisme" in *Architecture, Mouvement, Continuité* n°177, June 1970, p.51.
6. J. Cordier, *op. cit.,* p.52.
7. F. Jourdain, *op. cit.,* First article, p.247.
8. F. Jourdain, *op. cit.,* First article, ibid.
9. L. Magne "Les arts à l'Exposition Universelle de 1900: L'Architecture", in *Gazette des Beaux-arts,* XXIV (1900) p.67.
10. F. Jourdain, *op.cit.,* cont., p. 327.
11. F. Jourdain, *op.cit.,* cont. II, p. 345.
12. L.-C. Boileau, "Causerie. Le Pavillon Moët et Chandon, architecte Frantz jourdain", in *L'Architecture,* 1900, p. 251.
13. L.-C. Boileau, "Causerie. Les installations de la parfumerie", in *L'Architecture,* XIII (1900), p. 415.
14. F. Jourdain, "L'Art du Décor à l'Exposition Universelle", in *L'Architecture,* XIV (1901), pp. 29-30.
15. Ch. Genuys, "Les Essais d'Art Moderne dans la Décoration Intérieure", in *Revue des Arts Décoratifs,* XX (1900), p. 252.
16. F. Jourdain, *op. cit.,* cont., p. 330.
17. Ch. Genuys, *op. cit.,* p. 287.
18. Ch. Genuys, *op. cit.,* p. 33.
19. L. Magne, "Le mobilier moderne à l'Exposition Universelle de 1900", in *Revue des Arts Décoratifs,* XXI (1900), p. 219.
20. E. Gallé, "Le Pavillon de l'Union centrale des arts décoratifs à l'exposition universelle", in *Revue des Arts Décoratifs,* XX (1900), p. 219.
21. E. Gallé, *op. cit.,* passim.

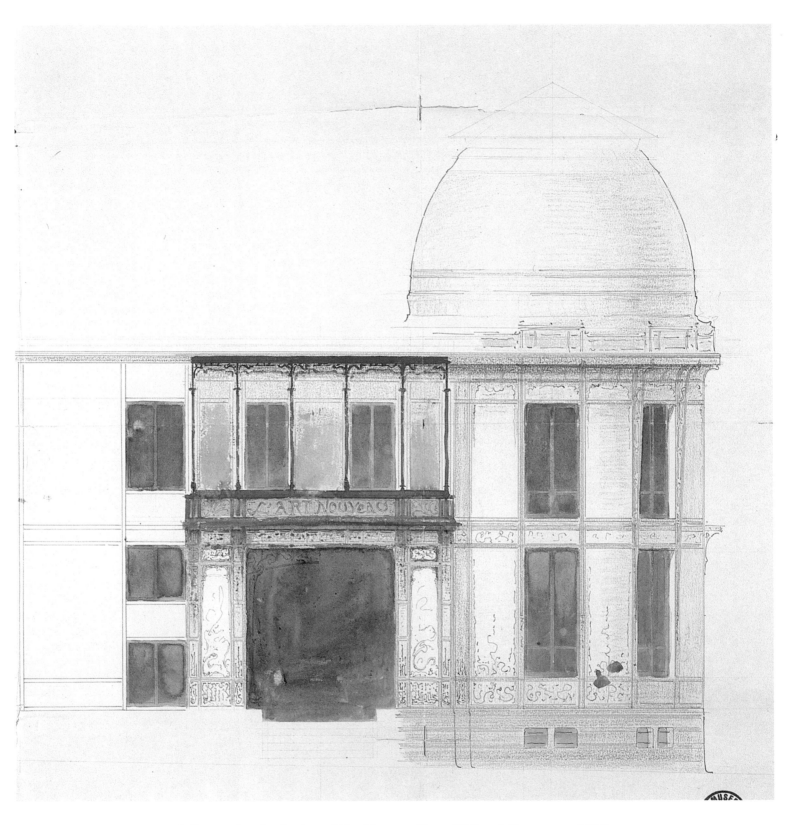

46. *First project for the shop « L'Art Nouveau Bing », 22 Rue de Provence and 19 Rue Chauchat, Paris 9ᵉ.*

III

ART NOUVEAU BING

47. *L. Bonnier. Project for the door of the shop «L'Art Nouveau Bing».*

A floral decoration composed of warmer tones, "brown, pink, yellow on a terracotta background merging into violet"[1] - walls covered with a plain "brick pink" material, were the introduction to the pavilion of Samuel Bing. "Under the trees of the Invalides, adjoining the Breton village, a light façade is revealed. Crowned by a frieze of orchids, panels in enchanting colours, with undulating lines, of rare harmony, women, flowers and symbolic landscapes, adorn it; windows define unlooked for features; it smiles and shines, joy and clarity: such is the Maison de l'Art Nouveau"[2] This pavilion was not conceived as a bazaar, but as a private house, with its furniture and everyday objects: the dining-room and bedroom were by Eugène Gaillard, a sculptor who turned to furniture. The carpets, the glass-work and other furnishings were the work of Georges De Feure, a designer who collaborated for some months with Bing. The most provocative and ingenious furniture was by an artist with an Italian name, Eugène Colonna, who also designed jewelry with great success.[3] These artists came from the world of the figurative arts and had no architectural training; they worked as a group, according to Bing's formula:

"And indeed M. Bing would be right in thinking, now that we are within sight of victory, that if reform in the crafts owes much to individual artists of high attainment, like Messrs Plumet, Tony Selmersheim, Henri Sauvage and others, it owes to him something much the same which, with irresistible force, made it popular in Germany and which in France lacked the impetus to gain recognition: a united effort, a collective will in which all are impelled towards the same goal".[4] The critics of the period struck the customary note of nationalism: "The first works of undeniable value to come from the workshops of Art Nouveau were the jewelry, Tiffany's settings in glass,

Bigot's ceramics and a few bits of gold or silver. Here there was certainly something new and fresh; but these were isolated objects, created at the whim of the imagination. Quite another thing is to design a scheme of decoration like the one which is seen today at the Maison de l'Esplanade des Invalides, given the aim which Monsieur S. Bing sought to attain: to produce a work truly French which would be a genuine expression of the sensibility of our race and not an adaptation of foreign principles".[5]

Samuel Bing was not French and his name was really Siegfried.[6] Born in Hamburg in 1838, he remained in Germany, employed in a manufactory of ceramics, until the end of the Franco-Prussian war, by which time we find him in Paris with French citizenship and a business in oriental art. After a journey to China and Japan, where he met Edward Moore, a director of Tiffany and a great orientalist, he returned to Paris, where he devoted himself to the importation of objets d'art from the East, more particularly Japan. In addition to his commercial activities, he became deeply involved in the cultural world and made many contacts, frequenting especially Vincent Van Gogh and the Goncourt brothers. In 1888 he founded the review "Le Japon Artistique", with Roger Marx and Edmond de Goncourt among the contributors.[7] Bing then went to the USA, opened a gallery in New York, renewed his association with the Tiffany concern and wrote a book on American architecture in which he thoroughly analysed the contribution of Henri Hobson Richardson and Louis Henri Sullivan. He wrote with remarkable penetration on American industrial art, from Samuel Colman and John La Farge to Louis C. Tiffany, son of the founder of Tiffany and Co. In 1895 he exhibted ten windows designed by French artists - among them Bonnard, Grasset, Sérusier, Toulouse-Lautrec, Valloton and Vuillard[6] - and executed by Tiffany.

Upon his return to Paris, Bing opened the Salon de l'Art Nouveau on 26 December 1895, at 22 Rue de Provence. This was an old two- storey private mansion renovated by Louis Bonnier, an architect who was not yet thirty years old. Bonnier had already distinguished himself by designing, in 1894, a few summer houses in the dunes at Ambleteuse, in which he demonstrated that he could take typical forms of traditional country houses and reinterpret them in a modern key. For the installation of the Salon de l'Art Nouveau, Bing had first called on Frank Brangwyn, who had suggested a mostly pictorial solution characterized by brightly colored ceramic facing or -as an alternative- less expensive cement rendering, continuous strips of friezes, mosaics and decorative panels. The work had already started when Bing decided to interrupt the execution of Brangwyn's design and ask Horta another one, provided he keep the already existing preliminary studies show that he suggested that the façade

48. *L. Bonnier. Transformation and decoration of the shop "L'Art Nouveau Bing», 22 Rue de Provence and 19 Rue Chauchat, Paris 9e.*

be covered by a metal superstructure in which his favourite theme of the stem would develop. Apparently Bing did not use Horta's design, but the latter may have shown it to Bonnier, who used to buy prints from him. Bonnier designed steel beams as architraves of the openings on the façade on to Rue Chauchat, as well as the main entrance flanked by vases of sunflowers and the entrance to the Japanese Gallery. Stimulated by Horta's example, Bonnier created a naturalistic idiom, in which the influence of Japanese prints is evident. This was particularly true of the entrance to the Japanese gallery,, where the gate featured an asymmetric arrangement of flower stalks, which was to become popular shortly thereafter on the cover of musical scores and theatre programmes designed by Georges Auriol and Henri Rivière. This idiom ruled also the ironwork of the balustraded gallery on the first floor of the cylindrical projection forming the corner of the building. Stained glass by Tiffany

enhanced the Art Nouveau style of decoration; there were designed by Pierre Bonnard, Eugène Grasset, Henri Gabriel Ibels, Paul Ranson, Ker-Xavier Roussel, Paul Sérusier, Henri de Toulouse-Lautrec, Félix Vallotton and Edouard Vuillard.

Edmond de Goncourt, who had hurled from the stage of the Théâtre Libre his notorious cry: "Down with progress!", was to write a few days later that this "salon" represented "delirium. .. the delirium of ugliness".[9] In contrast, Marie Nordlinger, who was to create enamels for Bing, inspired Marcel Proust to speak of a "crude blue, almost violet, suggesting the background of a Japanese cloisonné" or of "the polychrome enamel of pansies".[10]

It was Samuel Bing who made Henry Van de Velde famous, whose works "in spite of German, Austrian, Dutch and French imitations, remain worthy of respect; let us not carp at them for being Belgian, for therein lies their irrefutable merit, and would to God that we had had, at the time when Monsieur Bing brought them to our notice, works as characteristic of French taste".[11] It was also thanks to Bing that the French public discovered the works of its own artists, such as Alexandre Bigot's ceramics, the glass of Emile Gallé and Karl Köpping, René Laliques jewels, and the sculpture of Auguste Rodin, Alexandre Charpentier and Bourdelle, besides "the rural pottery of England, Flanders, the Nivernais and Berry", the wallpapers of Walter Crane and Voysey, William Morris materials, Tiffany glass, and the paintings of Louis Anquetin, Aubrey Beardsley, Pierre Bonnard, Eugène Carrière, Maurice Denis, Fernand Khnopff, Paul Sérusier, Paul Signac, Henri de Toulouse- Lautrec and Edouard Vuillard.

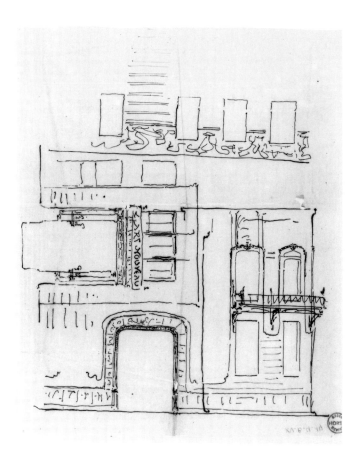

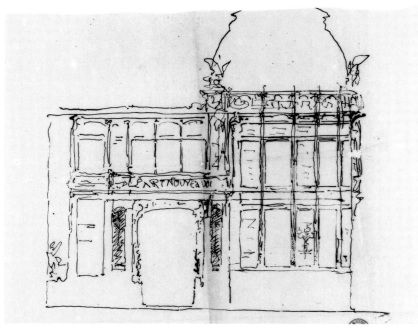

49. V. Horta. First projects for the shop « L'Art Nouveau Bing ».

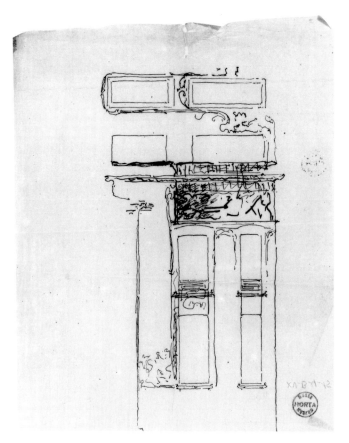

51-52. Colonna: living-room (above) and
G. De Feure: dressing- room (below) shown
in the Bing « Art Nouveau » pavilion, at the
International Exhibition of 1900.

The gallery of the Rue de Provence was a kaleidoscope of experiments in cultivated taste. Recalling this period, Bing commented shrewdly that the main threat had been success: "It aroused as much enthusiasm as indignation. Yet, its impact was enough to generate a large and adept following: artists inclining more towards fantasy than to practical things (table legs in the form of curvaceous nymphs or strange symbolic figures) and housewives devoting their otherwise frustrated skills to little works in leather and bronze. There lay here a certain danger for the survival of Art Nouveau. But a greater menace came from another direction, that of profiteers enrolling under the banner of Art Nouveau to defend their commercial interests. This phenomenon is common, but it was particularly apparent in the case of Art Nouveau. Industry entered with frenetic zeal into the production of objects of novel conception, based simply upon improvising anything which was different and first of its kind. Designers were required to draw lines intercepting at random and without method. It was not difficult to produce Art Nouveau of this sort. It was cheap and needed no preliminary study, choice materials or great care in execution. The public accepted everything as Art Nouveau. Little by little, however, people began to distinguish the real from the false and future critics will recognize the indelible imprint of our time, without expecting its artists, as did Hamlin, to try to adopt an absolute identity of style as in the past".[12]

In fact, according to Bing, it is essential that the principles which inspired Art Nouveau should not be confused with subsequent applications. He was firmly opposed to the habit of submitting all the products of Art Nouveau to a single summary critical assessment and in the end accused all critics of

50. E. Gaillard. Buffet shown in the Bing « Art Nouveau » pavilion at the
International Exhibition of 1900.

53-54. E. Gaillard. Dining-room (above),
and bedroom (below) shown in the Bing
« Art Nouveau » pavilion at the
International Exhibition of 1900.

55. L. Majorelle: stair rail. Chairs and settee
by G. De Feure.

49

having betrayed their professional ethics by not giving a lead to the public and guiding them through the ocean of new objects, utterly different from anything of the past and, above all, having no common denominator.

It is true that, when considered as a whole, Art Nouveau lacked any cohesive principle, since it was advancing over uncharted waters, where every artist was free to exploit his particular bent. Amid all these experiments critics were, according to Bing, under an obligation to indicate those who were aiming at a well- defined target, eliminating the misconceived attempts, imitations and commercial products, and salvaging from oblivion any that contained the germ of inspiration. This spirit of selection was to encourage Bing to take another step forward on the occasion of Expo 1900: the first had been as an importer of works of art and as a gallery director, the second was as an exhibitor and talent- scout in the field of interior design. He now took upon himself to put forward new names working in interior decoration and to persuade these artists to follow the same path as Van de Velde, and renounce the fine arts for crafts. "It is hard to imagine how one and the same man could combine this multiplicity of aptitudes, not to mention the prodigious activity needed to achieve, from his beginnings a few years ago, such a result today".[13] "An educated mind, exquisite taste", the "Revue des Arts Décoratifs" added enthusiastically, "a thirst for discovery and for pointing the way to artists and craftsmen, tact and discipline"; these were the reasons for Bing's success.

The "Architectural Record" asked him to define Art Nouveau in an article published in 1902. Once again he stressed the great dangers run by the new-born movement which, if it was to survive, had to follow very precise lines firmly directed by restraint and good sense, rejecting extravagances and exuberant fantasies, and obeying two cardinal rules: (1) every object must be closely linked to its function; (2) harmony must be attained through line and colour. When, in the same year, Alfred Dwight Forster Hamlin of Columbia University passed a very negative judgment on Art Nouveau in an article published in "The Craftsman,, Bing, while agreeing that Art Nouveau was a movement and not a style, dismissed Hamlin's contention that its followers were united only by their common hatred of historic styles. In his view it was essential to judge separately the original principle of the movement and the unlimited multiplicity of its applications, all individual and inevitably interwoven with the good, the bad and the indifferent.

For Bing, the real bond which united these innovators was their hatred of stagnation. It was true, as Hamlin maintained, that the movement's point of departure was negation, but this was in fact an energetic protest against the disruption which for a whole century had stifled this field of art. The pioneers of Art Nouveau tried to rekindle in the old system the little spark of life which had been transmitted from generation to generation until the sudden paralysis caused by the trauma of the French Revolution. They did not want to destroy the work of their predecessors, but to revive certain essential and forgotten principles. This meant subordinating every object to a strict logic in relation to its function and the material of which it was made. It was also necessary to emphasize the clarity of the organic structure and to accentuate in the architecture of every object the part played by each detail; finally, to shun like the plague the deceit of counterfeit luxury, which consists in changing the nature of materials and carrying ornamentation to the extreme.

NOTES

1 Gabriel Mourey, "L'Art Nouveau de M. Bing à l'Exposition universelle", in *Revue des Arts Décoratifs,* XX (1900), p. 262.

2 *Ibid.,* p. 257.

3 G.M. Jacques, "Exposition universelle": *L'Art Nouveau Bing,* in *L'Art Décoratif,* II (June 1900), pp. 88-97.

4 *Ibid.,* p. 92.

5 G. Mourey, *op. cit.,* p. 262.

6 On the subject of Samuel Bing, see Robert Koch, "Art Nouveau Bing", in *Gazette des Beaux Arts,* CI (1959), vol. LIII, pp. 179-190; Gabriel P. Weisberg, "Samuel Bing. Patron of Art Nouveau", in *Connoisseur,* 172 (1969), 692-694, pp. 119-125, 294-299; 173 (1970), 695, pp. 61-69; Gabriel P. Weisberg, "Samuel Bing. International Dealer of Art Nouveau", in *Connoisseur,* 178 (1971), 718, pp. 200-203; Yvonne Brunhammer, "L'Art Nouveau Bing", in *Art Nouveau Belgium/France,* exhibition catalogue, Institute for the Arts, Rice University, Chicago, 1976, pp. 130-132; and Gabriel P. Weisberg, *Art Nouveau Bing,* Paris Style 1900, New York. Abrams 1986.

7 Published between May 1888 and April 1891, the magazine *Artistic Japan* set itself – as stated in Bing's "Programme published in the first issue – "to initiate the public at large in the secret beauty of an art that, to this day, has made an impression mostly for its superficial qualities". It intended also to provide "the great number of people .... interested in the future of our industrial arts" with models drawn from the Japanese graphic and decorative arts. The thirty-six volumes featured plates, which made use of the high-quality chromolithography of Charles Gillot's workshop, and introductory texts written by such informed lovers of Japanese culture as Louis Gonse, Victor Champier, Lucien Falize, Edmond de Goncourt, Théodore Duret, Ary Renan, Philippe Burty, Ernest Hart, Seymour Trower, A. Lequeux, Gustave Geoffroy, Arthur Lasenby Liberty, Marcus B. Huish, William Anderson, J. Brinckmann and Samuel Bing himself.

8 Samuel Bing, *Artistic America. Tiffany Glass and Art Nouveau,* Introduction by Robert Koch, Cambridge, Massachusetts, 1970.

9 G. Mourey, op cit., p. 259.

10 George D. Painter, *Marcel Proust. A Biography,* New York, vol. II, p. 3.

11 G. Mourey, op. cit., p. 260.

12 S. Bing, «*L'Art Nouveau*», in The Craftsman, October 1903.

13 G.M. Jacques, op. cit., p. 91.

56-57. *L. Majorelle. Decoration of the Restaurant Lucas-Carton, 9 Place de la Madeleine, Paris 8ᵉ. Detail of the paydesk and of a bracket.*

58. H. Guimard. Oak grandfather clock.

59. G. De Feure. Corner table.

IV

FRENCH FURNITURE

GAILLARD, DE FEURE AND COLONNA

"Take for example - Lucien Magne wrote in the 'Revue des Arts Décoratifs' - one of the dining-room chairs designed by Monsieur Gaillard. It is simply composed of a seat and a back covered with tooled repoussé leather, supported on four legs secured by braces. The wood is walnut. The decoration in this instance is reduced to a minimum, since there is no carving nor mouldings, but only as moothing of the edges of the wood for bodily comfort. Yet, art is apparent in the curves of the assembled elements, in the form of the openings, and in the fastenings of the leather to the uprights and cross-pieces of the back and to the frame of the seat. By an ingenious system of jointing, the under-brace, which is an extension of the upright of the back joined to the two feet, allows the wood to be used in the direction of the grain, without the need for pieces of large section to effect the required curve".[1] Again, the dining-room exhibited in Samuel Bing's Pavillon de l'Art Nouveau occasioned the following comment: "Its furniture is strong, without exaggeration or heaviness, simply by the logic and sanity of its structure; there are sinews under these forms".[2]

A lawyer, then a sculptor for ten years, Eugène Gaillard renounced the fine arts to devote himself to the arts and crafts, and especially to furniture. Unlike the School of Nancy, he adopted a rationalist or rather purist attitude: "Ornamental detail would be all the better if it stemmed from a more natural growth without evoking, however, any too precise form of the plant or animal realms that could be identified by name".[3] He was a propagandist and a writer, fully aware of the competitive and social function of the decorative arts, and he denounced the capitalist interests which have brought about "the exploitation of styles" which "assembles against us vast and organized interests of the curio trade,

mock-antique, commercial collecting and archaeological pedantry.[4] Gaillard claimed that a work of art has a definite function, but he also understood fully the repetitive meaning of design: "An object belongs to the arts and crafts only if it allows for unlimited repetition with no appreciable loss of its essential qualities".[5]

Nevertheless, manufacturers and merchants made no serious attempt to popularize Art Nouveau at reasonable prices, hence the movement was criticized for producing either exceptional works at exorbitant prices, or kitchen furniture. The example of Gustave Serrurier-Bovy illustrates the failure of inexpensive furniture,[6] while the vogue for Art Nouveau was to pass so quickly that at the third Salon des Industries du Mobilier in 1908, the competition for inexpensive furniture took as its theme a bedroom in the style of Louis XVI. Resistance came from the antique dealers, fearing the loss of a market, from the manufacturers of fakes, architects accustomed to working in styles which did not easily harmonize with Art Nouveau furniture, and particularly from a middle class who did not want to break with the tradition of aristocratic taste, especially as the Revolution had inheri-

NOTES

1 Gabriel Mourey, "L'Art Nouveau de M. Bing à l'Exposition universelle", in *Revue des Arts Décoratifs*, XX (1900), p. 262.
2 *Ibid.*, p. 257.
3 G.M. Jacques, "Exposition universelle": *L'Art Nouveau Bing*, in *L'Art Décoratif*, II (June 1900), pp. 88-97.
4 *Ibid.*, p. 92.
5 G. Mourey, *op. cit.*, p. 262.
6 On the subject of Samuel Bing, see Robert Koch, "Art Nouveau Bing", in *Gazette des Beaux Arts*, CI (1959), vol. LIII, pp. 179-190; Gabriel P. Weisberg, "Samuel Bing. Patron of Art Nouveau", in *Connoisseur*, 172 (1969), 692-694, pp. 119-125, 294-299; 173 (1970), 695, pp. 61-69; Gabriel P. Weisberg, "Samuel Bing. International Dealer of Art Nouveau", in *Connoisseur*, 178 (1971), 718, pp. 200-203; Yvonne Brunhammer, "L'Art Nouveau Bing", in *Art Nouveau Belgium/France,* exhibition catalogue, Institute for the Arts, Rice University, Chicago, 1976, pp. 130-132; and Gabriel P. Weisberg, *Art Nouveau Bing*, Paris Style 1900, New York. Abrams 1986.
7 Published between May 1888 and April 1891, the magazine *Artistic Japan* set itself – as stated in Bing's "Programme published in the first issue – "to initiate the public at large in the secret beauty of an art that, to this day, has made an impression mostly for its superficial qualities". It intended also to provide "the great number of people .... interested in the future of our industrial arts" with models drawn from the Japanese graphic and decorative arts. The thirty-six volumes featured plates, which made use of the high-quality chromolithography of Charles Gillot's workshop, and introductory texts written by such informed lovers of Japanese culture as Louis Gonse, Victor Champier, Lucien Falize, Edmond de Goncourt, Théodore Duret, Ary Renan, Philippe Burty, Ernest Hart, Seymour Trower, A. Lequeux, Gustave Geoffroy, Arthur Lasenby Liberty, Marcus B. Huish, William Anderson, J. Brinckmann and Samuel Bing himself.
8 Samuel Bing, *Artistic America. Tiffany Glass and Art Nouveau*, Introduction by Robert Koch, Cambridge, Massachusetts, 1970.
9 G. Mourey, op cit., p. 259.
10 George D. Painter, *Marcel Proust. A Biography*, New York, vol. II, p. 3.
11 G. Mourey, op. cit., p. 260.
12 S. Bing, «*L'Art Nouveau*», in The Craftsman, October 1903.
13 G.M. Jacques, op. cit., p. 91.

56-57. *L. Majorelle. Decoration of the Restaurant Lucas-Carton, 9 Place de la Madeleine, Paris 8ᵉ. Detail of the paydesk and of a bracket.*

60. E. Gaillard. Chair.

61. E. Gaillard. Pedestal table.

62. E. Gaillard. Settee.

ted in the main an old-fashioned taste in furniture, to which the Napoleonic era had added the chapter of the "Empire" style.

Georges De Feure was the son of a Dutch architect and a Belgian mother. He began as a decorator, costumier and even actor. He was a friend of Claude Debussy, and in 1894 exhibited thirty-nine watercolours and paintings at the Galerie des Artistes Modernes in the Rue de la Paix. He was not concerned with industrial problems or social demands: he was an exponent of moderate symbolism, an interpreter of the feminine world in an idiosyncratic way, creating a type of woman not unlike Beardsley's, but with less sense of humour and a certain ambiguity in unearthing "rampant vice with the equivocal smile of virgins".[7] His women wore long veiled tunics with high necklines, barely suggesting the hips and heavily trimmed in gold.

For Bing's pavilion, De Feure also chose the theme of woman, but unlike Gaillard he did not design sensually intertwined lines and bedrooms. He preferred the intimacy of the boudoir and bath, and of dresses full of folds, flounces and secrets. His furniture reveals a frivolous world of little collections, trinkets and perfume. His work was well received and he separated from Bing; for seven years he worked independently, following his own inspiration and inventing something without precedent in the typology of the eighteenth and nineteenth centuries: "vide-poche" furnishing: "In a sensuous cloud of russet and buttercup, he half reveals the mystery of the cosseted retreat, the fastidious hiding-place, disclosing the disorder of delicate veils and scented gloves, the little purse with gilded stitching, the long hat-pins removed in haste. It is better than decorative art; it

is a poem of coquetry and elegant frivolity".[8]

In the course of a few years, after devoting himself with incomparable skill to painting, watercolours, gouache, pastels, lithography, posters, bookjackets, graphic arts, bindings, wallpapers, fabrics, jewelry and knick-nacks of every kind, De Feure tried to give himself a distinctive formal entity, setting aside certain Baudelaire-like affectations and symbolist ambiguities. His furniture and joinery now presented a clear differentiation between loadbearing elements and infill panels. He devoted particular attention to edges and joints, also enriching sometimes the panels and sometimes the supporting elements with carving in low-relief, while retaining a sense of restraint in the structure of the piece as a whole. In this he came close to the Italian Ernesto Basile (unless it was Basile who came close to him), displaying an architectural mastery which included an innate feeling for fine materials; beside lemon-wood and the almost magical marquetry of "vide-poche", we find silvered bronze keeping company with walnut, elaborately worked keys and hinges, scutcheons and drawer-knobs in the form of the service-berry.

Of Colonna, the third of the gifted trio of the Pavillon Bing, little is known, and his reputation relies on the recol-

lection of a few pieces, of which Roger H. Guerrand's judgment seems excessively harsh.[9] He had no ambition to create a personal style and appeared to have followed the Bing line with studied skill and perception. His inspiration was probably Van de Velde, but a Van de Velde without some of the heaviness and sound Flemish structural caution, and showing a grace and delicacy, approaching the almost impractical virtuosity of French furniture, the subtle resource of a Reisener. Just as slim ankles and hocks were considered the attributes of class in the shallow hedonism of the time, so Colonna's furniture aimed to demonstrate the pliancy of slender elegance; his pieces were a long way from evoking the anatomical preoccupations of Guimard or the solid constructivism of Gaillard, or indeed the discreet complicity with a patron conveyed by De Feure's furniture. Colonna limited himself to designing furniture with style, accentuating the formal and rather abstract lines of the Art Nouveau idiom.

PAVILION OF THE CENTRAL UNION OF DECORATIVE ARTS

More composite, not to say heterogeneous, the pavilion built under the direction of Georges Hoentschel put its trust in the three elements of rational construction: wood, ceramics and iron.

"What characterizes, the commentary on the exhibition notes, the works exhibited by Messrs Majorelle, Gallé, Damon and Colin, Bigaux, Gaillard and Bing, Genuys and Simonet, Plumet and Tony Selmersheim, Lambert, etc., is both the adaptation of furniture to programmes susceptible to variation from generation to generation, and the exploitation in decoration of the qualities of the material".[10] One of course finds the rejection of historicism and especially the replacement of a vocabulary borrowed from stone by one specifically related to furniture, a search for a new domesticity, middle-class sensibilities, and the growing contribution of the machine: "The spindle-cutter has replaced the moulding-plane and, in furniture without massive feet, machined mouldings bring out, by the play of light, the value of surface and mass".[11]

Mechanised production imposed

certain simplifications and brought with it a saving in materials, as well as a more accurate definition of their structural role. The choice of wood assumed increasing importance, as did

63. G. Hœntschel. Wood section in the Pavilion of the Union centrale des Arts Décoratifs, International Exhibition of 1900.

its intrinsic properties: malleability, resistance, character. "Protests are raised against the exclusively decorative approach of certain artists, which leads to facile success: the iris, mistletoe, holly, seaweed, thistle and various insects, which profusely adorn some pieces of furniture, are already being denounced as useless outworn motifs. A sense of the beauty intrinsic to the object, without external assistance, is awaking in us".[12] Decorative themes were transferred from the furniture to the walls.

Charles Plumet, Tony Selmersheim

and, most of all, Benouville follow this austere line. Instead of the traditional cornices, attention was directed to joints, extremities and casings. The naturalistic tendency, however, was represented by Emile Gallé: a tea-table supported by dragonflies, their bodies forming the legs of the tripod and the wings as brackets, was decorated in marquetry with butterflies and flowers. Another little table was called "skimming water", a sideboard "the white vine", a desk "forest of Lorraine". "It also marks the advent to the realm of furniture of the observation of nature, after the reign of false and conventional decorative elements. From the most modest examples, from a simple entasis to elaborate details, the decoration of furniture must reflect life. To all artificial combinations it will prefer natural truth. It will have character, in other words it will possess life-lines, specific features, drawn from the physiological characteristics of species of flora and fauna, appropriately adapted to each material, to construction and to use by broad and necessary syntheses".[13] And Gallé stated: "The forms provided by plants are by their very nature adapted to woods. They are infinite in their variety and beauty. They are decorative by nature, by virtue of the characteristic structure of the various organs and stages of growth, in countless families, genera and species of plants, each of which possesses, so to say, its general and its particular style".[14] "I have used this method", Gallé went on to say, "in a few subordinate parts of my modern furniture: the silhouette of the gentianella, the flowerhead of the alpine 'everlasting", displays of flowers and fruit, garlands in baskets of wild carrots with their fan-shaped leaves, the multifoil whorls of the hemlock, the thorny and stellate erygium, black masterwort, sea-holly, and sometimes the tree-frog, snout in

64. *F. R. Carabin. Sculpted chair*

65-66. *F. R. Carabin. Sculpted furniture.*

his imagination. More often than not they are non- existent flowers, but which, logically formed, might well exist. What is more, this non-existence allows more freedom in their composition, grouping and attachment. What need have we to recognize such and such a flower in a decoration? Isn't it enough that it should be lissom of line, harmonious in tone, agreeable to the eye? This imaginative gift, this liberty, we often find in Dufrène, but always with a concern to make the form realistic, and not illogical, as we too often see elsewhere".[16]

The debate with the School of Nancy, with Emile Gallé, Louis Majorelle and Victor Prouvé, who whom ornament superceded construction, guided Maurice Dufrène to a more balanced and rational concept of form in furniture, in which he turned from the tapers and curves habitual to Art Nouveau to a manner close in substance to the Gothic tradition. In the field of decoration he opted for a sort of abstract floralism, in which he explored in a significant way the relationships between proportion and rhythm, opposing Alois Riegl's Stilfragen with a skilful contrast between fluidity and distinct geometry.

To this return to order, to this linking of form and structure and above all of form to the capacities of the machine, which enabled Dufrene to assert himself in 1905 in the competition of the Chambre Syndicale de l'Ameublement, came opposition from the "coloristes" who were much influenced by the success of the Ballets Russes: "At first these were no more than entertaining stage-setters, humorous upholsterers, excellent at throwing a stick or gloves onto an armchair, disposing a fan or the 'Almanach des Muses' on a side-table, arranging lemons or melons in a Persian bowl, hard-boiled eggs on

air, or the pond-frog, have helped me with decoration when shaping the mouldings of some small pieces and of their metal hinges".[15]

This is not the place to examine in greater depth the personality of Gallé, which reflects the School of Nancy, but it is opportune to underline the poetic part which he played in the development of new designs for furniture, even if his inclination to dedicate to each piece an epigraph in verse did not fail to arouse pointed controversy. Gallé's experimentalism, with its naturalist basis, assumed ever more didactic and semi-scientific tones, although it was pointed out to him that "a bed is a bed, and not a poem", and it was not of much importance to know the botanical details of a plant to draw inspiration from it. "Leaves and flowers are grouped in harmonious lines", wrote "Art et Décoration", praising the work of Maurice Dufrène, "and in well-balanced masses, without the cares of botanical exactitude interfering in any way with

67. *M. Dufrène. Bedroom. (1906).*

a green dish. Jaulmes, Süe, Huillard appeared, and Nathan Groult, Baignières, Drésa, André Mare and Mallet-Stevens. The latter produced a skilful mixture of echoes of the Directoire, a resuscitated neo-Pompeian, Louis-Philippe redivivus, the languishments of the Ballet Russe, the sensuality of Persian dances, and indeed the dismal geometry of German music rooms.[17]»

The relationship between clothes and interior decoration was so close that a woman's dress was regarded as a kind of artist's brush-stroke to harmonize with her surroundings, so much so that a couturier, the better to display his creations, would attach a furniture shop to his workrooms.[18] In this way, rare materials and precious woods were sought, moreover artificial processes were introduced. Mathieu Gallerey finished wood to obtain the colour of the most valued species, and even went so far as to stain oak with ammonia vapour. Subjected to such influences, furniture-making became "more rag-trade than joinery" and interior decoration more and more ephemeral. It must also be said that after Expo 1900 furniture design proceeded on two planes. Furniture was either an isolated piece considered entirely on its own merit and, thanks to its superior design, suitable to be placed in a traditional setting; or an object which enhanced the scheme of decoration by coordinating the colours of the furniture and its surroundings, emphasizing the unity of the decorative arts and inspiring not only a close

collaboration between the woodwork, doors, windows and glass, but also of every other feature - from the fabrics to the wallpaper - in short, all ornamental objects. Moreover, as the Pavillon Bing showed, the revival of colour was particularly striking. The palette was enriched by "symphonies in white, grey, pale blue, colours of the soul, deliquescent fantasies which the diaphanous light freezes like a moonbeam".[19] Thanks to the enchanting experiments of the Pointillistes and after, painting guided the other arts towards clarity, vivid tonality, and contrast.

Architecture, on the other hand, with

its spatial articulation and typological variety, added to its themes: "But let us not forget that we have just come into a private house, with curiously arranged rooms, of round forms succeeding square, breaks in the continuity of galleries, alcoves lit from above and below, harmoniously disposed in a paeam of colours sung by the most varied materials".[20] The invention of multi-purpose furniture remained outside of these two trends and only exerted a marginal influence. It tended to undermine traditional typology, providing opportunities for that experiment with continuity in proximity which characterizes architecture. The temptation was great to harmonize furniture and panelling, try to resolve in an original fashion the problem of the angle, seek to establish correspondence between chair and window or between supporting elements and seats. "Modern furniture likes this solidarity with the room in which it is placed. Moreover, its concern for comfort often links it to other furniture to form a single entity, logic and simplicity being the dominant considerations. Thus the dining room sideboard doubles as a serving-table, a set of shelves is attached to a settee, a cabinet to a work-table... "[21] This led to many absurd exaggerations, useless combinations and a superficial rationalism. But the important thing was that the tradition of recognized furniture types had been broken and that the theme of continuity and the problem of interrelationship had acquired an added strength.

THE BOULEVARD AND THE DECORATION OF MAJORELLE

At the turn of this century Paris contained about five hundred restaurants and more than two thousand cafés. The logic of an integrated scheme of decoration greatly appealed to the catering trade. In the traditional café, white, gold, and red velvet were replaced by the warm tones of the woodwork of Majorelle, exponent of the Nancy School, which was to give its name to this particular vogue in Art Nouveau.

Louis Majorelle had made his mark by 1890 after taking part in different salons. Like Gallé, Majorelle could be considered a naturalist: "My garden is my library", he often jested. He resorted frequently to marquetry decorated with very simple figurative motifs. A long way from the didactic experimentalism, scientific qualms and positivist vein of Gallé, Majorelle initiated a carefully weighed reinstatement of traditional themes, using them as a cover for exercises in Art Nouveau. Success smiled on him, especially when he was able - as in restaurants and public premises - to display the abiding qualities of his individuality in uninhibited freedom. Art Nouveau spread to the "cafés and restaurants, instead of the boulevard".[22]

In 1898 he decorated the Restaurant Voisin by Louis Bigaux, in 1899 the Hotel Langham by the architect Hurtré and the painter Jules Wilhorski [23] and the celebrated Maxim's by Louis Marnez and Léon Sonnier. The Brasserie Universelle by architect Edouard Niermans, which he decorated in 1902, already marked a decline. His most satisfying achievement is the Restaurant Lucas-Carton at the Madeleine (which survives practically intact). And it is here, in the gilded tones

71. *Majorelle. Detail of a bracket in the Restaurant Lucas- Carton.*

72-73. *L. Majorelle. Restaurant Lucas-Carton. Details of the woodwork.*

△ 75. H. Sauvage. *Salon in the Café de Paris,*
41 Avenue de l'Opéra, Paris 8ᵉ. (1899).
Altered.

△ 76. L. Marnez. *Restaurant Maxim's, 3 Rue*
Royale, Paris 8ᵉ. (1899). After a photograph
of the time.

△   74 and 77. Hurtré and J. Wielhorski.
Restaurant La Fermette Marbeuf, 5 Rue   ▷
Marbeuf, Paris 8ᵉ, formerly Restaurant of the
Langham Hotel, Rue Boccador.   View of
the interior. (1899).

of sycamore and mahogany woodwork, in the delicate marquetry of the paydesk and in the exquisite appliquéd bronze ornaments with sculptured heads, that Majorelle´s style is shown at its most convincing. Linking the spaces together by a subtle interplay of mirrors, preserving a sense of intimacy by continuous wall-sofas, separating the tables by panelling, it gives every table a particular character, and offers a hospitable setting for fashionable and varied gatherings by its ready adaptation to differing circumstances, from the tête-à-tête occasion to the grand banquet.

"When a fashionable restaurant has to be tackled", "L'Art Décoratif" wrote in of 1899, "the matter demands extreme tact. The customers of such establishments would not tolerate the heavy-handed effects that are suitable for a brasserie; to know how to be discreet, to be private, is essential; yet the passing guests who come there to be shaken momentarily from the apathy of their normal habits, 'for a changé', must not feel as if at home: this would be pointless. What is required is a salon which is a salon, but not the one they see every day. One could not find an art that better fulfils these conditions than that of Monsieur Majorelle, to whom the Café de Paris has turned for the renovation of three of its salons. Monsieur Majorelle´s art is indeed one which epitomizes the required intimate atmosphere, and it is also rare".[24] In the same review, Jourdain wrote in 1901 on the subject of furniture: "In the decoration of his furniture Majorelle has reduced images from nature to sensible limits, and in the use which he makes of them he is guided by a sure sense of the fitness of furniture. If he takes, for example, the roots or stock of a tree-trunk as his point of departure in studying the form of the leg of a piece of furniture,

79. L. Cauvy. Prize project for a dining room; concourse of Art et Decoration Magazine.

his aim - as his compatriots' would be - is to recall the natural growth, while providing a purely technical substitute of faultless elegance and ingenuity".[25] At this period Majorelle organized his production on an industrial scale, and his workshops for cabinet making, carving, marquetry and bronze accessories formed an economically viable enterprise, so that he was able to sell his luxurious furniture at reasonable prices.

Majorelle's success and ability to please rendered a great service to Art Nouveau after the failure sustained at the 1900 exhibition, "a failure all the more painful to record because of the general enthusiasm which beforehand had instilled confidence, rather blind perhaps, but full of goodwill, in the integrity and sincere convictions of the artists'.[26]

Majorelle's success and ability to please rendered a great service to Art Nouveau after the failure sustained at the 1900 exhibition, "a failure all the more painful to record because of the general enthusiasm which beforehand had instilled confidence, rather blind perhaps, but full of goodwill, in the integrity and sincere convictions of the artists'.[26] Majorelle's achievement encouraged the large stores to display Art Nouveau furniture, and decorators

like Grasset taught at the Ecole des Arts Décoratifs. In 1899 Louis Magne was appointed to the newly created chair in arts and crafts at the Conservatoire des Arts et Métiers, which was accorded to Louis Magne, who has been variously quoted here. On the eve of the war, in 1914, the Municipal Council organized a competition, which was won by Tony Selmersheim, for the decoration of the office of the President of the Assemblée Nationale at the Hôtel de Ville. This was the last manifestation of the delicate pastel colours of Art Nouveau before the cataclysm engulfed Europe.

ART IN EVERYTHING

Dating from 1897, the Société des Cinq was founded by Tony Selmersheim. It was soon to become the Société des Six, comprising Félix

Aubert, Alexandre Charpentier, Jean Dampt, Etienne Moreau-Nélaton, Charles Plumet and, of course, Selmersheim himself. They were to work in close collaboration. In their programme they advocated a reappraisal of the decorative arts, rejecting any distinction between major arts and minor, opting for logic and sincerity and propounding an open attitude to collaboration. Soon, to avoid accusations of exclusivism, they adopted the title of "L'Art dans Tout", increased the number of their adherents (Henri Sauvage, Albert Angst, Louis Sorel, Jean Dampt, Jules Desbois) and welcomed every artist sincerely concerned with producing objects for which "the conditions of practical use and genuine art are equally assured".[27] The most significant realization of the Exhibition of 1899 was the dining room door by Dampt, which consisted of a plain frame of a darker wood and panels which revealed the natural pattern of the grain disposed symmetrically. The only figurative elements were vine-shoots and and a corn-sheaf, the panelling being completely bare.

Sauvage was among those who in 1900 joined the group, which was united by a common principle: the relationship between "reason" and "charm" implied the study of pure form, independent of any decorative consideration. In 1901 the bedroom designed by Plumet and Selmersheim showed how "the sweep of the curves creates in itself an attractive impression, the contours seeming to flow one from another, linked in the pliancy of a natural movement";[28] while "with Monsieur Sauvage we can identify once again this double character in our furniture: the sweep and sincerity of the architectural line, and the broad contribution of surfaces in which the chosen material can play its part".[29] The logic of the construction, its role and the care in execution came not only from a close analysis of artistic taste, but also from a cultural background which made Roger Marx, Jean Lahor (by his real name Henry Cazalis, a physician) and Frantz Jourdain the advocates of an art for the masses. Lahor wrote in 1901, "We want - and this is really one of the characteristics of Art Nouveau - art to be available to everyone, like light and air, and we want it to be everywhere, in the artisan's home and in ours, in the school and the college, in all those university barrack blocks, generally so ugly and always lugubrious, at the hospital, and in our railway stations, in short wherever a crowd assembles, especially perhaps a working-class crowd."[30] The Société Internationale de l'Art Populaire - founded by Lahor and including in its ranks Gallé, Grasset, Lalique, Roger Marx, Sauvage and the Belgians Adolphe Crespin, Victor Horta and Gustave Serrurier-Bovy - and the Société du Nouveau Paris - founded by Jourdain in 1903 and counting among its members Roger Marx, Jules Chéret, Hector Guimard, Auguste Rodin and Henri Sauvage - were the two short-lived groups which were to defend this programme, which in other respects proved so harmful to Serrurier-Bovy's career.

The teaching of William Morris was not enough, and Art Nouveau failed to bring about the democratic art in which its most ardent champions believed, even if a hint of snobbery lingered in their neo-Jacobinism. The boulevard remained a prisoner of its worldly vanities, reflected narcissus-like in its mirrors, shielded by its cosy panelling, cut glass and pretty flowered carpets, rejecting this gust of fresh air, a little like Proust who wore his astrakhan overcoat in summer "since, tortured by a whom, a what, a when, he caught a chill between two parentheses".[31]

NOTES

1. L. Magne, "Le mobilier moderne à l'Exposition Universelle de 1900", in *Revue des Art Décoratifs*, XXI (1901°, p. 8.
2. G. Mourey, "L'Art Nouveau de M. Bing à l'Exposition Universelle", in *Revue des Arts Décoratifs*, XX (1900), p. 263.
3. R.-H. Guerrand, *L'Art Nouveau en Europe*, Paris 1965, p. 142.
4. R.-H. Guerrand, *op. cit.*, ibidem.
5. L. Moussinac, *Le Meuble Français Moderne*, Paris 1925, p. 41.
6. On G. Serrurier-Bovy see J.-G. Watelet, *Gustave Serrurier- Bovy, architecte et décorateur*, 1858-1910, Brussels, Mémoire de l'Académie Royale de Belgique 1975 and J.-G. Watelet, Serrurier-Bovy. *From Art Nouveau to Art Déco*, London, Lund Humphries, Brussels, Atelier Vokaer 1986.
7. R.-H. Guerrand, *op. cit.*, p. 139.
8. J. Laran, "Quelques meubles de G. De Feure au Salon du Mobilier", in *Art et Décoration*, n° 10, October 1908, p. 132.
9. R.-H. Guerrand, *op. cit.*.
10. L. Magne, *op. cit.*, p. 7.
11. L. Moussinac, *op. cit.*, p. 34.
12. L. Moussinac, *op.cit.*, p. 35.
13. E. Gallé, "Le mobilier contemporain orné d'après nature", in *Revue des Arts Décoratifs*, XX (1900), p. 335.
14. E. Gallé, *op. cit.*, p. 341.
15. E. Gallé, *op. cit.*, p. 370-371.
16. M.P. Verneuil, "Maurice Dufrène Décorateur", in *Art et Décoration* n° 3, March 1906, p. 78.
17. E. Bayard, *op. cit.*, pp. 257-258.
18. E. Bayard, *op. cit.*, p. 260.
19. E. Bayard, *op. cit.*, p. 281.
20. E. Bayard, *op. cit.*, p. 284.
21. E. Bayard, *op. cit.*, p. 276.
22. S. Arbellot, *La fin du Boulevard*, Paris 1965, pp. 54 and sqq.
23. On the restaurant of the Langham Hôtel, Rue Boccador, see F. Weyl, "Décoration d'un restaurant", in *Art et Décoration*, V (1899), I semester, pp. 16-21. The installation of the restaurant of the Langham Hôtel has been reconstructed at the restaurant "Fermette Marbeuf", Rue Marbeuf.
24. Musée Grévin, "L'Art au Restaurant", in *Art Décoratif*, n° 4, January 1899, p. 161.
25. O. Gerdeuil, "Les Meubles de Majorelle", in *Art Décoratif*, n° 37, October 1901, pp. 19-20.
26. P. Olmer, *La Renaissance du Mobilier Français* (1860- 1910), Paris 1927, p. 22.
27. "La Société de L'Art dans Tout'", in *Art et Décoration*, vol. V, 1899, p. 82.
28. G. Soulier, "L'Art dans Tout", in *Art et Décoration*, vol. IX, n° 4, April 1901, p. 130.
29. G. Soulier, *op. cit.*, p. 136.
30. R.-H. Guerrand, *op. cit.*, p. 180.
31. S. Arbellot, *op. cit.*, p. 40.

80-81. H. Guimard. Castel Orgeval, 2 Rue de la Mare-Tambour, Villemoisson. (1904-05).
View from the garden (page 66). Entrance and turret (page 67).

V

HECTOR GUIMARD

TRAINING AND EARLY CAREER

Hector Guimard, in his essential development, is no child of the Ecole des Beaux-Arts: this premise is fundamental to a sequence of events linked together by a remarkable coherence or historic providence. At the outset Guimard seems to have had to recommend him only the engaging freshness of receptive youth and his natural talents.

Born in Lyons in 1867, he was scarcely fifteen when he entered the Ecole des Arts Décoratifs in Paris, where a young disciple of Viollet-le-Duc, Charles Genuys, was teaching and where he obtained his diploma in 1885. He then enrolled at the Ecole des Beaux-Arts, choosing the Atelier Libre of Gustave Raulin, founded in 1860 by Emile Vaudremer, who had been the spearhead of a provocative rationalism leading to a marriage between the idiom of Viollet-le-Duc and the institutional style of the big state commissions, notably correction establishments and schools. Raulin was not content to follow in the footsteps of his illustrious predecessor; he drew inspiration from Hector Horeau, the

glass-house builder, and performed important work for private clients. In 1889 Guimard was admitted in second year, but - like the Perret brothers - did not enter for the diploma, which was not obligatory at this time. Ten years earlier, Atelier Vaudremer included Louis Sullivan, who admired its critical spirit, while remaining convinced "that this great school, in its perfect flower of technique, lacked the profound animus of a primal inspiration".[1]

Guimard was among the finalists for the Prix de Rome in 1889, but was eliminated in the final test. Historical providence seems to have played some part here, for what could Rome have taught him? Would a thorough

knowledge of history have helped or hindered him? Instead, Guimard became a professor at the Ecole des Arts Décoratifs. The Director was Jacques-Auguste-Gaston Louvrier de Lajolais, an indifferent landscape painter, but an excellent educator. He had renamed his establishment, which was still known in Viollet-le-Duc's day as the Ecole Municipale de Dessin et de Mathématiques.

Guimard was given charge of the course in drawing and perspective for girls. The Director described him as "very intelligent, amenable and docile",[2] and he had some success with his students, although his duties - twelve hours a week for one term a year - were not demanding. Five years later Louvrier de Lajolais suggested that he should take on the course in perspective of his old studio master Genuys, but Guimard's teaching career was interrupted by his professional activities.

In 1887 he came third in a competition for a branch savings bank at Le Mans, and a year later he was placed among the first ten for the building of the Hôtel de Ville at Calais. In 1888 he was responsible for a "café-restau-

82. H. Guimard. Hotel Roszé, 34 Rue Boileau, Paris 16ᵉ. (1891). Façade.

83. H. Guimard. Private Mansion, 63 Avenue Charles-de-Gaulle, Issy-les-Moulineaux. (1893). Overall view.

rant" on the Quai d'Auteuil.[3] Aged twenty-two, he built for the Exhibition of 1889 a little pavilion rather pompously called "Pavillon de l'Electricité", and two years after this a small house, the Roszé house, at 34 Rue Boileau, in which it is already possible to detect signs of what were to be his favourite features: asymmetry, articulation of masses, conspicuous external handling of staircases by a staggered arrangement of openings, the pitched roof contrasting with the horizontal cornices of the pavilion or truss-roof covering the two other elements of the building, the preference taste for brickwork interrupted by a large stone arch in a bow- window, and the use of turquoise blue earthenware with elements of terracotta. This typical character was to appear in the most natural manner in two works of 1893: the house at 63 Avenue de Clamart (today Charles de Gaulle) at Issy-les-

84. *H. Guimard. «Pavillon de l'Electricité» at the International Exhibition of 1889.*

85-86. *H. Guimard. Hotel Jassedé, 44 Rue Chardon-Lagache, Paris 16ᵉ. (1893). General view and façade detail.*

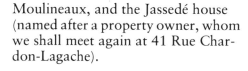

Moulineaux, and the Jassedé house (named after a property owner, whom we shall meet again at 41 Rue Chardon-Lagache).

The Jassedé house is remarkable for frequent recourse to iron and earthenware, but also for combining stone and brick with rustic rendering and exposed rubble masonry, and also for an oriental type of refinement, as - for example - in the bronze termination to a boundary wall and the little canopy over the entrance gate. Guimard's uninhibited freedom linked mediaeval echoes and English taste in his use here, for the first, time of a glazed canopy supported by a metal frame, which overhangs the balcony and protects the large opening of the sitting-room.

Without being true Art Nouveau, the ironwork followed no known prece-

*87-88. H. Guimard. Travel drawings. Country houses in Farnham (above)
and in the Isle of Wight (below). (August 1894).*

dent; its oriental influences were not those of Japan, widely represented in the figurative world of the French nineteenth century; his inspiration was more Thai in feeling. In short, it was a union of several eclecticisms. In the Jassedé house, Guimard solved for the first time the problem of interior decoration in a coherent and comprehensive way. He rejected historical eclecticism, which consisted in juxtaposing a Louis XIV bedroom, an Empire study and a Henri II dining-room: "Domestic ornamentation", he wrote later, "is purely deductive in kind; the lines of the most humble furniture should reflect the character of the whole dwelling, of the house conceived by an artist, for the harmony which determines the style is the indispensable condition for designing a home".[4]

The following year, 1894, may truly be considered decisive for Guimard, for he was now to become aware of his own potential. With the help of a travel bursary he went to England, where he showed a fresh interest in the chalet and the Scottish domestic revival. Far from being satisfied with John Ruskin's writings and the studies of Hermann Muthesius, he made several field trips, returning with an album of watercolours which bear witness to his flair for painting, the vitality of his draughtsmanship and the architect's keen interest in three-dimensional form and the "picturesque" relationships between the elements of roofs and vertical structures.

Guimard then went to Belgium and found in Victor Horta's Tassel house confirmation of that which he had been seeking until now, and indeed a new concept of the disposition of spatial elements, a structural fluidity which was entirely novel, and the use of iron both for loadbearing members and for interior decoration, in which the young Horta had shown great talent in his "première œuvre". The meeting between the two men will always be remembered for Horta's alleged advice : "Leave the flowers and the leaves, and grasp the stalk". Although in his "Mémoires" Horta, in his idiosyncratic, weary manner, seems to have regarded this meeting as a kind of sponsorship, he does not claim, as do the majority of critics, that this was Guimard's Road to Damascus. And indeed, when the main trends revealed by Guimard in his early career are analysed, one finds in them an eager interest in materials like earthenware, terracotta and stone, applied in an abstract context, and many allusions to the English picturesque style - characteristics foreign to Horta's more rigid training, which was born of his opposition to Alphonse Balat's rigorous classicism and advocated in private building the technique of metal construction already widely

89. H. Guimard. Hotel Delfau, 1ᵗᵉʳ Rue Molitor, Paris 16ᵉ. (1894-95).

applied in public architecture. Guimard regarded the Tassel house "as a kind of masterpiece synthetizing the manner of a genuine master. .. Yet Horta has not carried the application of his principles to the ultimate. He has accepted fireplaces, pieces of furniture, and wallpaper from England, designed by English artists. Monsieur Guimard did not believe it possible to achieve a total unity in a work, whatever its complexity, without designing everything down to the smallest detail. In

the Castel Béranger he designed even the stair- carpet."[5]

The meeting with the Belgian architect, who was slightly older than he, proved therefore both a revelation and a confirmation.[6] But there were some - with echoes of chauvinism - who considered it merely a passing fancy. In "Art et Décoration", for example, in 1899: "If the reader cares to compare Horta's style and that of Monsieur Guimard's designs, he will

be quickly convinced that the one comes from the other and exaggerates it without understanding its spirit, and I do not think that Monsieur Guimard in any way denies this origin. Without disputing Horta's merit, there was perhaps something better for a French artist to do than to go and seek inspiration in Belgium. We should have preferred to be witnessing an attempt, albeit incomplete, to revive the old French Style".[7]

It was also in 1894 that Auguste Vaudremer finished the new church at Auteuil. During the arguments conducted by the partisans of demolition or entire reconstruction of the old church, Guimard was commissioned to restore in a rather "pop" style certain features of the Romanesque chapel, so as to make of it a little monument of sorts dedicated to the Virgin. It is insignificant as a work, but important to him for the professional contacts which he made with the Historical Society of Auteuil and Passy, for whom he was working, and especially with Madame Fournier, who entrusted him with a block of flats in the Rue La Fontaine.

As in the case of the Delfau house in the Rue Molitor which, given the relationship between the two buildings, may be considered as a kind of preliminary project, the first drawings were characterized by neo-mediaeval feeling and an austere facing of ashlar. On his return from Belgium, however, Guimard succeeded in persuading his client to transform completely the design submitted to the municipality (and still preserved in its archives) and adopt an entirely new idiom. Thus, out of a commonplace six-storey house of thirty-six flats he was to make one of the more celebrated works in architectural history, giving to it, by a curious semantic intuition,

90. H. Guimard. Castel Béranger, 14 Rue La Fontaine, Paris 16e. (1895-98). First project, drawing of the façade.

90. *H. Guimard. Castel Béranger, 14 Rue La Fontaine, Paris 16ᵉ. (1895-98). First project, drawing of the façade.*

▷ 91. *H. Guimard. Castel Béranger. First project, drawing of the sections.*

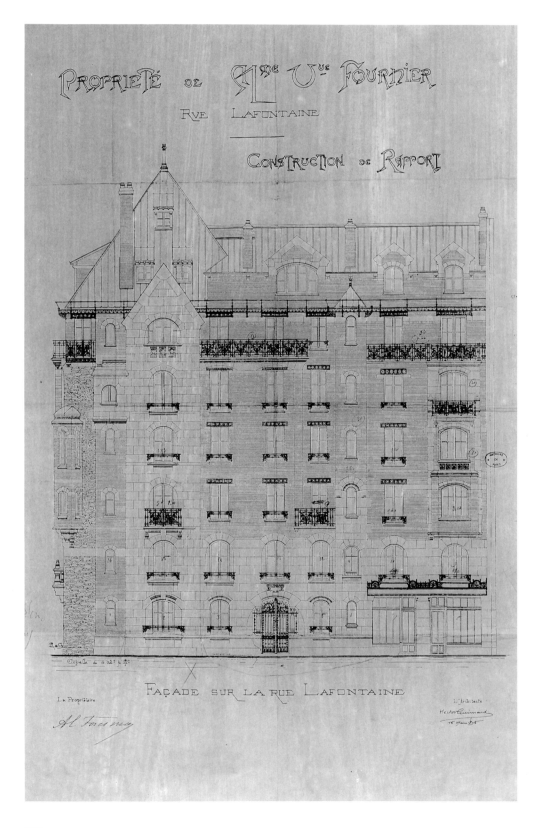

the name of Castel Béranger (after a little private road adjoining the site), which encouraged some who may have been startled by this intemperate intrusion into stylistic convention to call it "Castel dérangé". Compared with Belgian examples which, because of the individuality of the owners, were almost houses built to measure, the Castel Béranger was a simple block of apartments having the inherent problems of passages, landings, many staircases and an internal court, here sensibly left open to a little private road at right angles to the Rue La Fontaine.

In his design, Guimard tackled the problems of space and, above all, economic rentability with the same enthusiasm which he had shown in attending to all the details of the little chalets built by him up to now. To diminish the impression of mass, he continually varied his themes and thus allowed a sort of eclecticism to emerge out of his personal predilections, which included neo-mediaeval forms, the style and metalwork of Horta, a progressive rationalism and that indulgence in moments of unbridled fantasy and impulse which earned him the title of "Ravachol de l'architecture". To reduce expenses, Guimard embarked to a rather primitive extent upon the mass production of the elements of that remarkable vocabulary of decoration - to which he resorted, in a typically practical way, on a variety of jobs.

But we will examine in greater detail this building, which certainly deserves close study, when we analyse in a general way Guimard's idiom. For the moment it is interesting to note that the essentially innovative character of the work inspired both a positive reaction and a certain prudent caution. To have vanquished

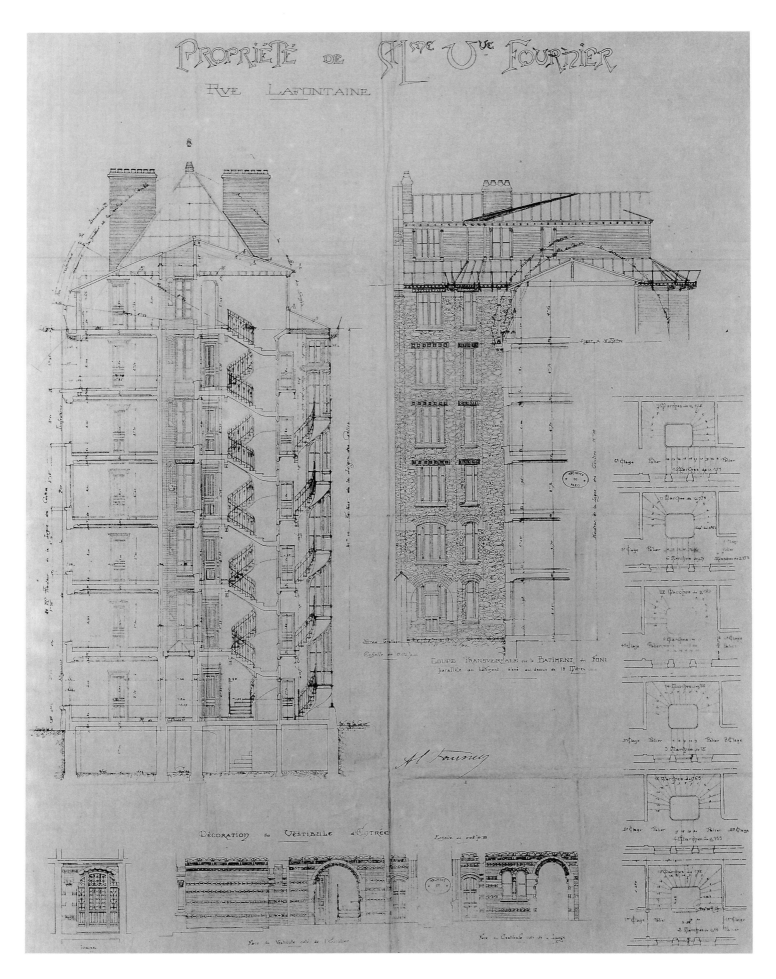

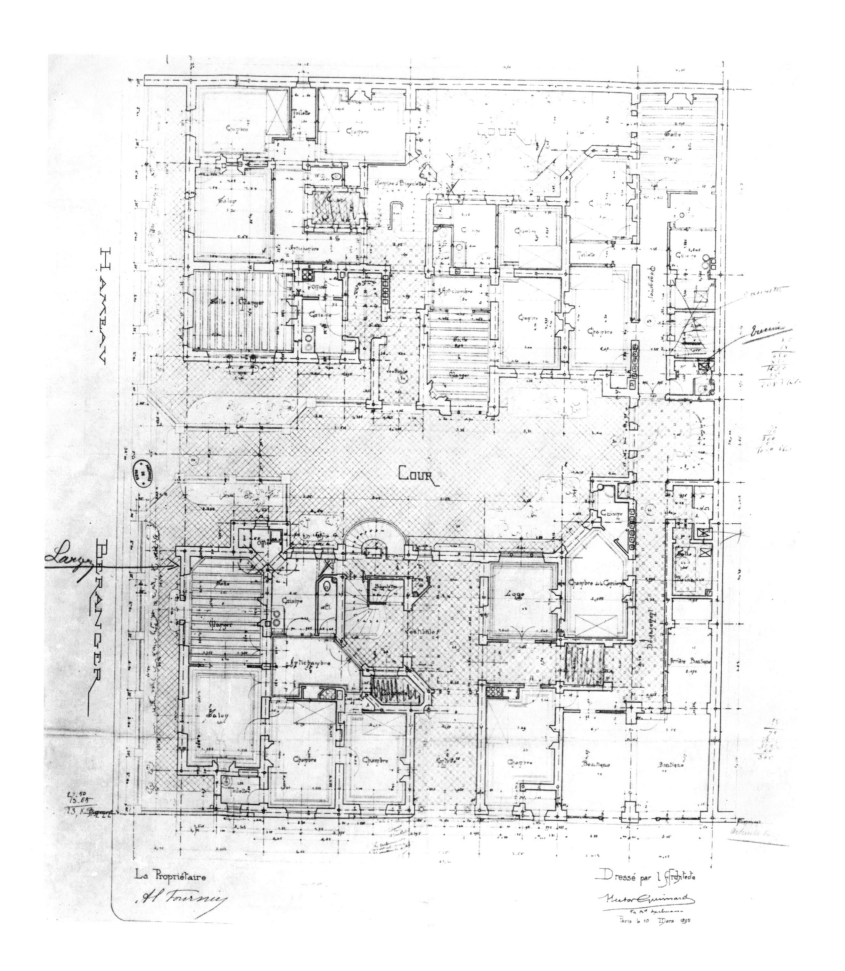

92. *H. Guimard. Castel Béranger. First project, plan.*

convention," observed the "Moniteur des Arts" of January 1899, "to have convinced an intelligent client, a woman in this case, fought and defeated the contractors, ousted the tradesmen from their normal age-old methods, upsetting their customary routine, that alone shows determination and energy which, disregarding other factors, exalt the man who is capable of it".[8]

Guimard appreciated the high risk which he ran in posing as an "revolutionary architect", for he might have found himself isolated. In "La Construction Moderne" of May 1899, we read that Guimard, in a talk given at the inauguration of the exhibition staged at "Le Figaro" relating to the Castel Béranger, explained his theories on the art and technology of building. He had developed rationalist ideas which guided him in the construction of the Castel Béranger, and he defended himself against the accusation of wanting to be new at any cost.[9] Another critic asserted that "he takes pride in the sound logic of his reasoning and discusses his method in lively style".[10] When he invited the journalist Louis-Charles Boileau to this lecture, Guimard wrote: "You have seen how nothing could be farther from my thoughts than to act the eccentric; I am the first to be surprised that with classical principles one could be so new. .. decoratively, my principles are perhaps new, but they are grafted on to those applied by the Greeks, especially in their native setting. I am not the cause of the new circumstances of our time, and - in short - I have only applied Viollet-le-Duc's theory, but without being hypnotized by mediaeval forms".[11]

Guimard understood that he had to exploit his success intelligently. Three

96-98. H. Guimard. Castel Béranger.
Entrance. Details of the ceiling and walls
(above) and overall view (below).

99. H. Guimard. Castel Béranger.
Perspective view.

100 H. Guimard. Castel Béranger. View
        from the courtyard.

101. H. Guimard. Castel Béranger. The
        main entrance.

years before, "L'Architecture" pointed
out that Guimard had allowed nothing
but a sketch of the entrance doorway
to be published, while promising to
produce a monograph on the building
as a whole. "I had to be content, after
special permission, to give an indication of the general outline of the
entrance door", the journalist wrote.
He then interviewed Guimard, who
declared: "All the models, drawings
and mock-ups have been done under
my care and are my property except
for Lincrusta-Walton's panelling in
the dining rooms, which I left at
home".[12] In discussing the work at
some length and praising the choice of
furniture, a writer in the "Revue des
Arts Décoratifs" of 1899 enumerated
all the points which were to occasion
the clearest reservations and the most
lively opposition: "At the present time
we have reached in art a period of
cacophony which corresponds approximately to the kind of intellectual
and moral anarchy amid which our
contemporary individualist society is
feeling its way. Let us not be too
astonished therefore at the
antics of artists in search of novel
formulas; they are merely the consequence of such anarchy".[13]

"Art et Decoration" published an even
more forceful criticism: "By yielding
to the fairly general feeling that a new
style is needed, Monsieur Guimard has
been led into creating a work which, in
being homogeneous, is not beyond
reproach: not only, as I said at the
beginning, because the style startles,
but because at a large number of
points it strays too far from what we
are used to seeing. Quality, you say;
flaws too, I reply. Its construction
produces rather the effect of the work
of a lost civilization seeking a sudden
return to the light of day".[14]

The description which follows sketches

a portrait of Guimard at one of his talks: "The lecturer himself is a young man, tall, dark, with very black curly hair and beard trimmed to a point, very elegant, of handsome appearance".[15] "Yes, yes, I know," Hector Guimard replied, performing wide circles with his huge arms, "I know what they say and I pay no attention. I shall stick to my goals, because I know that I am right. It is to nature, you see, that we must look for advice. When I build a house, when I design furniture or carve, I think of the splendour offered us by the universe, in which beauty appears in perpetual variety. Neither parallelism, nor symmetry; forms are engendered by ever-changing movements; you have an impression of unity achieved by infinite variety. And what decorative scheme could be finer, more intoxicating? Then consider just one of these plants which, assembled in masses, make a forest; see how each tree, each bush, differs from its neighbours: not one branch resembling another; no two flowers alike. And what a lesson for the architect, the artist, who knows how to look at this admirable repertory of forms and colours! As for construction, isn't it the branches of trees, and the stalks of plants, now rigid, now sinuous, which furnish us with models?"[16] Despite his moderation, Victor Champier concluded: "When Guimard grandiloquently expands his reforming theories, we can only leave him to it. No doubt there are plenty of follies in what he calls 'doctrines', but - in the end - what do words matter? It is the work that is the artist."[17]

While the Castel Béranger accentuated the fantastic side of his personality, Guimard was not content with defending its rationalism in his "talks", but he gave a concrete example of it with the completion of the Ecole du Sacré-

Cœur, Avenue de la Frillère. Built on a long and narrow site, it consists of a dwelling-house and a building of about 21 feet (7 meters) in depth and comprising seven rooms which face an open space. The structure is carried on one side on a blind wall, according to a principle dear to Guimard, and is oriented towards the little garden giving on to the street. The ground floor is completely open and the floors are supported, on the street frontage, against a wall incorporating a wide glazed bay. The class-room tract as a whole rest on a continuous steel beam, supported by two intermediate cast-iron V-shaped supports at the height of the portico, and by two other smaller sloping supports attached to the masonry abutments at either end. It is a faithful echo of Viollet-le-Duc's "Entretiens", even if the cast-iron is tapered and modelled to a very Guimardian design. The rather sharp-edged fluting pivots in a gentle spiral towards the top. Above the double-T beam with its exposed riveting, Guimard also leaves uncovered the structural elements of the floor. For the façade he makes expressive use of his technical expertise: the polychrome brick interlined with stone courses; the windows of the second storey with arches slightly depressed and strengthened by two slender brick mullions; the large triform windows of the first floor, which, with their iron colonnettes and the lintels with extruded elements of terracotta, recall Horta; the decorative grace of the ends of the flooring on which the butts of the secondary beams are picked out in white; and, finally, the terracotta facing of the little vaults resting on stone elements fixed to the inside of the flange of the beams.

It is certainly fortunate that this «exercise in the elements of construction has survived, in spite of demolition threats.

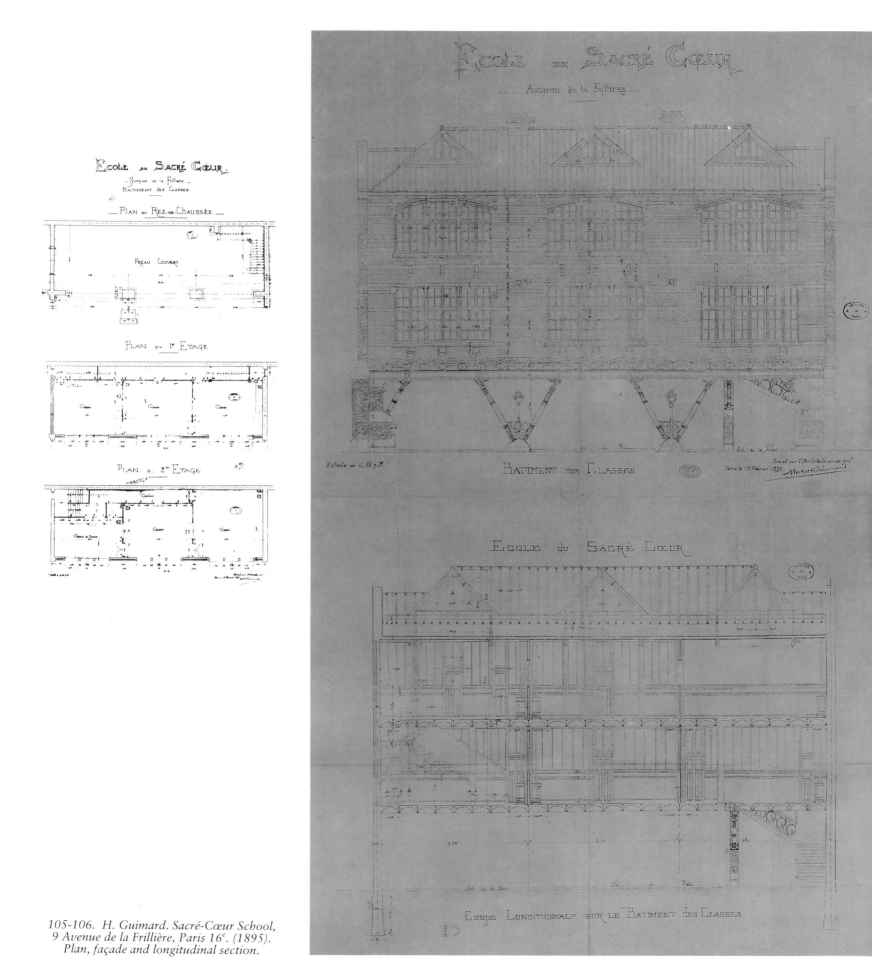

105-106. H. Guimard. Sacré-Cœur School,
9 Avenue de la Frillière, Paris 16ᵉ. (1895).
Plan, façade and longitudinal section.

But this can only make us regret all the more the loss of Guimard's most significant work, as much from the spatial point of view as for its structural importance. This was the Concert Hall dedicated to the "Blessed Humbert de Romans", general of the Dominicans at the time of Saint Louis. The building which Father Lavy was to commission Guimard to build for the teaching of religious music was to be his last job for the Catholic church.

The misty "rêveries" of the young architect did not befog the Dominicans who put their faith in his success and promising future. This attitude was typical of a progressive French church which, with the help of the foundation of the Société Immobilière of the Rue Saint-Didier, found sufficient resources to build a hall with 1800 seats, the largest in Paris after that of the Trocadéro.

The hall included a large organ, its loft also serving as a chapel, and a library. It also housed the central office of the "Dames Patronnesses". For the first time Guimard was faced with designing a roof of about 72 feet (27 meters) span. But he had the skill to create entirely original three-dimensional forms of economical regular plan, which provided a balanced distribution of space and ingenious contrivances to reduce the inequalities of the site in relation to the symmetry of the two axes of the principal hall. After having constructed a solid, finely modelled stone casing extending from the basement to the gallery, he fixed to it the roofing elements, comprising eight pillars corresponding to the angles of the irregular octagon. These pillars, in the form of a truncated cone, rose towards the ceiling where, by means of a system of branches and inclined members, they were linked to the horizontal fabric on which the roof rested. From what can be seen from the drawings of the scheme (for the hall was destroyed soon after 1905) and from some rather indistinct postcards, this structure was of quite extraordinary spatial significance.[18]

In the structure of the rafters "à la Viollet-le-Duc" and in their fan-like arched supports, Guimard introduced the pliant forms of the vegetable kingdom, but exploiting less the "stalk" than the trunk and branches of the tree. And it was both the absence of curves, i.e. of focuses of reflection, in the roof, and the distribution of sound-waves resulting from the remarkable arrangement of the pillars, which allowed excellent acoustics to be obtained. Nor was Guimard a prisoner of the daring symmetrical structural system which he invented; he treated the roof in sections in an unusual manner, adopting a different

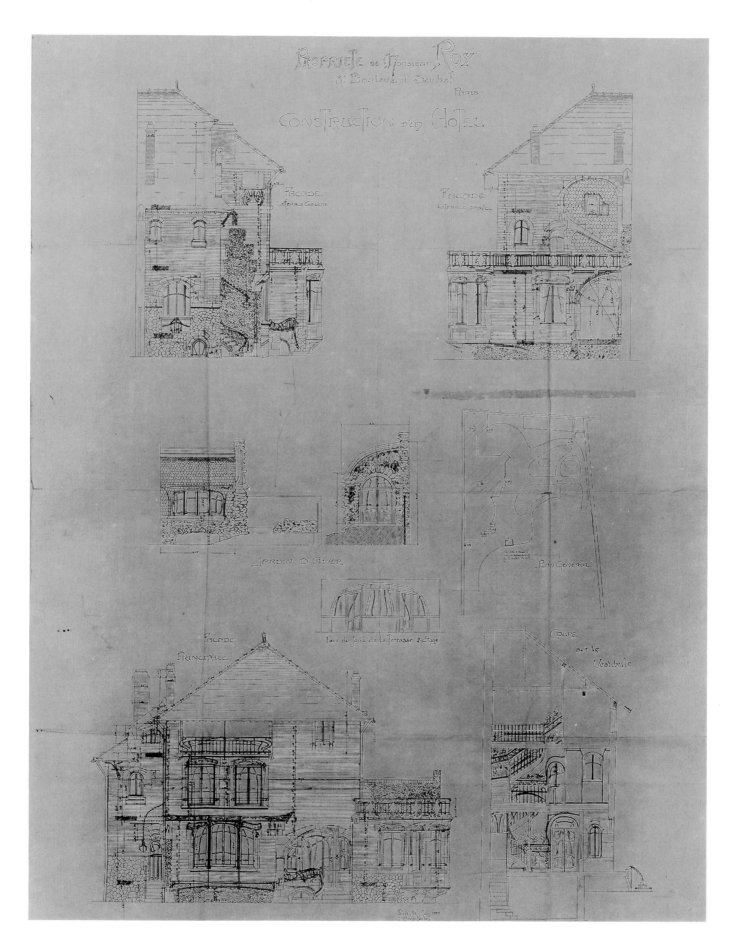

110. H. Guimard. Hôtel Roy, 81 Boulevard Suchet, Paris 16ᵉ. (1897). Demolished.

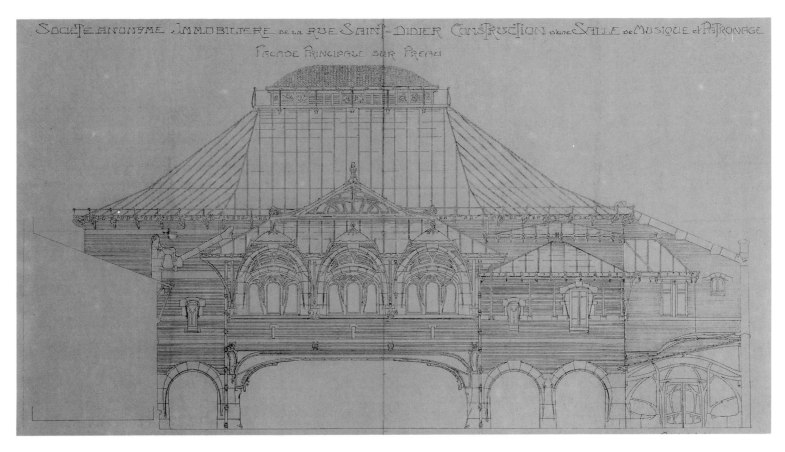

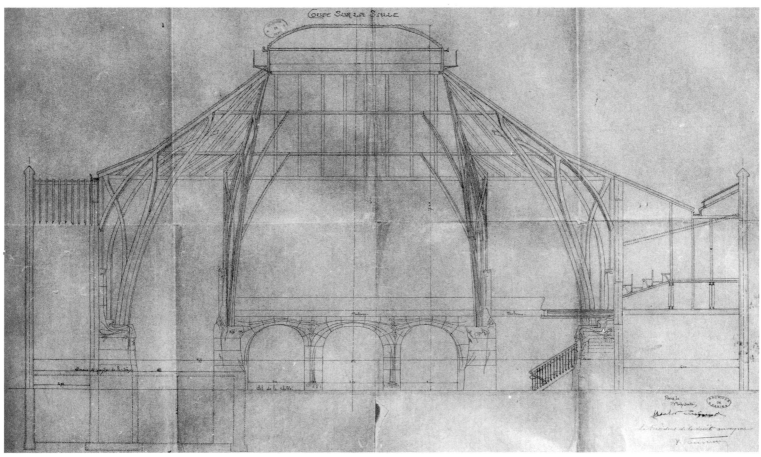

111-112. H. Guimard. Humbert de Romans Concert Hall, 58-60 Rue Saint-Didier, Paris 16ᵉ.
(1898-1901). Demolished. Plans of façade and section.

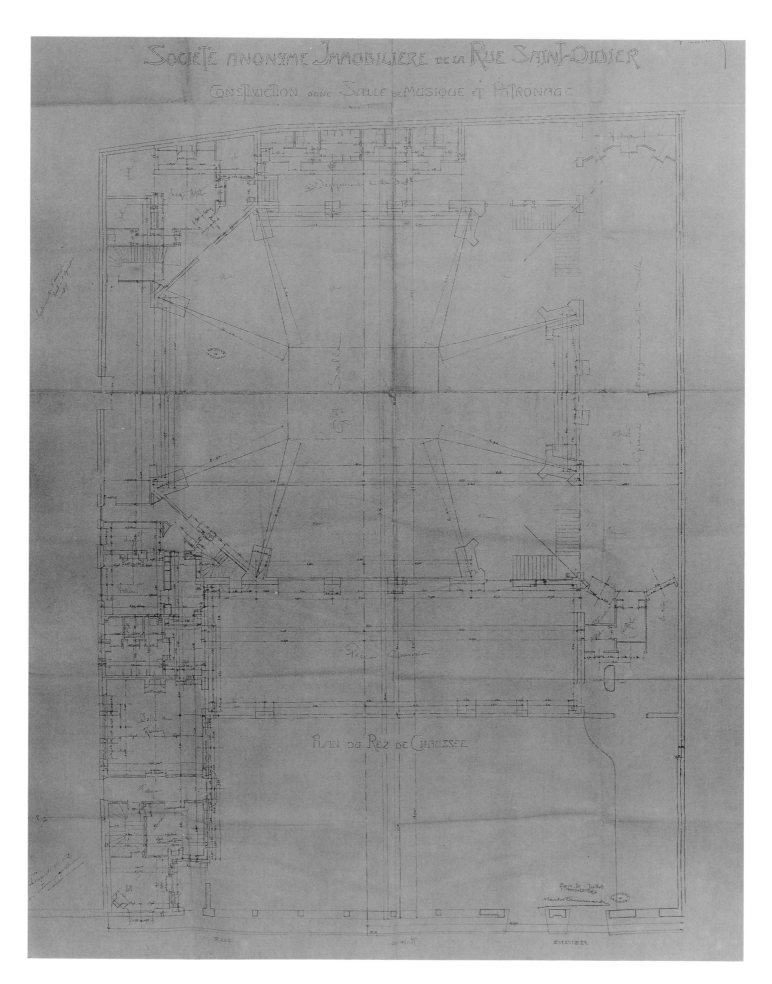

SOCIÉTÉ ANONYME IMMOBILIÈRE DE LA RUE SAINT-DIDIER

CONSTRUCTION D'UNE SALLE DE MUSIQUE ET PATRONAGE

PLAN DU REZ DE CHAUSSÉE

113. H. Guimard.
Humbert de Romans
Concert Hall.
Plan of the ground
floor.

114-115. H.
Guimard.
Humbert de
Romans Concert
Hall. Façade and
stairs to the
galleries.

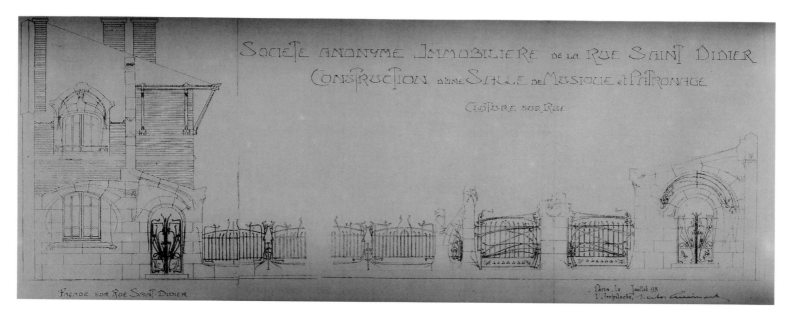

SOCIÉTÉ ANONYME IMMOBILIÈRE DE LA RUE SAINT DIDIER
CONSTRUCTION D'UNE SALLE DE MUSIQUE et PATRONAGE
CLOTURE SUR RUE

FAÇADE SUR RUE SAINT DIDIER

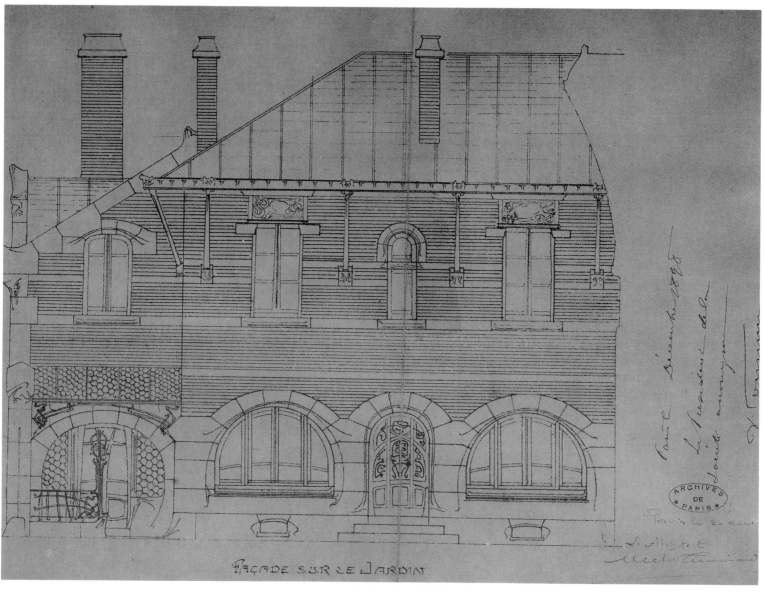

FAÇADE SUR LE JARDIN

116-117. *H. Guimard. Humbert de Romans Concert Hall. Drawings of the conciergerie.*

solution for the stage and the galleries, and allowing the light to enter by means of curious openings in the side facing the stage. "Lighting comes principally from above, where colours similar to the tones of the glass used in metro stations give a very soft light in the hall".[19]

The formal elements of the design show great freedom in combining Horta's taste for the fine handling of stone with the theme of continuity apparent in the strictly horizontal courses of the cladding, as well as in the Art Nouveau style of the iron work with its characteristic "whiplash" motif. The mahogany structural frame incorporating metal elements inevitably suggests Gothic timberwork, but in a context of uninhibited modernity. Although the documents which have come down to us are extremely sparse, it is possible to advance a general hypothesis and trace a sort of parallel between the importance for Guimard of the Salle de Musique Religieuse and that of the Maison du Peuple for Horta in Brussels - the more so in view of the coincidence of dates.

THE GUIMARD STYLE

Everyone of the artist's drawings, their simple technique well-fitted to his style, bears the inscription "Hector Guimard, style Guimard". Was this narcissism or a deep sense of deliberate isolation? There is no doubt that Guimard had a sharp eye for propaganda and exploited the slightest opportunity to gain publicity.

He also knew that his name evoked both the patient craftsman designing every detail and the man who had

118. H. Guimard. Monceau Metro station. Detail of the entrance: cast-iron decorations.

reinvented the language of architecture. An opportunity unique of its kind was presented to him in 1899, when the Metropolitan (railway) Company organized a competition for the entrance "pavilions" of metro stations, as well as for the two stations of the Bastille and the Etoile. The winners were Jean-Henry Duray, Charles Lemaresquier (both studio-masters at the Ecole des Beaux-Arts) and Pomier. Despite this result we can read in a contemporary review: "Of the thirty or forty designs submitted in the competition opened last year for this purpose, those which fulfilled the required conditions were of such a paltry artistic standard that the authorities shrank from using them. Monsieur Hector Guimard, whom the Municipal Council commissioned to

undertake the work after this failure, brought it to a very happy conclusion".[20] It was a victory over the academic world and an opportunity to show everybody that which was the Guimard style. Adopting a vocabulary which rejected any influences on decorative features from environmental considerations, Guimard provoked violent discussion, which began in particular with the Opera station, with its glass canopies and roofs supported by elaborate cast-iron elements bidding uncompromising defiance to institutional eclecticism. Here too, despite the simplicity of the theme and the restricted dimensions, as can still be seen today at the stations of the Porte Dauphine and the Place des Abbesses, Guimard resolved every problem in a practical way, but with irrepressible imagination, analysing and moulding each element according to its function with unfailing originality.

The lighting of notices and maps of the metro system, the discharge of rainwater, the supporting elements, the weather hoods and screens, the seating of the stanchions on the stonework and the balustrades, were all the occasion for reappraising the components of architecture and for replenishing his sources of inspiration from the realm of plants and from the bone-structures of animals.

Cast-iron can easily be produced in quantity, allowing appreciable economies and rapid execution. The marriage between glass and metal, and the rarity of an architectural idiom unconnected with any stylistic tradition, were the distinguishing marks of a work of fundamental value, a harmony untouched by classicism, and a modernity which, enhanced by the rich greens of the cast-iron panels, could

119-121. *H. Guimard. Bastille Metro station, entrance, (1900 - demolished), Etoile (1900-demolished) and Porte Dauphine (detail of the porch roof).*

124. *H. Guimard. Place des Abbesses Metro station. Entrance. General view.*

122-123. *H. Guimard. Hôtel de Ville Metro station. (1900), now on Place des Abbesses. Details.*

stand unembarrassed beside the austere circular toll-house, the Barrière of Claude-Nicolas Ledoux, at the "Entrée de Monceau". Cast-iron opened up certain possibilities, but it also had its limitations; that it is to say, it lacked qualities which are inherent in materials of greater resistance. Because of this, and in spite of a studied elegance in every element, Guimard's stations suffer from a certain timidity, a structural restraint, and make us think of forms roughly sketched, which have not yet attained their full potential. Such reservations notwithstanding, his challenge was strong enough to cause the most vigorous reactions. The municipal authorities proposed the construction of simple balustrades in place of the entrance "pavilions"; at the Opéra station it was decided to replace the cast-iron balustrade in the Guimard style by a stone one of utterly characterless monumentality. Passy turned its back on Guimard; the two stations at the Etoile were demolished, a new design of balustrade was commissioned from the architect Dervaux, and right up to the time of the well known exhibition at the Louvre - which was to establish Guimard among the pioneers of the twentieth century - the process of dismantling or replacing Guimard's stations continued, relegating most of the few that survived to the suburbs and rural obscurity.

From now on the public authorities no longer turned to Guimard and, as we have seen, the exhibition of 1900 gave little space to Art Nouveau architectu-

128. *H. Guimard. Workshop and town house for an artist, belonging to Mr Nozal, 12 Avenue Perrichont, Paris 16ᵉ. (1903).*

129-131. *H. Guimard. Hotel Nozal, 52 Rue Ranelagh, Paris 16ᵉ. (1904). Demolished. Drawing for the fence, elevation and plan.*

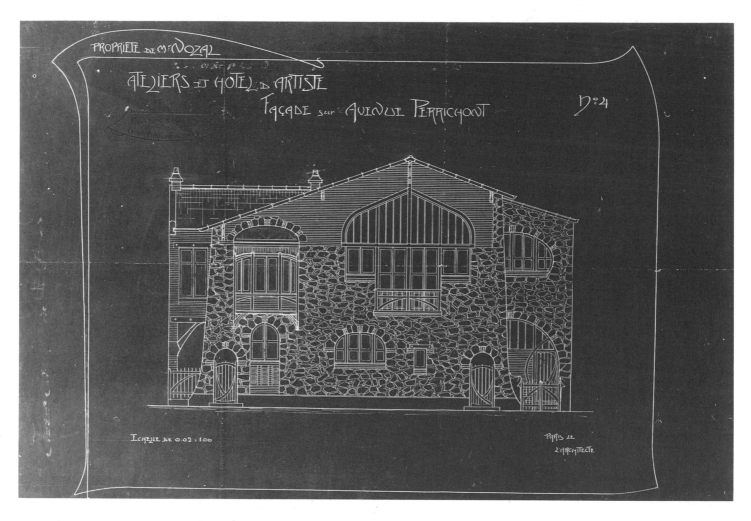

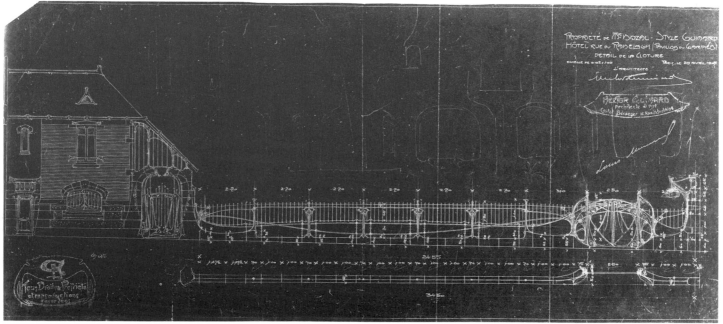

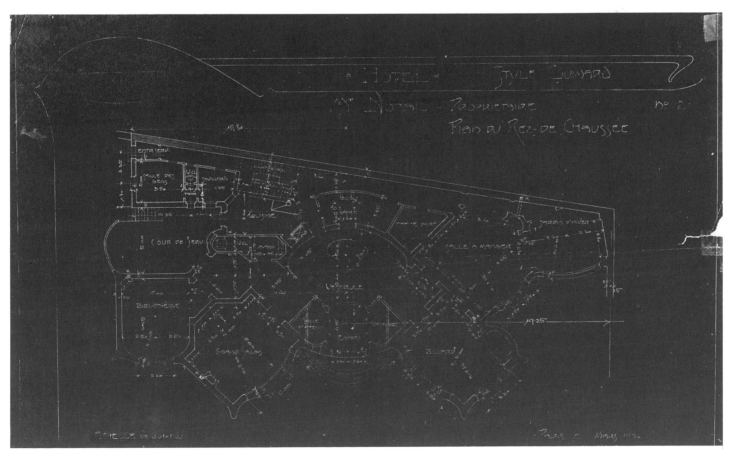

132. *H. Guimard. Hotel Nozal. Overall view of the façade.*

re. Guimard had therefore to work exclusively for private clients and, to avoid the problems which seldom fail to occur between the latter, the architect and the contractor, he decided in the end to combine the functions of the last two.

Guimard's most important contact was with the Nozals, a family of rich industrialists, who invited him to build successively a factory at Saint-Denis, a luxurious house in the Rue de Ranelagh (destroyed in 1957) and a villa oddly named "La Surprise", at the fashionable resort of Cabourg. Like

the Aubecq house by Horta, the fate of which fate it was to share, the Nozal house constituted the architect's supreme manifestation of masterly freedom in the handling of space and an expert blend of symmetry in the two wings converging at a forty-five degree angle towards the central hall, and asymmetry in the elements connected to them. This delicate spatial manipulation is reflected in each room and, in the grand tradition of French decorative art as expounded in the treatises of the eighteenth century, formed an architecture of its own with its particular symmetries, dominant axes and speci-

133. H. Guimard. Hotel Guimard,
122 Avenue Mozart, Paris 16ᵉ. (1905-1912).
Overall view.

fic themes, determined for the most part by the windows which, without assuming the true character of bow-windows, curved outwards in an inspired rhythm of measured continuity and serpentine movement.

The Castel Orgeval at Villemoisson, which fortunately survives thanks to the tenacious affection of its owners, is a living witness to a world now disappeared. Guimard returned here to his favourite themes: roughened unhewn stone and flowing lines broken only by large projections which make daring intersections in the surface of the roofs. The plan of the Nozal house was an extreme example of another of Guimard's predilections: seemingly supported by a rigid back-wall, it opened out like a balcony jointed into the wall-face.

This feature was to be taken up again in the Guimard house, a feat of ingenuity, which he built for himself out of sheer bravura. The triangular site is so small that it was hardly possible to construct more than two rooms of irregular shape on each floor. The house resembles a small tower block of four storeys plus an attic, with two of the sides of the triangle, those facing Rue Mansart and Rue Villa Flore (which is at right angles to it), presenting a broad front. The work reflects the out-going, expansive personality of the architect, immensely enjoying his success. His marriage to the American painter, Adeline Oppenheim, had assured his future material wellbeing. Built between 1909 and 1912, the Guimard house shows a measure of composure, of "settling-down", in his normally dynamic approach to design. His pursuit of continuity recalls certain similar experiments of Horta; the frequent recourse to bow-windows and to corbelling were due to the

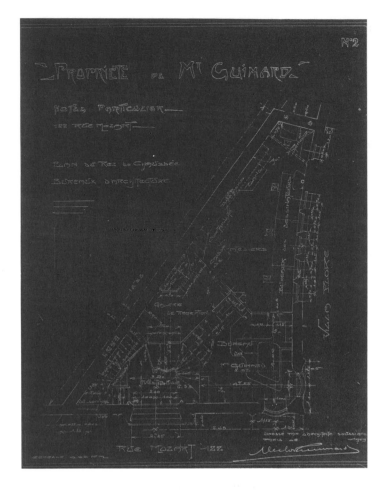

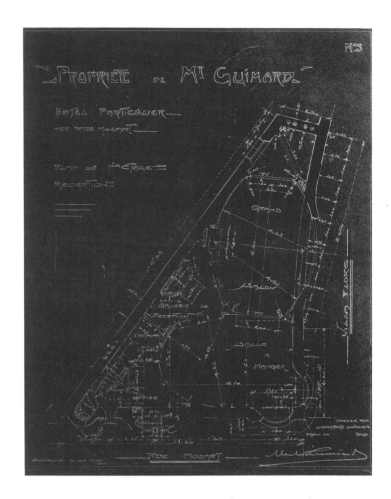

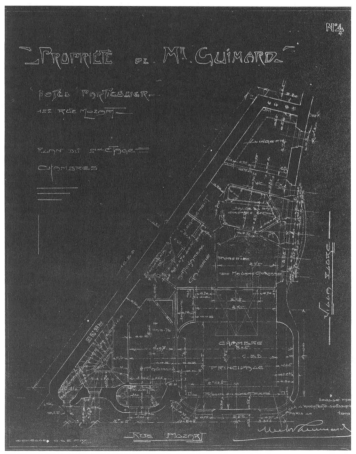

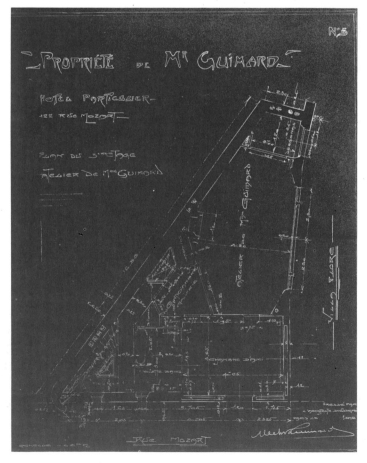

134-137. *H. Guimard. Hotel Guimard. Plans of the ground - 1ˢᵗ - 2ⁿᵈ - and 3ᵈ floors.*

138-140. *H. Guimard. Hotel Guimard. Plan and façade.*

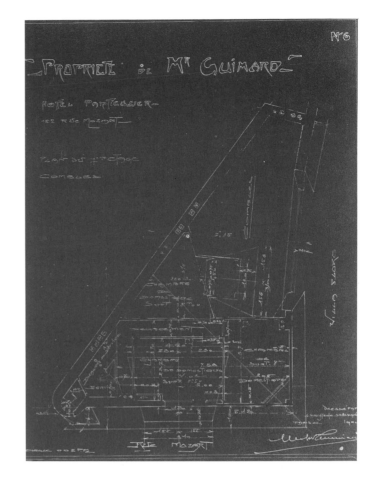

141. *H. Guimard. Hotel Guimard. Staircase.*

functional demands of the interior, very strict because of lack of space. The elegance of these vertical and horizontal associations in a consistently studied relationship between smooth-faced stone and yellow brick needs no comment, while the ironwork established to the full the maturity and refinement of the "style Guimard".

In the architect's work there are two other examples of this type of artist's house that is so common in Brussels: The first, the studio of Madame Carpeaux, belongs to the period when Guimard was training and therefore constitutes a precedent. The second, the Hôtel Mezzara in the Rue La Fontaine (1910-1911), is later and is notable for a deep concern for symmetry. Slightly set back from the street, it seems to display an introspective quality in the way in which the interior and exterior are related. This is apparent in the interplay of concave and convex elements, of successive recesses and salients, and by a kind of contraction which also seeks to resolve the contradictions between vertical and horizontal forms. For the rest, apart from a few exceptions, among which the Deron Levent house at Villa de la Réunion (1904- 1907), of exquisite refinement and exemplary restraint, was outstanding, Guimard devoted himself successfully to the building of co-ownership apartment and office blocks, either for his old client Jassedé, or by establishing, with the help of Nozal and the financial support of his wife, a construction company for the large scheme in the Rue Agar.

From the planning point of view, the Jassedé building shows the same regularity and refined taste as is exemplified by each of the flats. The latter are distributed from two ranges of oval staircases (placed at the two

142-144. H. Guimard. Hotel Mezzara,
60 Rue La Fontaine, Paris 16ᵉ. (1910-11).
Façade and staircase.

145. H. Guimard. Hotel Mezzara. Dining-
room.

internal angles and lit by an ingenious recessed arrangement of the courts). This rational, but resourceful, response to the exigencies of the site bears Guimard's stamp. It offered free rein to a characteristically subtle treatment of the elevations, this time marked by a graceful superimposition of balconies and bow-windows at the corner of the Avenue de Versailles. He created between them a variety of contrasting effects when seen from the principal street, while on the side facing the Rue Lancré he was content merely to exploit the overall continuity of a plain brick cladding interrupted by an oriental pattern applied to the metal architraves and balconies, for which

146. H. Guimard. Hotel Deron Levent, 8 Villa de la Réunion, Paris 16ᵉ. (1904-1907). Overall view.

147. H. Guimard. Group of buildings, 17-21 Rue La Fontaine, 8-10 Rue Agar, 43 Rue Gros, Paris 16ᵉ. (1910-11). Overall view.

he used cast-iron elements of his own design. This feature occurs again in the Rue Agar, although the treatment is very restrained and limited to the gentle curvature of the bow-window mullions. The accent of the ironwork is closer to Art Nouveau than is the idiom as a whole, which was ultimately to be distilled and simplified, even though, as in the much later Tremois building, Guimard accentuated the contribution of towers, tops and pinnacles in a sort of return to "flamboyant" fantasy.

In 1913, on the eve of the First World War, Guimard used reinforced concrete for the synagogue in the Rue Pavée,

148-150. *H. Guimard. Group of buildings,*
Rue La Fontaine, Rue Agar, Rue Gros.
Overall view and details of two cast-iron
balconies.

151. *H. Guimard. Group of buildings, Rue* ▷
La Fontaine, Rue Agar, Rue Gros. General
view.

152. *H. Guimard. Café-bar. Ground floor of the group of buildings. Rue La Fontaine.*

153. *H. Guimard. Immeuble Jassedé, 142 Avenue de Versailles, 1 Rue Lancret, Paris 16ᵉ. (1903-1905). Overall view.* ▷

154-155. H. Guimard. Immeuble Jassedé.
◁ Entrance and corner of the building. ▽

156-157. H. Guimard. Immeuble Jassedé.
Façade on the Rue Lancret and détail of the
windows.

158. H. Guimard. Postcards «The Guimard style». Castel Béranger, 14 Rue La Fontaine, Paris 16ᵉ.

159-160. H. Guimard. Postcards "The Guimard style". Humbert de Romans Concert Hall, 56-60 Rue Saint-Didier, Paris 16ᵉ. (1898-1901). Outside and interior views.

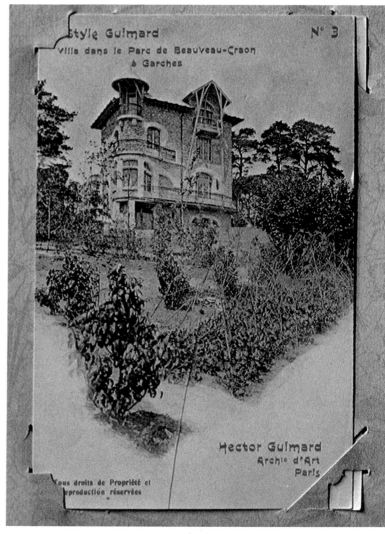

161. H. Guimard. Postcards «The Guimard style». Castel Henriette, Rue des Binelles, Sèvres. (1899-1900). Demolished.

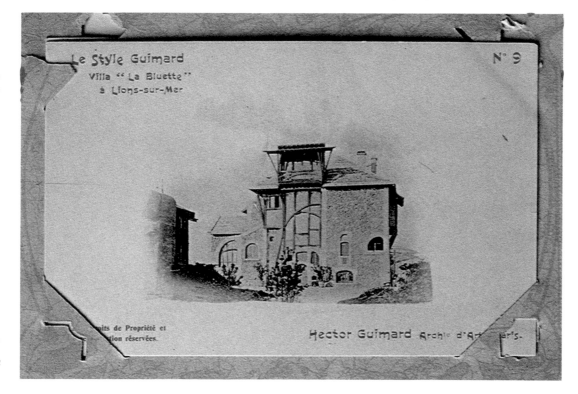

162. H. Guimard. Postcards «The Guimard style». Villa in the Beauveau-Craon estate, Garches.

163. H. Guimard. Postcards «The Guimard style». Villa La Bluette, Lions-sur-Mer.

119

164. H. Guimard. Trémois house, 12 Rue François-Millet, Paris 16e. (1909-10). Overall view.

165-166. H. Guimard. Trémois house. Details of the iron-work.

167-168. *H. Guimard. Pavilion, 16 Rue Jean-Doyen, Eaubonne. (C. 1907). Overall view and cast-iron balcony.* ▽

169-170. *H. Guimard. Grivellé house, 148 Quai d'Auteuil - angle to Rue Tesniers, Paris 16ᵉ. (1910).* ▷

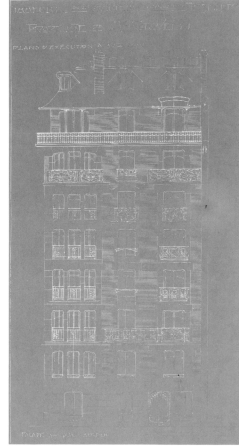

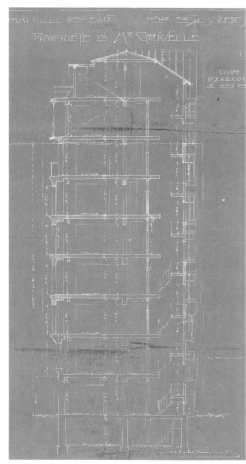

171. *H. Guimard. Town house, 7 Rue Pierre-Ducreux, Paris 16ᵉ. Plan (1914). Demolished in 1960.*

and thus joined forces in one respect with Anatole de Baudot, Perret and the pioneers of modern architecture. As so often, the plan indicates a compromise between regularity of structure and irregularity of site, the latter being very marked and slightly oblique in relation to the perpendicular line of the façade. Guimard explored the effect of narrow vertical openings, a kind of tall Gothic fenestration of which the bow-shape elevation made a re-entrant curve and a small salience, contrasting with the pitch of the roof and of the entrance canopy. There is no decoration or ironwork: the pattern of the stone emphasizes the rhythmic continuity of the narrow windows cut in the delicately curved surface, the practical result being perhaps more monotonous in its effect than intended.

The interior comprises nave and two lateral aisles, each of the latter having

173-174. *H. Guimard. Synagogue. Inside view and detail of the galleries.*

175. *H. Guimard. Synagogue.* ▷

*176 H. Guimard. Office building, Rue de
Bretagne, Paris 16ᵉ. (1914-19). General view.* ▷

two rows of superimposed galleries
carried on slender pillars. The building
is neo-Gothic in feeling, uninfluenced
by Art Nouveau, but with anticipa-
tions of Art Déco, which was to be a
guiding principle of Guimard's work
after the war. For him the war was not,
as it proved for Horta, a profound
crisis leading to a return to order, the
immediate abandonment of Art Nouveau and a descent into the academic
rut. With his practical sense Guimard
took advantage of the need to rebuild
what the war had destroyed to propa-
gate his methods of prefabrication,
although the only surviving evidence
of this is a house in the Rue Jasmin,
composed of prefabricated elements
and erected in a few days. Guimard
was by now in process of gradual
transition from Art Nouveau to Art
Déco, which resulted in his construc-
ting a very interesting building opposite his own house in the Avenue Mozart. Next came the fine block of flats
in the Rue Greuze and, still within the
ambit of partial prefabrication, the
experimental "La Guimardière" at
Vaucresson, demolished in 1969. In
this phase he was no longer alone;
with his friend Frantz Jourdain and
Tony Selmersheim and Henri Sauvage,
Guimard founded the Groupe des
Architectes Modernes, of which Michel Roux-Spitz also became a member.

In 1930 we find him still among the
avant-garde in a project for a monument to the fallen of the Marne. Yet
his vitality, his capacity for renewal,
the flair which dissuaded him from
abrupt changes and his faculty for
adaptation were never to be rewarded
by genuine comprehension or any
official encouragement. The economic
crisis forced him to slow down and
then to discontinue his activities as
architect and contractor. Faced with
the political tragedy of Munich and

the racial problems heralding the
Second World War, he decided to
make his home in the United States for
the sake of his wife, who was Jewish.
He died there, forgotten, in 1942,
without having had the chance to see
rise in New York the building for the
United Nations, for which he had
outlined his hopes in a pamphlet
published as long ago as 1915, describing it as "the sole possibility of
ensuring the rights of nations and the
security and peace of tomorrow"

ANALYSIS OF AN IDIOM

Audacity, impetuosity, enthusiasm are
implied in the terms most commonly
used in the rare examples of impartial
evidence that we possess of the character of Guimard. They describe a coura-
geous extrovert, whose convictions ill
fitted the traditional concepts associated with a pragmatic rationalism. In
Guimard, professional commitment
was incongruously linked to an acute
practical sense and a sure instinct for
self-publicity and the profitable opportunity. He was not content to dream,
but was bent on realising those
dreams; from being an architect, he
became his own contractor. He was

convinced that, apart from a few rare
instances, the only way to express his
ideas freely was to put them into
practice himself. Thus, the client's
contribution was limited to buying or
renting the site of the building, and his
influence on its design to the humdrum
task of financing it. The urge to exploit
every possibility of experiment distinguished Guimard from his colleagues
Victor Horta, Henry Van de Velde and
Paul Hankar. It explains the extraordinary variety of his architectural interpretation, which reflected not merely
experimentalism for its own sake, but
a deep desire to transform the conditions of man's habitat.

Horta worked within the framework
of a more clearly defined architectural
idiom, for clients who in the main
seem to have been progressive and
enlightened. Hankar drew upon a
mediaeval vocabulary which he expressed in terms which were a blend of
historicism and Art Nouveau; Van de
Velde worked with perception and a
hint of snobbery for a particular
clientèle, the fashionable intelligentsia.
Hector Guimard, however, wanted to
work in every sphere of the human
habitat, whether urban or rural: the
chalet, the "castel", the luxurious
villa, the janitor's lodge, the private
residence, the humble dwelling in its
isolated village setting, the block of
flats or offices under co-ownership,
pretentious or modest. He exhausted
therefore the gamut of architectural
interpretation at his disposal, within
the constraints of building regulations
and by-laws and the tastes of a middle-
class patronage which for the most
part has remained anonymous.

Apart from the Guimard house, the
studio of the Carpeaux house and the
Mezzara studio, he displayed little
interest in the type of the artist's house
or the "maison manifeste", of which,

177. H. Guimard. Town house, 3 Square Jasmin, Paris 16ᵉ. ▷
(1924-26). Detail of the façade.

▽ 178. H. Guimard. Apartment block, 36-38 Rue Greuze, Paris 16ᵉ. (1925). The angle of the building.

▽ 179. H. Guimard. Apartment block, 18 Rue Henri-Heine, Paris 16ᵉ. (1926).

180. H. Guimard. Town house with a workshop, belonging to Mrs Cappeaux, 39 Boulevard Exelmans, Paris 16ᵉ. (1894-95). Overall view.

as we have already noted, so many examples existed in Brussels. He was much attracted by the chalet or cottage, and it is appropriate here to quote Ruskin: "The French cottage cannot please by its propriety, for it can only be adapted to the ugliness around; and, as it ought to be, and cannot but be, adapted to this, it is still less easy to please by its beauty. How, then, can it please? There is no pretence to gaiety in its appearance, no green flower-pots in ornamental lattices; but the substantial style of any ornaments it may possess, the recessed windows, the stone carvings, and the general size of the whole, unite to produce an impression of the building having once been fit for the residence of prouder inhabitants; of its once having possessed strength, which is now withered, and beauty, which is now faded. This sense of something lost, something which has been, and is not, is precisely what is wanted".[21]

One might add to this the concept of the lost "castel", fallen from the wonder of the middle ages to the commonplace level of middle-class use. But it was towards the English model, "pretty from its propriety", that Guimard was to turn. The idiom which he was to employ had already appeared in Ruskin's writings: "The

third and last distinctive attribute is sensuality. The word may sound alarming, so it must be explained. First, each line is voluptuous, floating, and undulating in its form, deep, rich and adorably versatile in its colour, soothing in the effect it produces like lingering and wild music; the eye lights upon it as on a whorl of clouds without any intrusive act coming to break or thwart the spell". But it was not only a matter of agreeable sensations and of sensuous surrender; Guimard also propounded a form of logic very much his own, an appeal to reason which

was also the reason of nature: "Since in nature, according to Monsieur Guimard, one of the most ardent protagonists of French modern art, any object what ever always has a form appropriate to its purpose, it is in the material it self that we must look for decorative form. In this way we become creative - but not by copying nature, which is nonsense - and extract from it what is totally new. .."[22]

THE LESSON OF VIOLLET-LE-DUC

"This method of construction in iron and masonry fulfils the conditions which, in our opinion, should characterise such works. Thus the iron framework is visible, independent, and free to expand and contract, so that it cannot cause dislocation of the masonry, whether through oxidation or variation in temperature. The masonry, while concrete in parts, yet preserves a certain degree of elasticity, owing to the small arches which carry the whole. As the vaulting is of inconsiderable depth in proportion to the width of the interior, it allows of large windows comparatively elevated, so that a minimum of materials is required and only thin walls, which (excepting the points of support) may be partly built of rubble stone; in the ironwork, the use of bolts, which are liable to be injured or broken, is avoided, bolts being employed only for fastening the tie-rods to the braces or collars."[23]

And again: "Let it be well understood, once for all, that architecture cannot array itself in new forms unless it seeks them in the rigorous application of novel methods of construction; that casing cast-iron columns with cylinders of brick or coatings of stucco, or building iron supports into masonry, for example, is not the result either of calculation or of an effort of imagination, but merely a disguising of the actual construction; no disguise of the means employed can lead to new forms".[24]

These principles served as the foundation for Guimard's and Horta's methods. In fact their application by Guimard, starting with the Sacré-Cœur, was purely experimental. The use of V-shaped columns in cast-iron is clearly indicated by Viollet-le-Duc on page 63 of Lecture XII and taken literally by Guimard, whether for the disposition of static elements, or for their structural advantages, at any rate so far as the plastic pattern of cast-iron was concerned: "The supporting struts or slanting columns are of cast-iron, resting in shoes likewise of cast-iron connected by a tie-rod. The feet of these supporting struts are spheroidal, and sink into two cups sunk in each shoe. The tops of these struts have tenons fitting into spheroids surmounted by dwarf shafts, which again tenon into the cast-iron capitals, each of which carries the springer of three arches".[25]

Guimard drew his inspiration directly from the "Lectures", and from the

181. H. Guimard. House of the potter Coilliot, 14 Rue de Fleurus, Lille. (1898-1900). Façade.

diagonal articulation of the pavilion on page 284, for the Nozal and the Geneva houses, whose timber framing curved inwards towards the exterior (fig. 16, p. 342, Lecture XVIII) already foreshadowed the Coilliot house at Lille. During his formative period Guimard turned often to mediaeval precedents, which coexisted happily with the rationalism taught by Viollet-le-Duc. But apart from specific quotations, suggestions and an element of fantasy already mentioned, it does not appear that Guimard could be credited with a more accurate knowledge or

exact analytical grasp of Gothic idiom, of which Viollet-le-Duc's "Dictionary" constituted an incomparable monument. In Guimard, instinct, freshness and vitality were not inhibited by history; his attachment was spontaneous, which gave his mediaevalism an ingenuous quality. Yet the forms evolved in a coherent manner and this harmony was apparent as much in the general plan as in the smallest detail. One may fittingly emphasize this vitality which naturally led him to adopt a simplistic Gothic style, in particular on the iconographical level. Just as Gothic buildings are peopled with monsters and the architectural framework sometimes presents zoomorphic and anthropomorphic features, so Guimard, starting with the Castel Béranger, and thanks to the ductility of cast-iron, peopled buildings with sea-horses, insects or shapes calling to mind that of bones and crustaceans. In practice the forms and structures of Guimard's idiom, the thickening in section of reinforcing ribs and the concavity of elements supporting smaller loads, were directly inspired by lobsters' claws, which in a certain sense may be said to exemplify one of many ironical aspects of the "style Guimard".

THE TREND TO INFORMALITY

A single thread seems to have linked Guimard to Antoni Gaudí, then to Hermann Finsterlin, Rudolf Steiner and, finally, to architectural informality. This tendency is visible in almost all Guimard's decorative motifs. Indeed, the floral and vegetal decorations, the notorious Horta "stalk", gave place rather to an effusion of zoomorphic and plant forms expressed in terms of uninhibited freedom.

Examples were soon to proliferate from the ornamental facing of the entrance of the Castel Béranger, in which a earthenware decorative pattern is applied in a lattice framework of metal whiplash curves and undulating folds, which overflow into seeming viscous drops or end in plunging flounces. In the metro entrances even the most obvious allusions to plant life appear surreptitiously to seek an escape from an absolute realism by assuming a kind of plasticity. In the Castel Orgeval the rubble masonry outlines a cavity above the entrance like that of a grotto. The exploration of "continuity in continuity" relationships, of which the Guimard house was one of the most conspicuous and coherent examples, produced similar results.

As a general rule the same approach must be recognized in the way surfaces and roofs are related, and in the movement of masses, in the free-standing house or in the decorative details of urban blocks for which the building regulations were more stringent. Such features are more easily perceived when the freedom of treatment becomes more provocative, as it was for the corner of the Jassedé building in the Avenue de Versailles or in the enumerable details of metalwork grilles and elaborate cast-iron elements.

In October 1900 "L'Art Décoratif" published an article, which gives us an idea of the effect produced on his contemporaries by Guimard's idiom: "We know Guimard's modelling practices, imprecise, baffling, perplexing the eyes familiar images". The paintings decorating metro stations did not escape criticism: "In painting, these deliberately elusive lines without representational or geometrical sense. .. tire the eye and are very far from resting it".

The "Magazine of Art" analysed in a more accurate manner the relationship between naturalism and abstraction in Guimard's vocabulary: "His aim has been to avoid any ornamental motif borrowed directly from nature or, more specifically, flora. Here we shall find no decoration assuming the forms which exist in nature, neither flowers nor vegetation. Monsieur Guimard is only interested in line; it is from the 'line' or from the arrangement of several lines that he draws all his effects. I confess my inability to share the artist's opinions in this regard; it seems to me indeed that by this means he deprives appliqué design of some of its most interesting resources, notably those which we so much admire in the Japanese and in certain French artists, such as Majorelle and Gallé. In fact the influence of nature is so great that Monsieur Guimard, despite his wish to stick to abstract lines, has sometimes been dragged far away from his principles."[26]

But where the abstract factor becomes the only possible interpretation, or at least the most interesting, is in the analysis of the furniture. True, there was the great tradition of Louis XV, the extraordinary capacity of French cabinet-makers, the widespread taste for the signed piece, which Carabin, for example, sought to exploit with ingenuity and spontaneity. Guimard's approach was to be more subtle, and he already revealed his attitude in the furniture made for the flats of the Castel Béranger. Then, with the help of master-craftsmen and fine, close-grained mahoganies, he achieved sections of ever diminishing size. The little armchairs and those designed for writing-tables were almost always authentic masterpieces, whether for the logical coherence with which the sections expanded towards the joints, for the extreme tenuity of supporting members, or for the mouldings sometimes extending across plain surfaces and at others gathered into delicate folds and clustered bands, or culminating in decorative features of still greater refinement.

Guimard, however, was accustomed to think in terms of cast-ironwork and did not appreciate the logic of assembling pieces of wood of dimensions fixed by custom and worked in accordance with immutable tradition. Among the latter may be mentioned the distinction between front and back legs, the second forming a single component with the chair-back (i.e. the vertical element) and with the joints of the chair-back and the stretchers supporting the seat (i.e. the horizontal elements). For Guimard, the design formed by the grain or the fragmentation necessary to the construction of the piece had to be ignored, for what counted was his insistence on continuity and on creating abstract figures which were not amenable to the solution of continuity. In spite of many reservations, contemporary critics recognized some merit in the

186-189. *H. Guimard. Chairs and chaise longue. (C. 1904).*

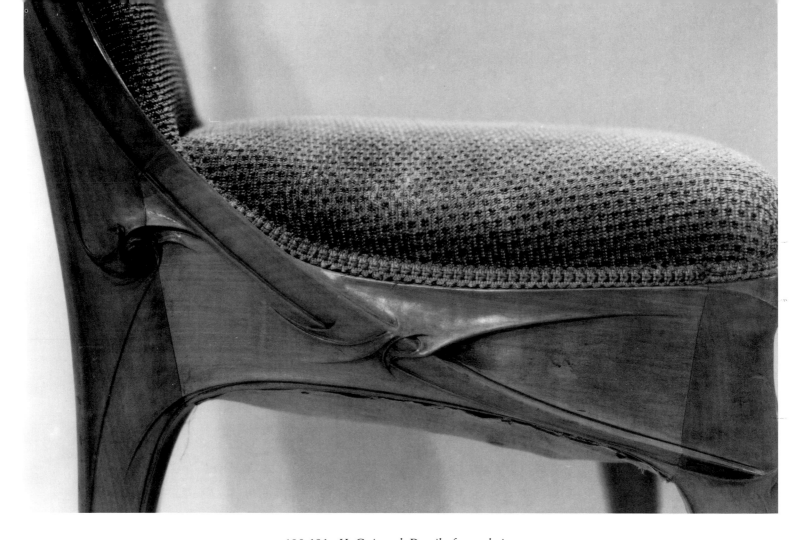

190-191. *H. Guimard. Detail of two chairs.*

*192. H. Guimard. Fire guard for the Hotel
Nozal. (C. 1904).*

unaccustomed slenderness: "The
comment is fair enough. The truth is
that a special effort has been made to
generate the different parts of a piece
of furniture like plant stems growing
from a trunk, and so give the appearance of life to an artificial creation."[27]

This is why, if the chairs were genuine
masterpieces, quite as much cannot be
said for the storage furniture, in which
the same problems occurred as in any
mural architecture: those of an exposed frame with storage surfaces and
decoration that was excessive in certain cases, as - for example - on the
drawers, various salient details and the
unit tops. But this is a fate common to
all furniture design, from the antique
to the modern, and Guimard's furniture remains something more than a
series of mere unique pieces; by virtue
of their exquisite refinement, they are
objects which can never be reproduced.

194-196. *H. Guimard. Wardrobe in the*
master bedroom, Hotel Nozal. (about 1904).
Overall view and details.

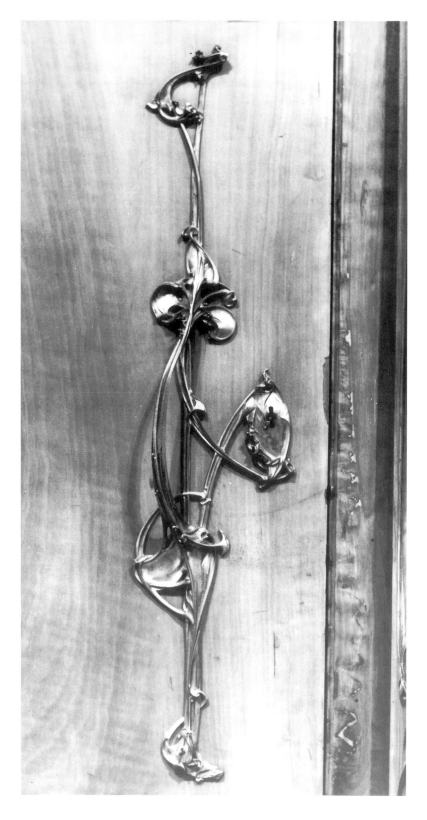

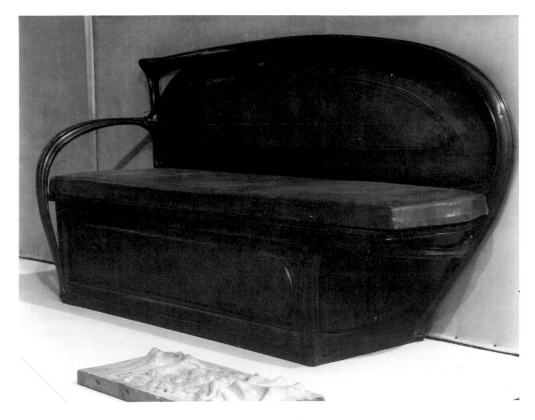

197. *H. Guimard. Sofa.*

198. *H. Guimard. Bed for the master bedroom. Hotel Nozal.*

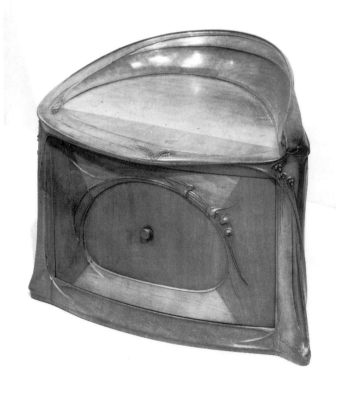

199. H. Guimard. Corner window. Detail.

200. H. Guimard. Cast-iron umbrella-stand.

201. H. Guimard. Bedside table in the bedroom in the Hotel Nozal. (C. 1904).

203. H. Guimard. Corner window.

202. H. Guimard. Chair.

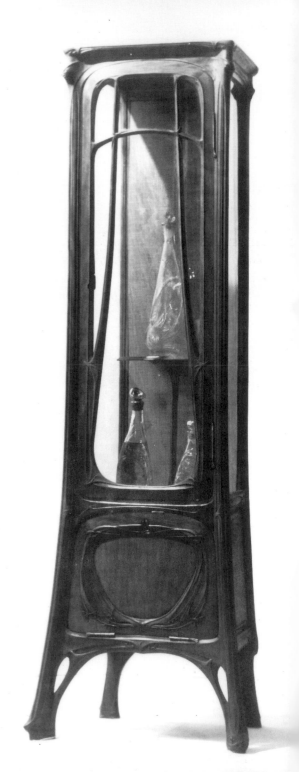

206. *H. Guimard. Woman's desk. (C. 1909).*

207 H. Guimard. Guimard's desk for his office in the Castel Béranger. (C. 1897-1899).

208. *H. Guimard. Plateau. (C. 1909).*

209. *H. Guimard. Vase. (C. 1898).*

210. *H. Guimard. Easel frame. (After 1909).*

211. *H. Guimard. Vase.*

REPETITION AND PREFABRICATION

If the high standard in the quality of its surroundings - the Nozal house comes to mind - justified the extreme refinement of this furniture, Guimard was nonetheless a pioneer in the field of prefabrication and the mass-production of design elements. He wrote in "La Construction Moderne" of 16 February 1913: "How can architects be reproached for always reproducing the same motifs, when the trade only stocks Louis XVI patterns? If the architect wants to design everything down to the smallest details of construction, the cost of models represents an expenditure of time which renders his task impossible. To solve such problems, the building industry would have to replace their patterns and assemble catalogues of new models which, designed for the practical needs of our modern buildings, would complement one another in expressing a new outlook, that of our time." And he added: "I have no wish to pass over their names in silence. You will allow me to acknowledge the sacrifices made by the Fonderies de Saint-Dizier for cast-iron, the firm of Vital Evrard and the De Villiers company for marble, the house of Brun Cottan for ironmongery, Gillet for ceramics, Sigg and Godmann for glass, Parlant and Biron for carpets, etc. If my colleagues care to glance through the album of the Fonderies de Saint-Dizier, Haute-Marne, they will see the considerable effort made by this company to provide modern building with every essential component."[28] Clearly, Guimard felt no need to divorce publicity from theory; his pragmatism made him eager to design for his friends of the Saint-Dizier foundry details for use in funerary architecture, and handles, screens for balconies and a variety of

212. H. Guimard. La Guimardière, Rue Lenôtre, Vaucresson. (C. 1930). Demolished.

other furniture for buildings. Moreover he used them himself in important jobs, from the Jassedé house to the flats in the Rue Agar.

Thus, as Guimard found solutions to the problem of mass-production of components which had to be modelled under the strict supervision of an architect, he found that cast-iron and tiles were the most suitable materials. The concept of repeatability and continuity which characterized his designs led also to the use of prefabricated components, submitted certainly to precise specifications, but starting from dimensions and sections supplied by the industry.

Even though the number of Guimard's admirable drawings reproduced here

is limited, they clearly emphasize that the factor of repeatability was to influence the formulation of his designs and even his draughtsmanship. While Horta stuck closely to a linear presentation of his designs for ironmongery, based upon the function of elements of specified section, Guimard drew his furniture and ironwork with charcoal. He drew in quick strong strokes when he gave pride of place to the line but, when he wanted to indicate a continuous motif in relief, he used his thumb to prolong the effect in charcoal, which produced subtle shades of chiaroscuro, an impression of continuity and a somewhat facile elegance. They are less an architect's drawings than a sculptor's, exploiting areas of deep shade, and the strong lines that show absolute mastery of the form created. Apart from the mechanical reproduction of elements of high formal value, Guimard thought also in terms of prefabrication, at least insofar as the experiments of the immediate post-war phase and of the Guimardière were concerned. He envisaged the use of such durable materials as glazed and unglazed earthenware, which could be used for both decorative and structural purposes and provided components of a high architectural standard and modest cost.

The point is not to claim that Guimard was a pioneer of prefabricated construction, nor to make him one of the precursors of any other specific tenet of the modern movement, but simply to record his acute sense of the relationship between practice and production, between an architectural idiom and the "consumer", between the privileged classes and the extension of Art Nouveau to the middle ranks of French society. In this lay to a large extent his ready approachability, his inspired pragmatism which achieved certain results, even if he was ahead of his time and for that reason he was rarely valued at his true worth. He was to survive the crisis caused by the war and the disappearance of Art Nouveau. It was perhaps because Horta was too uninterested in the connection between the one-off piece and the standard product that he was almost paralysed by that same crisis.

FREEING THE STRUCTURAL FRAME

When Guimard was not preoccupied by the problem of continuity, which since ancient Rome has been dominated by brick, or when he did not turn to that impressive severity of stone dear to the Gothic age (and which he handled with immense vitality and a sharp eye for innovation), he displayed a predilection for exposing the structural system.

This preference was especially apparent in the 1910s, at the time when Art Nouveau was losing its momentum in the decorative sphere. Guimard had already revealed this tendency in his faithful revival of the theories of Viollet-le-Duc in the Ecole du Sacré-Cœur and in the exposure of the structural framework of the two semi-detached pavilions of the Hameau Boileau. Next, in the house of the ceramist Louis Coilliot at Lille, he drew attention to the timber frame by making its transverse section a main feature of the façade, in an entertaining exercise in asymmetry between a pointed arch and a pillar conspicuously placed off-centre. For the Castel Henriette he went back to a free interpreta-

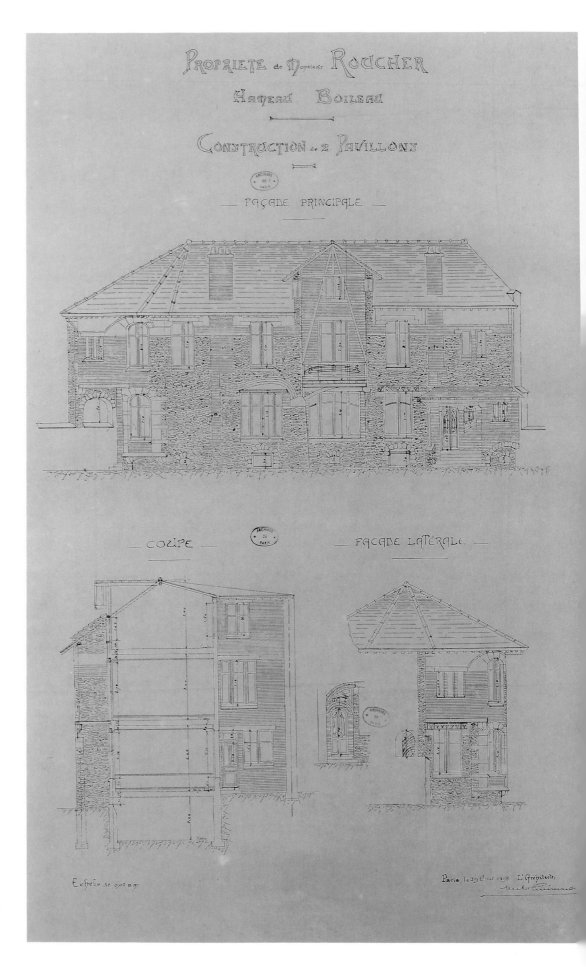

tion of the Gothic frame with a coarse rubble infill. We have already seen that, for the Humbert de Romans concert hall, Guimard designed the loadbearing frame as an evocation of a forest, and an indispensable element of the spatial structure; but some lesser works should not be underestimated, such as the Chalet Blanc at Sceaux (1908), or the more constricted attic-balcony of the chalet in the Rue de Crillon at Saint-Cloud (1913). In the latter case the curves and branches of timber extending outward from just above the rustic masonry of the ground floor to the overhanging balcony, which they partly support, clearly show style and vigour. The loadbearing structure of the house resembles a cluster of trees stretching out towards the sun from the twilight of the interior to sustain the balconies and bow-windows.

Although the impulse to reveal the internal structure was still embryonic and timid, it was already emerging as the single authentically valid principle in this episode of architecture. According to his colleague Plumet, architecture - as Guimard conceived it - was "the artistic expression of the needs of the individual in society" and, he optimistically added in "La Construction Moderne" in 1907, "you will therefore allow me to suggest that, if the struggle between the classics and the innovators is unequal, it is strongly in favour of the innovators; indeed the former stand for the past, meaning death - but I want to acknowledge their status, for they represent an established position, honours and authority; while the innovators represent merely the whole of life - for them, that is enough".[29] Guimard's line, which was echoed in his buildings and, above all, in his attitudes, collided head-on with the narrow-mindedness

215-216. H. Guimard. Castel Henriette,
Rue des Binelles, Sèvres. (1899-1900).
Demolished.

217. H. Guimard. Castel Val, 4 Rue de
Meulières, Chaponval.

218. H. Guimard. Castel Eclipse, Versailles.
(C. 1901).

219. H. Guimard. Villa in the Beauveau-
Craon estate, Garches. Façade overlooking
the garden.

220-221. H. Guimard. Chalet blanc, 2 Rue
du Lycée, Sceaux. (C. 1908). General view
and detail of the balcony.

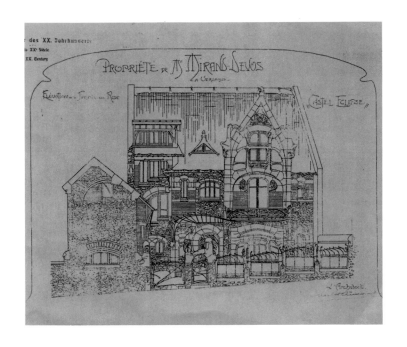

and ingrained prejudices of middle-class society, of which he was the representative. Despite the adaptability to new ideas apparent in his last works, his critical success, tempered by a lukewarm recognition of his abilities as an innovator, was not to increase. His great qualities and strong personality had to find expression in a hostile context, but he was able to

222-225. H. Guimard. Projects for chalets. (C. 1904).

break out of his isolation and follow his bent in freedom. Suffice it to remember the answer which he gave to tenants of the Castel Béranger, who had asked him to change the wallpaper and interior decoration; refusing to do so, he said that "if they wanted to be housed as everywhere else, they were under no obligation to choose the Castel Béranger".[30]

NOTES

1. L. Sullivan, *Autobiographie d'une idée*, Roma 1979, p. 254.
2. *H. Guimard, Bibliographie,* collapsed by R. Culpepper, Paris 1975, p. 74.
3. C.E. Curinier, *Dictionnaire national des contemporains*, Paris s.d., vol. IV, p. 101.
4. A. Blondel, "Guimard, architecte de meubles", in *L'Estampille*, May 1970, p. 40.
5. L.-C. Boileau, "Causerie", in *L'Architecture,* 15.1.1899, p. 128.
6. On the relantioship between Guimard and Horta see V. Horta, *Mémoires,* edited by C. Dulière, Brussels, Ministère de la Communauté Française, 1985, pp. 146-147, 286-287, 294, 308.
7. F. Molinier, "Le Castel Béranger", in *Art et Décoration*, January 1899, pp. 76-81.
8. M. Méry, "Le Castel Béranger", in *Le Moniteur des Arts*, 7.1.1899.
9. In *La Construction Moderne,* 6.5.1899., p. 375.
10. L.-C. Boileau, "Causerie", in *L'Architecture,* 1899, p. 122.
11. Ibidem.
12. L.-C. Boileau, "Les maisons de M. Guimard, rue La Fontaine", in *L'Architecture,* 10.2.1899, p. 388.
13. V. Champier, "Le Castel Béranger et M. Hector Guimard, architecte", *in Revue des Arts Décoratifs,* January 1899, p. 7.
14. E. Molinier, "Le Castel Béranger", in *Art et Décoration*, 1899, vol. V, pp. 78-79.
15. L.-C. Boileau, "Causerie", in *L'Architecture,* 15.4.1899, p. 127.
16. V. Champier, *op. cit.,* p. 10.
17. V. Champier, ibidem.
18. The most complete iconographical sources of this demolished building are A. Mangeot, "La Salle de concert Humbert de Romans", in *Le Monde Musical,* 15.12.1901; F. Mazade, "An Art Nouveau edifice in Paris: the Humbert de Romans building, H. Guimard architect", in *The Architectural Record*, 1902, n° 2, pp. 50-66; H. Guedy (edited by), *L'Architecture au XXème siècle,* I volume, Paris, Librairies-Imprimeries réunies, s.d., pl. 76-80.
19. In *La Construction Moderne,* 16.1.1901, p. 81.
20. G. Bans, "Les gares du métropolitain de Paris", in *Art Décoratif,* n° 25, October 1900, p. 38.
21. J. Ruskin, *La poesia dell'architettura,* Milano 1909, p. 25.
22. Ibidem.
23. E. Viollet-le-Duc, *Entretiens sur l'architecture,* vol. II, Paris 1872, p. 83.
24. E. Viollet-le-Duc, *op. cit,* p. 67.
25. E. Viollet-le-Duc, *op. cit.,* p. 82.
26. H. Frantz, "The Art Movement", in *The Magazine of Art,* 1901, vol. XXV, pp. 86-87.
27. E. Molinier, "Le Castel Béranger", in *Art et Décoration*, 1899, pp. 77-78.
30. "Chronique de l'Art Décoratif", in *Art Décoratif,* 7 April 1899, p. 42.

226-227. F. Jourdain. Expansion of La Samaritaine department store. Façade overlooking the
Rue de la Monnaie. Todays' overall view and detail.

VI

FRANTZ JOURDAIN:
A CONTROVERSIALIST

Frantz Jourdain's significant part in the cultural life of Paris during the first twenty years of the century was due less to his own architectural creations than to his unconditional support, with his writing and organizational ability, of every artistic manifestation by the avant-garde. Louis-Charles Boileau, a conservative critic, defined Jourdain, with a touch of malicious irony, as "the advocate of the'young" infatuated with Modern Style", the "valiant champion of artistic causes, more often engaged in lambasting classical principles, liberal as they are, and lavish with choice bouquets for the most trifling flirtations with Art Nouveau".[1] A brilliant and pugnacious writer gifted with an acute critical penetration and sharp prose, Jourdain included among his friends Emile Zola, Alphonse Daudet and the Goncourt brothers. He was not a theorist with a taste for aesthetic speculation, but rather a militant critic and virulent polemic, more successful with pamphlets than with essays.

He was ahead of his time and quick to detect an authentic quality of innovation as he assessed cultural fashion and picked out the real values in some artistic disputations shunned by established critics.

This ability was reflected in the controversies aroused in the early years following the creation in 1903 of the "Salon d'Automne", organized by Jourdain to welcome artists ostracized by the official salons. That same year and under his chairmanship, the first retrospective exhibition of Paul Gauguin was organized; the following year five rooms were devoted to the works of Pierre Puvis de Chavannes, Odilon Redon, Auguste Renoir, Henri de Toulouse-Lautrec and Paul Cézanne, whose paintings had been consigned, only a little earlier, to the attic of the wife of Emile Zola, his one-time fellow student at Aix-en-Provence. The constant campaign waged by Frantz Jourdain in the interests of the avant-garde embraced all forms of representative and decorative art. This endeavour caused Jourdain to become involved in a contention with the teaching system of the Ecole des Beaux- Arts, and to be continuously soliciting, in his capacity as chairman of the society "Le Nouveau Paris" and the union of the arts press (jobs assigned to him in 1903 and 1906 respectively), the support of public opinion, and not only of specialists, for the avant-garde and the establishment of the "Salon d'Automne" as an alternative to the official salons.

His collaborator, Robert Rey, has provided us with an account of Jourdain's childhood and early studies: "Frantz Jourdain's father was a singer. His wife accompanied him on his tours, and this explains how Frantz came to be born in Antwerp on 3 October 1847. His father's voice had deteriorated and he had to give up the stage soon after his son's birth. This marked the beginning of gloomy days. .. The mother returned to Paris with her son.... His miserable cosseted childhood was watched over with impassioned devotion by his mother. .. a poet and musician. She had known Chopin, Georges Sand and corresponded with Marceline Desbordes Valmore. Some of her romances - the'Amandier fleuri ' - achieved near-fame... She founded the 'Ami du Foyer ', a journal of poetry and moral uplift.... He was sent as a day-pupil to the lycée Henri IV... He felt lost when away from his mother's dovecote; the ragging became a torture to him. It was at this time that he came to know a man who made an indelible impression on his young mind, and whose influence on his ideas and affections was to remain. There were agencies. .. which supplied visiting tutors. His mother applied to one such. .. A young man introduced himself. .. His name was Jules Vallès."[2] Under the guidance of this exceptional teacher, who exercised a considerable influence upon his future literary ambitions and political orientation, Frantz Jourdain overcame the trauma produced by his first contact with the lycée, and enrolled at the Collège Stanislas, where, in 1861, he obtained his baccalauréat. Following a brief experience in an import-export business, he began to attend the studio of Honoré Daumet, a member of the Institute and architect of the Château de Chantilly. In 1866, he passed the entrance examination and was officially admitted to the Ecole des Beaux-Arts. The Franco-Prussian war put an end to his studies. He enlisted as a volunteer, was wounded in action and awarded a medal.

Jourdain's experiences at the school in the Rue Bonaparte provided the theme of an autobiographical novel ("L'Atelier Chantorel"), published in 1893 at the insistence of Edmond de Goncourt. This irreverent satire on the Atelier Daumet marked the start of his opposition to the academic world. Interspersed with racy titbits, Jourdain's novel exposed the method of teaching at the school, the cultural standards of Daumet-Chantorel (whose motto was: "Swot up your orders, gentlemen, they are the grammar of our art, one cannot have enough of them"), the

studio life, the conformity of the students and the oppressive professional hegemony of the school, for which "it was indispensable to have the status of first-class student, to be a grand-prix winner or at any rate 'ranked" in order to be welcomed in a city or state office, or to find a lucrative position with a reputable architect".[3]

As for the characteristics of the studio master: "Monsieur Chantorel was the mirror of his work. .. Since he was modestly gifted, he was forced to make greater efforts than others to reach the glittering prizes. His reliability and energy made up for the brilliant qualities which he lacked. .. As a young man he had gained the Prix de Rome. The stay in Italy stirred his enthusiasm for the classical, he accepted without hesitation its familiar, dutifully studied beauties. His disciplined mind never questioned the reason for his admiration. .. His competition entries, immaculately presented and executed, attracted the Institute's attention for the considerable work put into them and the impersonal character of this designs, steeped in blind allegiance to the traditions of the house".[4] And here we have his students: "These young people had not been thrust into architecture by an overwhelming sense of vocation. Most were sons of the well-heeled middle classes, who had chosen a career promising to be profitable, graced with an agreeable air of self-esteem and sugared with preliminary

studies of not too demanding a nature".[5]

The principal preoccupation of such students, who "had little to endure from a regime which encouraged mental laziness", was "to collect the awards essential for the 'first class'". "A few days before the competition they would thumb through the photographs of designs which had previously gained a mention, to ascertain the judges' preferences. No strain on the imagination was needed; a good memory, resourcefulness, some familiarity with the pencil and with Indian ink, and one could be certain of winning a prize... Under the brash indifference of the student lurked the atavism of generations of bourgeois, with their vices, their appetites, their prejudices, their ancestral decadence. .. Their fetishism for the established order in everything, everywhere, whatever the implications, was only equalled by their hatred of evolution and their terror of changes introduced into time-honoured usages. Their beliefs were trivial, but their inflated attitudes engendered an uncompromising respect for such solemn words as 'society ', 'property ', 'the law ', 'antiquity ','academy ', 'family ', 'duty '."[6]

Apostasy was not tolerated in this segregated world: "Galvanized by the inspiration and independence of Labrouste, one studio had protested against the domestication of art and had energetically insisted upon intellectual freedom and the rights of individuality. .. The 'Ecole' outlawed this revolutionary minority."[7]

Conformity and mimicry, "architectural hypocrisy" and graphic exhibitionism concealing an absence of ideas, expressed themselves in competitions on absurd themes, "indefinable and sexless, which could have been thought up equally well on the moon as on the earth, in no particular epoch and in a civilization of freaks, among a population of phantoms".[8]

In this atmosphere of "bureaucratizing inspiration", the chief character, Gaston Dorsner, gradually rebelled against classicism: "Blindly, the young man had accepted the teaching offered to him. .. He had been taught that there were five orders. .. The novice had therefore started to copy and study the orders. .. in Vignola, the copy being pitted with compass-pricks and spotted with the ink-stains of several generations. .. The imagination atrophied during this exercise in mnemotechny, which, however, had the advantage of being clear, simple, and within the capacity of every brain, and which also allowed a complete temple to be reconstructed from the discovery of a fragment of base or capital, so immutable and tightly interlinked were the laws of this architectural vocabulary. .. Yet a disquieting note disturbed his serenity: These empirical formulae without which it was impossible for the designer to express himself, these unchangeable, eternal principles of almost divine tradition, were not to be found in a number of the monuments which had delighted his childhood and youth. Certainly he could see the orders on the Madeleine, the House of Parliament, the Stock Exchange. .. and in other buildings inspired by classical antiquity, but he was utterly confused when confronted by the Sainte-Chapelle, Saint- Germain-des-Prés, the Hôtel Cluny, Notre-Dame. .. And what about the architecture of the Moors, Persians, Arabs, Chinese, Japanese, Indians?. .. In a word, no more orders! Sheer madness, foolish anarchy, an epileptic Saint Vitus's dance, a silly negation of everything, or simply another idiom. ..? Had only Greece

and Rome kept the flame of truth burning? Like a religion, architecture had been enmeshed in the absolutism of a dogma and had consigned to oblivion the beliefs and endeavours of several million intellects, imposing the implacable catholic interdict: Outside the Church, no salvation!. .. This claim to shackle humanity for ever seemed to him both monstrous and grotesque. What? For everyone a single idiom, an unalterable syntax, when people and things are continually changing, when every race has its particular temperament, when each society shows different tendencies, when each climate stipulates distinctive needs? What? Inaction when a scientific discovery or political upheaval can alter our thought and behaviour, even the physiognomy of a nation? What? Ossification of an art which has most faithfully reflected men's souls, whose desires it has understood, whose wills it has strengthened, while supporting their struggles, guaranteeing their victories and recording their history in pages of devastating candour? The falseness of the doctrines which had intoxicated him revolted him now."[9]

The best pages of the novel are devoted to the desanctification of the classical code and to a lucid refutation of the historical conventions upon which it rests, while others, more general and briefer, describe an alternative to the didactic system of the "Ecole" and

propose on the cultural level a mediaeval eclecticism associated with a positivistic trust in teaching characterized by a more relevant presentation of technology and science: "He became increasingly convinced that it is impossible to become a great architect, without proving oneself as a competent 'builder '.... The decoration and structure of a building must be tackled together as a single concept: the one explaining the other, defining it, adorning it, without mendaciously disguising it; working and acting together to diminish and soften the roughness of matter and idealize the harshness of reality. To be concerned only with the external design, the image, in the belief that, beneath the conventional muscular system, the skeleton will take care of itself, is to omit the very essence of an art which is the expression of social needs and the composite effect of the normal aspirations of humanity".[10]

The "Atelier Chantorel" reopened the dispute between the partisans of Gothicism and classicism which, apart from arguments over style, had revealed a conflict "between those who passionately advocated that architecture be thrown open to such new techniques and materials as iron and glass, and those who stubbornly defended the continuance of the pompous world of Vitruvianism".[11] The quarrel had begun in 1846-47, at the time of the foundation of the mediaevalist "Société Catholique pour la Fabrication, la Vente, la Commission de tous les objets consacrés au Culte" and the submission of Gau's design for the church of Sainte-Clotilde. It found a sensational epilogue some twenty years later, in the bosom of the Ecole des Beaux-Arts - the intellectual lynching of Viollet-le-Duc.[12]

That a pioneer like Frantz Jourdain,

153

who had often anticipated subjects of controversy which were later to polarize the attention of artistic circles in France, was late in raising a similar theme (which incidentally was to be evoked in various articles published at the turn of the century in reviews closer to Art Nouveau) by no means indicated an inability to catch glimpses of original developments through the mists of French architectural discussion. Indeed he clearly recognized that, apart from the mediaevalist movement, there were no alternatives to academic classicism with its national implications, and that new trends could not blossom without the cultural and professional monopoly of the Ecole Classique having to be considered. This conflict was bound to entail opposition to the cultural policy of state education in the arts. In 1896 Frantz Jourdain published a collection of articles entitled "Those honoured and those who are not...", in which he proposed that the Legion of Honour be awarded to a group of writers and artists unconnected with academic circles. Thus he gave to his uncompromisingly anti-academic polemics the force of an indictment of state policy in the artistic field, which was to become a recurrent theme in his writings.

"L'Atelier Chantorel" was not limited to a record of the continuing polemic directed against the classical and mediaeval lobbies, nor to sustaining, in the manner of those advocating a technical solution to architectural problems, a mediaevalist movement which, in its recent manifestations, had found a way of reconciling technological experimentation with the retention of the stylistic characteristics of national tradition.

It is also possible to detect a degree of agnosticism in relation to the subject of style, which related already Jour-

dain's belief (explicit in later writings) that a dependent relationship existed between technological innovation and the satisfaction of new social needs on the one hand, and the adoption of a new architectural idiom on the other. Paradoxically, this stylistic indifference was to prove only a marginal, or negligible, influence on the perpetuation of the anti-classical campaign by the modernist reviews. The latter were to present a Nessus tunic to the classical camp in their dialectical opposition; more often than not they reduced the terms of intellectual debate to a chauvinistic affirmation of a continuing national tradition (i.e. mediaevalism) preordained to deny the contribution of international Art Nouveau architecture and the validity of the "Ecole Classique" - from now on directed, thanks to the teaching of masters like Julien Guadet, towards an evolving historical classicism which, in the work of the Perret brothers and Tony Garnier, would inherit the great tradition of French structural engineering.

Jourdain's anti-academicism avoided these pitfalls to the extent that it tended to steer clear of mediaevalist nostalgia. He claimed to diesbelieve in the historical relevance of a "problem of style" and in its solution by a rapid succession of social and technological changes, determined by a pluralism of factors transcending and invalidating any a priori aesthetic attitude: "Styles

have succeeded each other naturally... and there has never been any idea of exhuming one in order to give it an artificial life... The new style will take possession of contemporary society gradually, without shocks or violence. It will not be imposed upon us by formulae, nor by arguments... The revolution in our everyday practices will bring about a revolution in exteriors and in architectural forms... The new architecture will insinuate itself among us first of all through the many manifestations of contemporary industry, by way of a thousand details in domestic life and the innumerable needs of society which, being of recent creation, do not have to undergo painful comparison with the past... Architecture will know how to... ennoble the prosaic nature of current requirements, adapt to the beneficent demands of progress, profit dutifully from the advice of science, eagerly pursue the invaluable collaboration of industry, and be persuaded that Art is in everything".[13]

This ideology of progress formed - starting with the publication of "L'Atelier Chantorel" - the eclectic element in the framework of avant-garde art, which sustained a wide variety of manifestations and refused to restrict its assessments to the exclusive furthering of one particular trend; it was a rejection of the sectarian attitude typical of avant-garde groups, which was a mere reflection of its reaction against the exclusive character of official culture. The same ideology defined Jourdain's approach to Art Nouveau, which he regarded as a phenomenon that included many different interpretations of form and was in constant evolution. He rejected that which was a codified stylistic formula in Art Nouveau but supported that which was experiments with solutions to architectural idiom released from any constraints: "Modern style has been characterized in two words by stigmatizing it as 'whiplash art"... This amusing aphorism ... does not seem to me mathematically accurate. What is the relationship between Monsieur Guimard's Castel Béranger and Monsieur Bonnier's Pavillon du Creusot? Where is the connection between Monsieur Plumet's houses and Monsieur Provensal's designs? What is the bond between the conceptions of Monsieur Benouville and those of Monsieur Risler? Where is the point of contact between Monsieur de Baudot's rationalism and Monsieur Sauvage's imagination? Were one to use a telescope that brought the moon within a metre's distance, it would be difficult to detect the smallest sign of a 'whiplash" in the works of Messrs de Baudot, Gout, Chaïne, Guillemonat, Sorel, Sauvage, Risler, Bonnier, Choupay, Lavirotte and as many others. The essence of the contemporary style is a hatred of old formulae, a desire not to revive the past, a thirst for the unseen, a determination to return to the study of nature; in short, it is the triumph of individualism, which - to my eyes - is the only justification for art; it is an anarchic theory which, exasperated by antiquated social mechanisms, seeks to abolish everything in order to resume a natural state and build the temple of the new era on virgin soil. For the dissidents of today there is, properly speaking, neither code nor grammar, neither master nor servant; each follows where his temperament leads him, without taking instructions or accepting orders. Hence those curious divergences in outlook which prove the breadth of the vision. To remain logical to itself, the modern style must be constantly modified and must not give its entire allegiance to any distinctive principle; it has to march with the century, the year, the month, in order to survive; it would be regarded as equally impotent as classicism if it

stuck rigidly to its earlier experiments, however interesting they may appear. Evolve or perish, Michelet wrote."[14]

These ideological signposts indicate the unchanging principles sustaining most of Jourdain's literary production and his attempts to promote the modernization of the artistic institutions of the state and their replacement by new and more dynamic establishments. From such endeavours came the foundation in 1902 of the society "Le Nouveau Paris" - the president of which he was to become and which was conceived in opposition to the "Vieux Paris" - and the "Salon d'Automne". The aims of the "Nouveau Paris", created with the assistance of Jules Chéret, Auguste Rodin, Adolphe Willette, Albert Besnard, Alexandre Charpentier, Georges Bans, Alfred Bruneau, Henri Turot, Théophile Poilpot, Fernand Hanser, Charles Plumet, Henri Sauvage and Henri Guimard, were "to bestow a little beauty and charm upon the brutish essentials of our modern requirements and renew, in short, the invigorating traditions of the past which found a way of translating the most distressing materialities of life into works of art".[15] Despite the nostalgia implicit in George-Eugène Haussmann's methods, in which the society was steeped (and the interpreter of which Jourdain had sometimes become), the activities of the "Nouveau Paris"

produced hardly any noteworthy results; its efforts were largely confined to protests addressed to the Municipal Council (for example, when in 1904 the designs for the Opéra Métro station submitted by Guimard were rejected) and to proposals for new decorations on the occasion of popular festivals in Paris.[16]

The Salon d'Automne made a much greater cultural impact. Its foundation brought to an end a long series of partly successful attempts undertaken by Jourdain to revitalize the organization behind the two official salons: the Salon de la Société des Artistes Français, established in 1673, and the Salon de la Société Nationale des Beaux-Arts, founded in 1890 following the secession of the first. In 1892 the Société Nationale des Beaux-Arts decided to add a section of objets d'art to its yearly exhibition; it seemed that the establishement was eventually changing attitudes at the instigation of intellectuals such as Jourdain, who advocated a larger role for the arts and crafts in the salons. The Salon of the Artistes Français quickly followed suit.

This reform, however, was not complemented by a radical refurbishing of the contents. While it was tolerated in the arts and crafts section, Art Nouveau was banished, with rare exceptions, from the architectural exhibits. While the Société des Artistes Français maintained close ties with the Ecole des Beaux-Arts, the Société Nationale displayed some readiness to welcome the architectural work of Sauvage, Plumet, Pierre and Tony Selmersheim, Guimard and Lavirotte; nonetheless it continued to relegate Art Nouveau to a secondary place. The criteria of selection for the painting section continued to be even more rigid. The desire to see the creation of a "salon wide open to ... constant evolution with no bias in interpreting trends, a salon accessible to every innovation, any experiment and all endeavours, a salon sincerely and intelligently eclectic",[17] remained unsatisfied. Outlined in "L'Atelier Chantorel", the idea of founding a new salon had its origin there, but it was not realized until 1903, and then through a happy combination of circumstances: "To my great surprise", Jourdain recalled, "I had a visit from Yvanhoè Dambesson, a distinguished poet and Deputy Keeper of the Petit-Palais. .. With enthusiastic and generous warmth, he detailed a plan for an artistic organization, vital, modern, clever and daring. .. and, very kindly, proposed that I take on the chairmanship of the new salon. .. We did not wait. .. At once we arranged meetings on the mezzanine floor of a little café in the Place Blanche; we drew up the hell of a list of members. .. We recruited the malcontents, the converts, the ambitious, the ingenuous, the sincere, the knowing, the timid, the fanatics, the failures, the shrewd, the unscrupulous and the victimized. When one founds something . .. that thing must exist. .. The 'Salon d'Automne' was founded. .. Sauvage, who had answered the first bugle-call sounding the fall-in,. .. undertook to enlist in our interests one of his clients, Jansen, the tapestry-dealer in the Rue Royale who, without hesitation . .. agreed to be our backer and general administrator".[18]

The Salon was the child of improvisation and artistic and financial independence from the state authorities; it was to become in a few years one of the most influential institutions of French art and constitute Jourdain's principal contribution to furthering the work of the avant-garde. It had immediate repercussions: The following year, the Société des Artistes Décorateurs inaugurated its own salon at the Petit-Palais, thus presenting a picture which

contrasted little with the productions of Art Nouveau.

Jourdain joined other associations, among which mention should be made of "L'Art pour Tous", created by the art critic Louis Lumet and the mechanic Edouard Massieux in 1901. Its purpose was to promote the artistic education of the masses and bring art within everybody's reach through lectures and guided tours of museums and artist's studios.[19] He was also a member of the "Société internationale d'Art populaire, a group organized by Henri Cazalis, the purpose of which was similar to that of "L'Art pour Tous"; the "Société des Logements hygiéniques à bon marché", an association for the building of salubrious, low-cost housing, of which Jourdain was to become president in 1904; and the "Société nationale de l'Art à l'Ecole, created in 1907, the purpose of which was "to make children love nature and art, make school more attractive and contribute to the development of art appreciation as well as moral and social education among the young", through "the (interior and exterior) beautification of school buildings, the permanent or temporary decoration of schools, the distribution of school-related pictures (books, prizes, etc.) suitable for the children's age and level, and the introduction of children to the beauty of line, colour, form, movements and sounds".[20]

The direct and coherent character of the polemical writer and activist on behalf of avant-garde art is not apparent in Jourdain the architect, who seems to have struggled on in an atmosphere of disillusioned professionalism, from which he often appears to have deliberately kept aloof. In fact his heterogeneous and eclectic architecture confirmed the sour judgment of the critic L.-C. Boileau, to whom Jourdain was "a revolutionary when holding a pen in his hand" but "almost a conservative when holding a pencil".[21] Two works designed for the Exposition Universelle of 1900 to underline the contradiction between the two facets of the architect's personality: the Moët et Chandon pavilion - a modest exercise in the Louis XVI style which Jourdain described as "a little horror" because the time schedule imposed on him had been inadequate;[22] and the design for the Perfume section which, despite concessions to "Art Nouveau", disclosed echoes of Louis XV. Roger Marx, an admirer of the work, noted: "France has always been entertained by displays of ingenuity. .. There is a tenaciously held predilection for those semblances of construction - trellises. .. Their suitability is never more clearly justified than in celebrating the flower and the virtue of its essences. The plant wreathes and entwines the frail aerial architecture; it climbs and rampages along the laths. .. The exact point at which a perfect combination achieves the most graphic effects . .. none sees better than Monsieur Frantz Jourdain. .. With him the spirit of our eighteenth century is reborn a little; but, to his exemplary credit, Monsieur Frantz Jourdain only exploits tradition to revitalize it. .. The cloister and the salon have become, at the touch of Monsieur Frantz Jourdain's baton, the theme of a symphony in yellow major, in which every shade has been tried, from creamy white to orange, from jasmine to nasturtium;

except for the awnings and cable mouldings, which are mauve, flowers and woods blend in a delicate gilded harmony, and the displays of perfumes leave a memory of an exquisite smiling winter garden lost in the desolate steppes of the Champ-de-Mars".[23]

Jourdain's production, varied as it may be, betrays the characteristics of a professional routine redeemed by a technological grasp of architectural problems which attained its most convincing expression in buildings of a utilitarian purpose. Scantily reproduced in the reviews of the period, the architectural work of Jourdain - who had begun his career by using money he had inherited to purchase a practice in the Rue Richer, "its business modest but sound" and "the clients of which were above all preoccupied with obtaining on the best possible terms work without charm but at least without pretension"[24] - distinguished itself by an uncommon skill in applying the results of research into new materials: iron and reinforced concrete. These qualities, which are to be found also in the successful restoration of the châteaux of Vertheuil in Charente, La Roche-Guyon in Seine-et-Oise, and Châteauneuf-sur- Sarthe in Maine-et-Loire, are particularly apparent in such buildings as the factory which he built in 1888 at Pantin, the printing works in the Rue Cadet in Paris, the villa at Bouffemont in Seine-et-Oise "in limestone and brick, with tiled roof, exposed timber and iron, and its only decoration in the colouring of the materials"[25] and the residence of the master-smith Schenck, built in reinforced concrete in 1894 at 9 Rue Vergniaud, in Paris.

The extension of the Samaritaine department store provided Frantz Jourdain with the great opportunity to show his qualities. [26] Earlier he had

228. F. Jourdain. Expansion of La Samaritaine department store, façade on the Rue du Pont-Neuf. (1905-07). Altered. Detail of the façade.

been induced to tackle the theme of the department store when his friend Emile Zola had invited him to make an imaginary plan for his "Bonheur des Dames". The design for this "Temple of Temptation" conceived by Jourdain for the novel published by Zola in 1883 already included some architectural and typological traits which were to predominate in La Samaritaine and in a good number of Parisian department stores: "The new formal entrance. .. high and deeply recessed like a church porch, surmounted by a group depicting Industry and Commerce grasping hands among a confusion of attributes, was sheltered by a vast canopy, its bright gilding seeming to illuminate the pavements in a shaft of sunshine. .. When the shoppers raised their heads, they saw stacks of merchandise, through plate-glass, which - from the ground-floor to the second storey - exposed the building to the light of day. .. In the centre, on the axis of the formal entrance, a broad gallery stretched from end to end, flanked to right and left by two narrower galleries. .. The open courts had been

glassed in and transformed into halls; and iron staircases rose from the ground floor to the two floors above, with ironwork bridges from one side to the other. The architect, luckily intelligent, a young man in love with the new age, used stone only for the basements and angle-reinforcement, and then assembled the whole structural frame in steel, together with the stanchions supporting the system of beams and girders. The cambered elements carrying the floors and the partition walls of the interior were of brick. Space had been saved everywhere; air and light entered freely; the public circulated comfortably under the wide-span trusses. It was a cathedral of modern commerce, strong and light, made for a nation of customers".

Jourdain's description evoked such a modern concept of a department store that Zola, in a letter to his friend, had to express some reservations: "Your magnificent dream of a great modern bazaar does not apply entirely to my store. Firstly, my scenes take place before 1870 and I cannot make an anachronism without stirring up all the critics.... Ah, what a beautiful stage set I could make with your bazaar...." [27] Although Zola was forced perhaps to modify the preliminary picture of the "Temple of Temptation" outlined by Jourdain, the ideas contained in that picture were not lost. Jourdain himself was to admit later that the department store he had described to Zola, which was "a entierely imaginary construct, became real with the 'Samaritaine, thanks to the open-mindedness and trust of the most intelligent and least traditional among his clients." [28]

Ernest Cognacq, founder of La Samaritaine, also seems to have belonged to Zola's world of "Les Rougon-Macquart". Cognacq was made in the image of Octave Mouret (of the "Bonheur des Dames"). The son of a Clerk of the Court and a ship broker, he was born in 1839 at Saint-Martin-de-Ré. His father's insolvency reduced the family to a desperate economic state. The young Ernest had to give up his dream of becoming a naval officer. After working as a clerk with a draper at La Rochelle, then at Bordeaux, he settled at fifteen in Paris. Completing his apprenticeship with various drapers, he established in 1847 a modest shop in the Rue Turbigo, "Au Petit Bénéfice". The business failed and Cognacq had no other choice than to take a stall in the local markets. An itinerant salesman, he finished up by renting a room in a little café at the corner of the Rue du Pont-Neuf and the Rue de la Monnaie. He had laid the foundation-stone of this commercial success. In 1870 he bought the premises of the café and set up shop under the sign of "The Woman of Samaria". He was now on his way up. In 1871 La Samaritaine occupied an area of nine feet by twenty five (six metres by eight), and employed two assistants. In 1926, when the construction of a new store was begun according to the design of Sauvage and Jourdain, it had been transformed into an impressive company which provided work for a staff of 8000.[29]

The collaboration between Jourdain and Cognacq was a matter of chance, as Marcel Zahar noted. Cognacq who "was occupying a humble shop in a building in the Rue Pont-Neuf ... had just become the tenant of the premises next door and asked the architect of the house for permission to have an opening pierced in the party wall. Monsieur Frantz Jourdain agreed; but happening to pass by the site, he was filled with justifiable indignation; for there in front of him casual labourers recruited by Cognacq ... were hacking

229. F. Jourdain. Expansion of La Samaritaine department store. (C. 1907). Dome on the corner to the Rue de l'Arbre-Sec and the Place de l'Ecole.

wildly at the wall with picks and, in their ignorance, threatening to bring the whole building down. Monsieur Frantz Jourdain conveyed his professional opinion in spirited terms. After endless stormy discussions, peace and order were restored; and a few years later Ernest Cognacq knocked on the door of this severe critic and invited him to undertake the new Samaritaine".[30] Rey's evidence dates Jourdain's appointment as architect of La Samaritaine as 1883.[31]

Meredith L. Clausen gave a summary of the successive stages in the execution of this complex: "In 1904, Cognacq established a general plan for the extension of the "Samaritaine. Facing the first store on Rue de la Monnaie, the future stores 2 and 4 would stand between the Rue de Rivoli on the north and the bank of the Seine on the south. The main façade of the third store

would be in the Rue de Rivoli. As a result, the stores 2, 3 and 4 would create almost 375 feet (125 meters) of glazed surfaces on this main thoroughfare. The acquisition of land in the very desirable area of the central market was so slow that the extension plan took almost thirty years to be completed: It was not finished before 1933. Long negociations with the municipality started in 1902, because the extension of the second store was to eliminate a public street, Rue des Prêtres Saint-Germain-l'Auxerrois. But these negociations were even more comprehensive. In 1904, after several years of bargaining, a first agreement was struck. By a decision without precedent – which cost Cognacq a large amount of money – the municipal council authorized the construction of an underground gallery, under the Rue de la Monnaie, to connect the buildings 1 and 2. This was the first stage of the plan. Construction work on the second store began a year later, in April 1905. Frantz Jourdain started with the portion facing the first store, in the Rue de la Monnaie, and at the same time on the opposite end of the site, in the Rue de l'Arbre-Sec. As soon as the old buildings in the Rue des Prêtres were demolished, the east and west portions of the building were connected. The west cupola – one of the two that were to crown the façade in the Rue des Prêtres – was completed at this stage. Jourdain returned then to the central portion of the building to fill in the part between Rue de la Monnaie and Rue de L'Arbre-Sec. At the same time he was building the large, two-storey high underground gallery under the Rue de la Monnaie – which linked the two stores and ran the length of the whole street – and completed the second cupola in the Rue des Prêtres, on the corner of the Rue de la Monnaie. This work was finished in August 1907. The final part of the second store, along the Rue Baillet, was added in 1909-10 (plan of 1908)".[32]

The first significant commission was the plan for extending La Samaritaine, in place of twenty-three old houses of a group bounded by the Rues de la Monnaie, des Prêtres-St-Germain, de l'Arbre-Sec, and Baillet.

All that is left today of this imposing structure is the skeleton, practically stripped of the original decoration,

230. F. Jourdain. Expansion of La Samaritaine department store. Overall view of the façade. Altered.

231. F. Jourdain. New façade of La Samaritaine department store, Rue de Rivoli, Paris 1er. (1912). Demolished.

which reflect Jourdain's adherence to the idiom of Art Nouveau. If it is true, as Walter Benjamin perceptively noted,[33] that Art Nouveau "is the last attempt by art to break out of the ivory tower in which it is besieged by technology" and that "the new elements of iron construction, columns and load-bearing forms, are putting 'Liberty style' to the test", because it "is striving, through decoration, to win back these forms for art", one can say that very few works illustrate this attempt so forcefully as La Samaritaine.

Clausen justly pointed out that the "Samaritaine presented a synthesis of "the enthusiasm for modern technology, concern for the working class, and fascination for that which is new and exotic", which derived in great part from the Exhibition of 1900. [34] The "Samaritaine was also the product of the great tradition of French steel engineering, which had already proved itself at the Exhibition of 1889 and which Jourdain greatly admired. [35] The use of steel structures for the construction of department stores had several precedents in the nineteenth century. It was only with Art Nouveau, however, that the steel framing was made visible on the façade instead of being hidden behind stone architectural facings borrowed from the neo-Baroque or the neo-Renaissance. Victor Horta's "Innovation" in Brussels (1901-03) constituted a significant step in the renewal of department stores. According to Clausen, "Jourdain went even further than Horta", who had "left the metal exposed.... but not the structure, hiding "the elements of the simple metal structure.... behind flowing and decorative metal shapes". He added, "instead of concealing the horizontal character of the grid as Horta had done,... Jourdain allowed for the expressive quality of the structure itself and its repetition of rectangular elements. This was unheard of in Paris. Jourdain's exposed steel structure, the dominant horizontality in the grid, the ceramic panels and, most of all, the three-part windows.... call to mind the influence of office buildings by the Chicago School of architecture, and of Louis Henry Sullivan in particular. The first bays of the Schleisinger-Mayer store built by Sullivan (which later became the Carson Pirie Scott building) had the same characteristics; they were built in 1899 and construction work was completed in 1903-04". [36]

Recourse to an iron structural frame - frankly exposed in the elevation - offered on the one hand the advantage of reducing to a minimum the points of support, while giving maximum flexibility to the plan and "allowing air and light to enter abundantly as it should in such an establishment"; [37] but it also necessitated "a softening of the possible rigidity of such a system of construction". [38] The answer proved to be in a complex decorative apparatus: "The webs of beams and stanchions are decorated, on the upper parts, by friezes and panels of encrusted lava which are weather-resistant, dispensing with all joints and largely inaccessible to dust. .. and smoke...; lower down, the panels are made of hard wood by Vicado, carved by Janselme; they rest on bases in Bigot's ceramic ware and frame copper plaques chased and hammered by Schenck, and gilded mosaics". [39] The striking polychromy contributed to the conceal the "rigidity" of the structure. This polychromy was essentially based on the contrast between the blue beams and stanchions and the orange background of encrusted lava panels, upon which multicoloured blossoms framed the names of the various articles sold in the store.

Decorative requirements were not limited to cladding the skeleton frame with ceramic facing materials - as was the custom in contemporary steel and reinforced cement construction. Decoration also strove to shape the metal according to the vocabulary of Art Nouveau. In practice, the stanchions terminated in plant-like capitals, formed by a covering of metal coils bolted to the web and to the flanges of the beams. The ribs and lantern of the dome, since demolished, displayed an even greater virtuosity in the handling of metal. The dome itself, with its "virile and daring" silhouette, surmounted the cylindrical feature at the angle of the Rue de l'Arbre-Sec and the Place de l'Ecole and in the evening was illuminated by the light shining through glass bricks in the cupola. The dome apart, another conspicuous formal element was provided by the large bow-window which broke the uniformity of the façade at the point where the Rue de la Monnaie widens by merging with the Rue du Pont-Neuf, and marked the great hall which originally extended the full depth of the building. The sign bearing the name of the firm was designed by Eugène Grasset. It is all that remains of the exuberant decoration of this window. [40]

With regard to the extension of La Samaritaine, the critics of the time were unanimous, less about the originality of the architectural idiom, but more over the technological experimentation, which had brought to the fore some particularly interesting solutions in the installation of services (air- control and ventilation, heating, rainwater down-pipes, etc.); among such, the pipe-runs were housed in the cavities of the stanchions, while the electrical system made it possible to operate all the blinds of the display windows from a single control-point.

Many critics had reservations over the design of the decoration. Pascal Forthuny, for instance, in "La Gazette des

232-233 *H. Gutton. Grand Bazar in the Rue de Rennes, Paris 6ᵉ. Demolished. General view and interior detail.*

Beaux-Arts", which was very conservative in outlook, criticized Jourdain for "responding to the monotonous architecture of the diehard traditionalists by an architectural impetuosity in which iron clambers capriciously and fantastically up walls, an entertaining exercise in improvisation which has little in common with the rationalism the apostle of which Monsieur Jourdain declares himself to be"; but he recognized some extenuating circumstances, such as the affirmation of a "schismatic credo, conceived in the lyrical enthusiasm of a spirit in revolt" and, for this reason, "without the restful and consoling serenity which can only be inspired by acts of faith, gradually elaborated in hearts at peace with themselves and entirely sure in their beliefs".[41] Frantz Jourdain replied to these objections through the columns of "La Construction Moderne", referring to the persuasive role which should be one of the architectural characteristics of department stores, and maintaining "that one must not forget the function to attract which a department store is called upon to fulfil" without "fear of being conspicuous". In this way, "the glamour, the violence if you like, of this decoration, may be unusual perhaps, but it is studied and thoroughly thought out"[42] and it complied with the brief.

During the years of building the extensions, the store had become an experimental ground for new materials: reinforced concrete and iron. Opposite the Potin building - a significant expe-

161

234-235. R. Binet.
Renovation of the Grands
Magasins du Printemps,
58 Boulevard Haussmann.
Paris 9^e. (1910-11).
Burnt down in 1921.

riment in the plastic potentialities of concrete - the architect Henri Gutton had completed the Grand Bazar in the Rue de Rennes in 1906. He had already attracted notice in his native Nancy by his construction of the Graineterie Job. Like La Samaritaine, the Grand Bazar featured an exposed steel structure, dark green in colour, with wide glazed surfaces framed - on the mezzanine and third storey - with infill panels faced with black marmolite picked out in gold. The pioneering experiments of Jourdain thus had immediate repercussions.

Among other works influenced by Jourdain, mention should be made of Charles de Montarnal's commercial building "Aux 100.000 Chemises" (1906), at 26 Rue Louis-Blanc, which revealed a structural approach similar to that of the Samaritaine in its wide glazed surfaces framed by a metal structure. Jourdain's influence could also be felt in the renovation work by René Binet of Paul Sédille's "Printemps" department store, which was done between 1910 and 1911. The new interior arrangement created by Binet evoked the spatial characteristics of the "Temple of Temptation" described in Zola's Au Bonheur des dames, while lifts were made visible and their movement became part of the buil-

236-237. F. Jourdain. Apartment block, 16 Rue du Louvre, Paris 1ᵉʳ. (1912). Overall view and detail.

ding's architectural character, according to a theme already developed in the Samaritaine.

The successive designs which he carried out for La Samaritaine, added nothing to the themes already developed in previous extensions. The Rue de Rivoli elevation - dated 1912 and subsequently demolished - was a kind of sheath, with a metal skeleton, placed as a veranda in front of the existing building. A series of three windows, faced on the inside by ceramic panels with floral motifs by Bigot, opened above a canopy decorated by a metal pattern entirely in relief, and welded to a projecting roof protecting the display windows of the ground floor and mezzanine. Here too, as for the bow-window of the Rue de la Monnaie, the façade was surmounted

by a tympanum on which the name of the company was inscribed on a background bordered with garlands, and the stanchions and beams of which formed webs faced with encrusted lava and featured the same designs and colours as that used for the general design completed in 1907.

Cognacq decided to add to the main store of the Samaritaine, which was intended for the working class, a new store for more affluent customers, near the Opera, on the corner of the Boulevard des Capucines and the Rue Danou. He turned again to Jourdain, who submitted the outline of a design in 1914, with G. Bourneuf. Started in 1914 and completed in 1917, the Samaritaine de luxe featured wide glazed surfaces with a metal frame covered by flowery decoration, calling to mind the extension in the Rue de la Monnaie. Clausen observed, however, that "this was the extent of the resemblance. While he had avoided all masonry on the façade in the Rue de la Monnaie, Jourdain used a lot of stone on the façade on the Boulevard des Capucines. Instead of a simple grid dominated by horizontal axes emphasizing the regular metallic structure of the Samaritaine, the façade of the Samaritaine de luxe was more traditional in its general proportions, vertical

axis, symmetrical arrangement of
voids and solid spaces. Ornamentation
was less excessive, more elegantly
restrained and colours were less striking".[43]

The building at 16 Rue du Louvre is
noteworthy for the attempt to absorb
the salience of the columns of the
bow-windows and balconies into a
close plastic relationship, but without
attaining the moulded smooth surfaces
characteristic of Xavier Schoellkopf.
There remain only faint echoes of the
decorative exuberance of Samaritaine,
in the high-reliefs with floral motifs

*238-239. F. Jourdain. La Samaritaine de
luxe, 27 Boulevard des Capucines, Paris 2ᵉ.
(1914-17). General view and detail of the
façade.*

which adorn the entrance and the
balcony consoles, and in the ceramic
mosaics on the lintel of the mezzanine
windows.

After the war Jourdain's production
was never to reach a level of quality
comparable with that of La Samaritaine, but his role as a committed contro-
versialist did not flag; indeed in 1928
he launched an appeal to intellectuals
all over Europe to mobilize public
opinion on behalf of Le Corbusier's
(Pierre Jeanneret) design for the building of the League of Nations in
Geneva.[44]

NOTES

1 L.-C. Boileau, Causerie, in *L'Architecture*, XIII (1900), 28, p. 251.
2 R. Rey, *Frantz Jourdain*, Paris, La Connaissance, 1928, pp.206-8.
3 Frantz Jourdian, *L'Atelier Chantorel*, Paris, Charpentier, 1893, p. 176.
4 Ibid., pp. 81-82.
5 Ibid., p. 85.
6 Ibid., pp. 187, 105.
7 Ibid., pp. 187-188.
8 Ibid., pp. 186-187.
9 Ibid., pp. 112-114, 116-117.
10 Ibid., pp. 173-174.
11 L. Patetta, *La Polemica fra i Goticisti e i Classicisti dell'Académie des Beaux-Arts*, Francia, 1846-47, Milan 1974.
12 An interesting account of this episode, in the form of a dialogue between Gaston Dorsner and his friend Fabien, a former student at the Ecole des Beaux-Arts, occurs in L'Atelier Chantorel (op. cit., pp. 231-234):
« — Eh bien, poussez avec moi jusqu'aux Beaux-Arts.
Fabien prit la posture d'un malade qui vomit:
— Voilà l'effet qu'ils me font, vos Beaux-Arts; le diable m'emporte si j'y mets les pieds.
Les deux jeunes gens dégringolèrent l'escalier et, une fois dans la rue, filèrent rondement vers la Seine.
— Vous y avez cependant passé, par la boîte?
— Dans ma belle jeunesse, en 1863, l'année où l'on a vilipendé Viollet-le-Duc.
— Assistiez-vous au fameux chahut?
— Parfaitement; impossible de contempler spectacle plus bête, plus lâche et plus ignoble.
— Vous connaissez le parti-pris de l'atelier pour tout ce qui touche à l'Institut; je n'ai jamais appris, d'une façon précise, comment les choses s'étaient passées.
— Rien de plus simple. Quand Niewerkerke réorganisa l'enseignement artistique, il chercha à le soustraire à l'influence académique. Les mesures appliquées offraient une planche de salut à la jeunesse et lui permettaient de quitter le bourbier où elle patauge.
— La meilleure organisation eût peut-être été de fermer l'Ecole.
— D'accord, mais nous sommes trop encroûtés pour accepter les bienfaits d'une mesure aussi radicale. En somme, les peintres, les sculpteurs et les graveurs, après avoir grogné pour la forme, plièrent l'échine devant le nouveau règlement. Quant aux architectes, s'ils avaient été écorchés vifs, ils n'auraient pas crié davantage.
— Pourquoi?
— Vous vivez avec eux et vous me posez une pareille question? Parce que le restaurateur de Notre-Dame était accusé d'avoir activé le mouvement, parce qu'on le soupçonnait de vouloir introduire rue Bonaparte, à côté du Grec, du Romain et de l'Italien, l'étude du passé sans distinction de styles. Et puis... et puis, Viollet-le-Duc a retapé des monuments gothiques, il a suscité une poussée d'opinion en faveur d'une des plus glorieuses périodes de l'art français, il a contrecarré le vandalisme des cacatoès qui opèrent sous la coupole, il a arraché à l'Empire quelques millions pour empêcher nos monuments de disparaître et, dame, les camarades ne lui pardonnent pas de tels crimes. Ils préfèrent un tesson de vase étrusque à une statue de Chartres, et ils placent Percier et Fontaine qui ont jeté dans le tombereau du démolisseur les autels de Saint-Denis, fort au-dessus du vaillant défenseur de nos ruines.
— Mais en dehors de l'architecte et de l'archéologue, l'écrivain est de premier ordre. Son dictionnaire est l'œuvre d'un penseur, d'un philosophe, d'un érudit, d'un artiste hors pair. Et c'est une pareille personnalité qu'on a injuriée.
— Traînée dans la boue, mon bon. Est-ce qu'ils lisent d'ailleurs, les architectes?
— Oh! s'ils lisaient, je le reconnais, ils ne comprendraient pas et le résultat serait identique.
— En tout cas, le mot d'ordre fut arrêté: le moyenâgeux n'achèverait pas son premier cours. Comme pour *Henriette Maréchal*, on mêla étroitement la politique à ma révolution artistique, bien anodine pourtant, qui se préparait. Les fanatiques, voués au culte de la religion *quatre colonnes et un fronton* organisèrent l'attaque, et embrigadèrent les moutons de Panurge qui, le jour dit, s'empilèrent dans l'hémicycle. L'entrée du professeur fut saluée par une bordée de sifflets. On le cribla d'injures, on lui jeta des sous et des trognons de pomme, on fit éclater des pétards et des pois fulminants, on entonna des chœurs, on déploya le *Grand Journal* dont les immenses feuilles élevèrent une barrière entre l'orateur et l'auditoire.
— Et ses amis, ses partisans toléraient ces lâchetés?
— Nous étions écrasés par le nombre; vingt à peine sympathisaient à des tendances que l'École entière repoussait avec la fureur des brutes brisant le premier bateau à vapeur. Au fond, ces gamins échappés du collège ignoraient absolument de quoi il s'agissait, et les doctrines en présence étaient de l'hébreu pour eux; ils gueulaient pour gueuler et embêter le pion, voilà tout. Calme et crâne, le maître tenta de s'expliquer. Avec l'habileté que vous connaissez, il dessina quelques croquis au tableau; mais le tumulte s'accentuant, tumulte outrageant et humiliant, il quitta la place. Une bagarre s'engagea dans la cour, je faillis être assommé; des sergents de ville durent intervenir pour dégager Viollet-le-Duc qui tint à rentrer à pied chez lui. Sur le quai, le flot des manifestants se divisa; une partie de la foule se rua derrière Niewerkerke qui avait voulu payer de sa personne en assistant à la bataille. Très chic, ma foi, ce gaillard-là! Je le vois encore, le cigare aux lèvres, la badine à la main, traverser d'un pas tranquille le Pont des Arts pour regarder le Louvre, pendant qu'une meute d'infirmes, autour et derrière lui, gesticulait, menaçait, vociférait et hurlait: Vive l'Institut!
— Mais après?
— Au second cours, le chahut continua; impuissant à placer un mot, Viollet-le-Duc jugea de sa dignité de ne pas s'imposer et céda. »
13 F. Jourdain, "L'Architecture de demain", in *Propos d'un isolé en faveur de son temps*, Paris n.d. (1914), pp. 82-84, 89, 98.
14 F. Jourdain, "L'Art du décor à l'Exposition universelle de 1900", in *L'Architecture*, XIV (1901), p. 2.
15 F. Jourdain, "La Maladie du passé", in *Propos d'un isolé en faveur de son temps*, op. cit., p. 65.
16 F. Jourdain explained the purpose of the "Société du Nouveau Paris" in several articles, among which "Paris! Beau Paris", in *Touche à tout*, 15 March 1910, pp. 329-334; "La Maladie du passé", in *La Revue*, XLIX (November 1912), pp. 168-178; "Le nouveau Paris", in *Feuilles mortes et fleurs fanées*, Paris, La Jeune Académie, 1931, pp. 121-124.
17 F. Jourdain, *Le Salon d'automne*, Paris 1928, p. 8.
18 Ibid., pp. 10-13.
19 See Louis Lumet, *L'Art pour Tous*, Paris, E. Cornélie & Cie, 1904.
20 See Ch.-M. Coyba, Léon Riotor, Frantz Jourdain, Roger Marx, André Mellerio, Georges Moreau, G. Qué-

nioux, Auguste Chappuis, *L'Art à l'école*, Paris n.d. (1907). The architects Charles Plumet, Louis Feine, Charles Sarazin and Henri Sauvage were also members of this association. Jourdain was vice-president and later president of its commission on architecture, the secretary of which were Sauvage and Sarazin. The latter's commitment to "art in schools" was expressed in the furnishing and decoration of the classroom exhibited at the Salon d'Automne in 1907 and in the design of a country school for boys and girls, published in L'Art à l'école, op. cit., p. 49.

21 L.-Ch. BOILEAU, "Causerie", in *L'Architecture*, XIII (1900), p. 430.

22 Ibid., p. 254.

23 Roger Marx, *La Décoration et les industries d'art à l'Exposition universelle de 1900*, Paris n. d., pp. 44-46.

24 R. Rey, op. cit., pp. 28-29.

25 Ibid., p. 42.

26 Meredith L. Clausen wrote the most significant essay on the Samaritaine by Frantz Jourdain: "La Samaritaine", in *Revue de l'Art*, 1976, 32, pp. 56-76. On the history of this department store, see also F. Laudet, *La Samaritai-ne*, Paris, Dunod, 1933.

27 Quoted in M.L. Clausen, op. cit., p. 64.

28 See F. Jourdain, "Feuilles mortes et fleurs fanées", op. cit., p. 64.

29 For more biographic notes on Ernest Cognacq, see F. Laudet, op. cit., pp. 1-10; P. Jarry, *Les Magasins de nouveautés*, Paris 1948; Francis Jourdain, *Né en 76*, Paris 1951, pp. 255-269; Pierre Cabanne, *Le Roman des grands collectionneurs*, Paris 1961, pp. 107-124.

30 M. Zahar, "Les grands magasins", in *L'Art Vivant*, IV (1928), pp. 921-922.

31 R. Rey, op.cit., p. 39. Selon F. Laudet (op.cit., p. 19), the association between Jourdain and Cognacq goes back to 1888. It should be noted that Jourdain did some work on the Cognacq house in 1891 (see M.L. Clausen, op. cit., p. 75, fn. 51).

32 M.L. Clausen, op. cit., p. 58.

33 Walter Benjamin, *Schriften*, Frankfurt a.M., 1955.

34 M.L. Clausen, op. cit., p. 68.

35 See F. Jourdain, "Les Conquêtes de la science". L'Architecture, in *L'Architecture*, XIII (1900), pp. 378-379.

36 M.L. Clausen, op. cit., p. 66.

37 E. Uhry, "Agrandissement des magasins de la Samaritaine", in *L'Architecte*, II (February 1907), p. 13.

38 Ibid. 39. Ibid. 40. Francis Jourdain, the son of the architect, worked on the decoration covering the beams and pillars. It seems that Grasset was responsible for the big sign of the Samaritaine and the decoration of the tympana above the doors (see M.L. Clausen, op. cit., p. 59).

41 Pascal Forthuny, "Dix années d'architecture", in *Gazette des Beaux-Arts*, I, (1910), pp. 433-434.

42 D.A., "Magasins de la Samaritaine à Paris – Nouvelle façade sur la rue de Rivoli", in *Construction moderne*, 3rd series, VII (1911-1912), p. 316.

43 M.L. Clausen, op. cit., p. 60.

44 See C.L. Anzivino and E. Godoli, *Ginevra 1927 – Il Concorso per il Palazzo della Società delle Nazioni e il caso Le Corbusier*, Florence, Modulo Editrice 1979, pp. 94-95.

Antichambre

Concierge

Salle à Manger   Salon

241. *H. Sauvage. Villa Majorelle, 1 Rue Louis Majorelle, Nancy. (1898-1901).*

240. *H. Sauvage and Ch. Sarazin. Project for a town house on the corner of a street.*

VII

HENRI SAUVAGE

Of all the protagonists of Art Nouveau architecture in France, only Hector Guimard and Henri Sauvage escaped the reactionary cultural decline which occurred on the eve of the First World War. The conflict was still barely over when Guimard demonstrated a considerable capacity for innovation in the office block of the Rue de Bretagne (1914-19), while Sauvage had shown from the earliest years of the century an ability to avoid the repetition of certain formulae and keep up-to-date with the idiom and tenor of his production, all of which pointed to an innate forward- looking disposition that was to reach its full potential by the l920s. Despite the unevenness of his post-war work, which oscillated between Art Déco formalism (manifest in the construction of the Gambetta and Les Sèvres cinemas and the new central building of La Samaritaine, erected in collaboration with Frantz Jourdain), an International Style mannerism resembling in some degree that of Robert Mallet-Stevens and the better achievements of Michel Roux-Spitz, and a "Neue Sachlichkeit" structural severity best expressed in the buildings of the Decré department store at Nantes (1931)[1] and in some early experiments with prefabrication, Henri Sauvage was to remain until his

death in 1932 among the front-runners of the Modern Movement in France. Although Sauvage was ignored, or only mentioned in works devoted to the history of modern architecture for his stepped houses in the Rues Vavin and Amiraux, he attained - unlike Guimard -a considerable critical success in his day, even on an international level. The attention accorded to him by critics for his activities in the years 1920 to 1932 partly accounts for the indifference shown to his early Art Nouveau works.

Born in Rouen on 10 March 1873, Henri Sauvage settled in Paris after attending the lycée in his native town. He took the entrance examination of the Ecole des Beaux-Arts in 1890. The young student of the Pascal studio quickly developed a keen dislike of academic teaching. Five years after

joining the Ecole in the Rue Bonaparte, he took part, like his friends Henri Provensal, Gabriel Guillemonat and Ernest Herscher, in an exhibition of avant-garde architecture in the Le Barc de Boutteville gallery, in the Rue Le Peletier. His frequent visits to the studio of Alexandre Charpentier, whose son-in-law he was to become, were to influence his cultural training decisively. The sculptor numbered among his friends such personalities as Auguste Rodin, Félix Aubert, Dampt, the architects Frantz Jourdain and Charles Plumet, and Emile Zola. The young Sauvage found in this circle, which inspired the Groupe des Cinq, the intellectual roots of his anti-academic attitude.

After forsaking the Ecole des Beaux-Arts in 1895, Sauvage began to attract critical attention with a range of Art Nouveau furniture exhibited at the Salons of the Société Nationale des Beaux-Arts. Thanks to the Loïe Fuller theatre of 1900-01, at the Exposition Universelle de Paris, and to the Villa Majorelle at Nancy, Sauvage soon occupied a high place in Art Nouveau architecture in France. For these two works the architect followed the suggestions of two exceptional clients, representative of the small independent employer who was to determine the professional sphere of Art Nouveau architects in France - a country which had not experienced any understanding between the intellectual avantgarde and leading capitalists who elsewhere favoured the new style. With the exception of the collaboration between Guimard and Paul Nozal, French Art Nouveau architects did not include in their clientèle representatives of industry, finance and the top bureaucracy, similar to the Güell and Batllo families in Cataluña, Ernest Solvay, Georges Deprez and Edmond Van Eetvelde in Belgium, Emil Rathenau, Peter Bruckmann and Karl Ernst Osthaus in Germany. On the other hand, they could count on a good number of intellectuals, artists and businessmen connected, in one way or the other, with Art Nouveau: Paul Mezzara, Bigot, René Lalique, Madame Carpeaux, etc. The essential character of this clientèle, which became identified as a cultural élite, and the lack of support from a wider section of society, accounts for the limited diffusion of Art Nouveau architecture in France.

Two figures stand out among Sauvage's first clients, who played a significant role in the development of Art Nouveau in France; Louis Majorelle and Loïe Fuller. While the work of Louis Majorelle, who made furniture designed by Sauvage and commissioned him a house at Compiègne in 1908, has been the object of close critical analysis, Loïe Fuller's deep influence on Art Nouveau remains largely unexplored. The sculptor Pierre Roche described her unhesitatingly as an "artiste décorateur", crediting her with bringing about "a complete revolution in theatrical decoration" and "opening up a new road for modern decorators".[2] The interest aroused in artistic and intellectual

circles in Paris by the dancer's first appearance at the Folies Bergères in 1892 confirmed that there was nothing exaggerated in Pierre Roche's claim. Her figure, neither slender nor lissom, was enveloped in veils concealing a tendency to plumpness. Within a few years, it was to become one of the commonest iconographical themes in the repertoire of Art Nouveau artists, even abroad. From the posters of Georges De Feure, Jules Chéret, Alfred-Victor Choubrac, Charles-Louis Lucas, Pal (a pseudonym for Jean de Paléologue), Manuel Orazi and Henri de Toulouse-Lautrec to the sculptures of Pierre Roche, Théodore Rivière, Bernhard Hoetger and Raoul-François Larche and the drawings of Koloman Moser, Marie-Félix-Hippolyte Lucas and Toulouse-Lautrec again, this physical opposite to Art Nouveau's eternal feminine seems to have fascinated many artists.

But Loïe Fuller was not only the product of a cult, the living symbol of a style, the favourite model for feminine silhouettes which, reproduced by the thousand, invaded middle-class homes. She was also the bearer of an aesthetic message, the repository of a concept of art which successfully conquered intellectuals and artists, and imbued Art Nouveau. Stéphane Mallarmé dedicated prose and verse to her; Igor Stravinsky admired her for her performance in the ballet "Feux

d'Artifice"; Anatole France said that she was "perhaps without knowing it" the custodian of "a complete theory of knowledge" and "a complete philosophy of art";[3] Henri Van de Velde stressed the tonal resemblance between her dancing and the "new style".[4] But it was Roger Marx in particular who illuminated in a penetrating manner - he devoted to her various articles and a monograph illustrated by Pierre Roche - the many and complex influences of Loïe Fuller on contemporary artists. An exponent of Art Nouveau, Roger Marx wrote: "A similar fervent and passionate cult of nature determines the harmony between the movement and the lights in the rays of which it is magnified. Every theme created is borrowed from the natural world and the elements, from the atmosphere, the stars in their courses, the phases of the year. Here is the justification for the semblance of a meteor, a bird, an insect ... the explanation for the creation of those 'girl-flowers' already present in the dreamworld of Walter Crane. ... The enchanting phantom glides through the polychrome waves of the electric glow; it skims the ground with the lightness of a dragonfly, hops and delicately settles like a bird, brushes with fluttering wings like a bat".[5] Woman-flower, woman-bird, woman-dragonfly, woman-butterfly: the themes of metamorphosis which characterized the work in precious metals, the jewelry and glass of Art Nouveau were all found in the sinuous dancing of Loïe Fuller, evoking a "vegetation of fantasy and impassioned love, which brings together, in one symbol, nature and being, and lights up the frail substance of flowers with a woman's smile".[6] The voluminous veils of the dancer traced vigorous lines, rising to extraordinary heights with the help of discreetly placed slips of wood and a series of ventilators;

242. H. Sauvage. Loïe Fuller Theater at the International Exhibition of 1900.

they were shot with streaks of changing light which Roger Marx saw as foreshadowing the opalescence of Lalique glass and the shifting transparency of the vases of Gallé and the School of Nancy.

Apart from this resemblance in forms, the Loïe Fuller myth was fed by implications which touched the core of the movement's aesthetic ideology. "In every scene she reappeared, the same yet different, aspiring, displaying an inventive originality that baffled imitation. .. Such complicated performances were not attainable. .. without patient preliminary effort; hence. .. the total novelty of the creations, often of genius, . .. hence, the day and night rehearsals, in the course of which the artist took on the difficult role of the engineer, assuming the direction of stage-hands and electricians, and obtaining and leading a coordinated effort so that, in anticipated succession, movements, lines and colours were correlated simultaneously".[7] In Loïe Fuller's dancing, the "search for that which is new" and the technical experimentation contributed to the

perfect union postulated by Van de Velde, for whom the "doctrine of the nine" would surely have recognized the rationality of the forms and their correspondance to technical fact. In Roger Marx's biased interpretation, the quest for originality and the winning back of technology for art were the basic elements which made Loïe Fuller the precursor of the aesthetic ideology of Art Nouveau. Besides, the component parts of the dancer's stage experiments - "her studies with mirrors, her researches into the projection of painting, polarized and reflected

light, dust floating in the air, the luminous rays that flash through chemical solutions, in short - fluorescence"[8] - were explicitly recognized by the critic as the sources of an artistic renaissance which went beyond the boundaries of stage perspective: "It was the province of the artificial vibrations and light waves to heighten visual sensibility already stimulated by the analysis of brightness to which Impressionism had pointed the way; a painterly technique strove to reproduce the flashes, clashes and fusion of tones, flaring, provocative, as on certain 'flambé' vases, by virtue alone of proximity and contrast. Unsuspected problems of balance appealed to the sculptor at the same time as an entrancing variety of disregarded movements was disclosed for his attention. What indeed could not be learnt from the flow and folds - the liquefaction - of flying draperies! . .. There was not an decorator, in quest of a future style, who did not draw from this repertory of innovative decorative themes - so true was it that to all who brought life to inanimate matter, to every poet of design and form, and of light and shade, there streamed a wealth of bountiful inspiration."[9]

The veils tossed by Loïe Fuller in her dances provided the theme for her theatre, one of two designed by Sauvage for the Exposition Universelle of 1900. The other, intended for puppet shows and situated close to the Alexandre III bridge, was a minor work - composed of a varnished orange-wood structure and panels of stretched fabric, with simple decorations inspired by the circus and variety stage - which demonstrated its ephemeral character by undisguised echoes of Luna Park. We have preserved few memories of these theatres, now demolished. A few photographs of the Loïe Fuller theatre survive. They show the façade built in collaboration with the sculptor Pierre Roche: "Generous draperies are spread, gathered, and then lifted to expose the entrance, only to drop once more and extend their serpentine folds; the edges, fluted at ground level, are drawn taut at the angles and twist into spirals."[10] At the entrance two caryatids represented the dancer, draped in "tissues billowing into volutes" in the "lissom play of flexions, points and girations". The same Loïe Fuller was represented in the form of a statue poised above the entrance, "whose pose is so vivid that one might call her a great bird beating the air with its wings as it takes flight!"[11] Conceived as a curtain, the façade "serves as overture and frontispiece to the show performed inside".[12] It was, therefore, an exercise in architecture for advertisement, in which the homage to the owner's art was translated into advertising adapted to the characteristics of a theme, and the value of which lay largely in demonstrating the narrow line separating the evocative symbolism of Art Nouveau from kitsch" - in spite of the enthusiastic approval of Roger Marx and Frantz Jourdain.[13]

A similar concern to express a personality trait of the client through architecture was interpreted in a far more praiseworthy way by the building of the Villa Majorelle at Nancy, the capital of Lorraine. The city was in course of becoming one of the most important centres of Art Nouveau in Europe, because of the flourishing state of the decorative arts, but also due to the architectural works of Emile André, Georges Biet, Lucien Bentz, Henri Gutton, Eugène Vallin and Lucien Weissenburger. "Sauvage knew how to give the Nancy villa its true character", Frantz Jourdain emphasized. "We clearly recognize the house of sensitive and perceptive artist, with refined tastes, a cultivated mind and discerning eye, who had little regard for the strictures of others or for fashionable snobberies, and who wanted to add beauty to the comforts of life".[14] Built in 1901-02, the villa perfectly illustrates the method of design propagated by Art Nouveau, which was based on the exposure of the interior structure on the elevation: "The four façades", Jourdain observed, "are different, for reasons of logic and not as a whim; they are the result of a mathematical resolution of the problem presented; and the lack of symmetry allows the plan to be read and the interior distribution to be accurately observed. .. but it informs the whole design with wit and imagination".[15] The various functions of the interior rooms and their distribution were indicated in the exterior design by the pleasing proportions and the variety of the bays, and also by the articulation of masses in which echoes of mediaevalist civil architecture persisted. "By juxtaposing the façades to the plans and making the first subject to the second, the architect renewed", Jourdain added, "... the sacred tradition of the Greek and Gothic styles, the tradition of true classicism which permits no cheating, no deception. This respect for truth he applied just as rigorously in his decoration, which was impeccably rational, and was conceived. .. all together, with the construction, as the consequence of an idea and the corollary of a theorem."[16] No detail escaped the architect's control. Each element of the construction enabled him to prove his decorative virtuosity and the technical mastery which was a constant feature of his work. The skilful integration of widely different materials (stone, brick, iron, wood, ceramics, etc.) never seemed artificial; on the contrary, the skilful use of technical and expressive characteristics in each of these materials instilled in the whole a rational variety of form. "Sauvage", Jourdain said, "appears ... to push his love of equality to its ultimate limits. .. the down-pipes which are usually disowned and sometimes hidden . .. assume the place which is proper to them. .. externally, so as to prepare for any possible accident in case of damage in a hard frost. And the jointing fitments inspired the his imagination to provide charming decorative motifs which . ... brighten the coldness of walls and prove that in art there are neither nobles nor commoners, neither privileged nor outcast."[17]

244. H. Sauvage. Dresser in the Café de Paris, 41 Avenue de l'Opéra, Paris 8ᵉ. (1899). Demolished.

Victor Prouvé, who executed decorative paintings, Jacques Grüber, who signed the stained-glass windows, and Louis Majorelle himself, who was in charge of the wood- and ironwork of his own studio/house, all contributed to make of this villa a total work of art (*Gesamtkunstwerk*) in Art Nouveau. Among the more significant elements of this concern for detail, which combined formal invention and technical skill, were the canopy over the main entrance, the balustrade of the steps linking the garden to the salon, the metal supports, resting on stone consoles and carrying the wooden balcony of the studio and, above all, the tall chimneys of glazed stoneware adorned with crocketing (designed, like all the other such elements, by the potter Bigot) whose only equivalents were the chimneys by Antoni Gaudi for the Vicens house and the Palau Güell at Barcelona.[18]

While he was still gravitating within the orbit of Art Nouveau, Sauvage furnished, again about 1900, two remarkable proofs of this talent as a decorator by rehabilitating two of the rooms of the Café de Paris and the premises of the tapestry dealer Jansen in the Rue Royale in Paris. In the rooms of the Café de Paris (1899), Sauvage completed the work begun by Louis Majorelle and he showed his

affinities with those who believed in unifying the design of furniture and mural decoration. An example of this integration is provided by the dresser resting on a base which is a projection of the skirting, and by the stays which buttress the consoles and shelves and are directly connected to ribs on the wainscoting. Sauvage distinguished himself by his intelligent interpretation of the themes of "continuous furniture" and multi-purpose furniture which were, in the work of many designers and even occasionally in that of protagonists of Art Nouveau, expedients for displaying their virtuosity under the pretext of a multi-functionalism of no real practical use. The decoration of the Café de Paris proved that much of Sauvagés furniture was intended to serve a variety of purposes; but here sensible control over the design led to genuine functionalism. Working in one of the temples of fashionable Parisian life, he succeeded in creating an impression of luxury without making concessions "to expedients rejected by logic and good taste". "Everything derives here from sound construction," G.M. Jacques noted, "without frills, purposeless parts and decorative additions... each piece... is an essential element of the whole. In this unity, from which the purely decorative component is deliberately excluded, the luxurious character is

245. H. Sauvage. Chimney piece in the Café de Paris.

the result of the uncommon richness of forms."[19] While intended exclusively to emphasize the wooden fillets - which divide the ceiling from the walls - or to mark the separation on the frieze between the walls and the ceiling, the floral motifs are also subordinated to the structural concept of the whole.

In the design for the tapestry dealer Jansen (c. 1902), the store space was divided into various areas by partitions in which the wooden ribs, carved with foliage, framed panels faced with a fabric of floral design. The bathroom

deserves particular attention: Once again assured of Bigot's collaboration, Sauvage experimented in the many possibilities offered by glazed earthenware. "The walls of the room are entirely covered with ceramic tiles, with a bolder relief running along the base.... The grey and yellowish tones of the scheme as a whole are enlivened with streaks and patches of a more strongly coloured enamel in shades of green and blue, in which the process of firing can be better appreciated. Ceramic tiling is also used for the floor, and ceramic ware for the bath itself."[20] By using all the properties of ceramics,

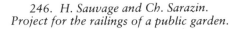

246. H. Sauvage and Ch. Sarazin.
Project for the railings of a public garden.

247 H. Sauvage and Ch. Sarazin.
Project for a public bath on the sea-side of
Alger. (C. 1902).

Sauvage designed fixtures which formed a monolithic whole with the walls, with the exception of a marble table placed in front of a large mirror. Next to the mirror, in a frame of three compartments, two ceramic brackets emerged from the wall and continued the decoration of the wainscot, surmounted by reliefs representing female figures enveloped "in flowing undulations". The same theme was repeated on the main wall by the substitution of a door for the mirror and of two cupboards with glazed doors, with reliefs by Frantz Jourdain. Finally, a recess incorporating two seats separated by a small table, and panels of translucent glass concealing lamps and decorated with coloured reliefs designed by Alexandre Charpentier, ensured the diffused, polychrome lighting of the bathroom.

Sauvage's contribution to Art Nouveau consisted also in a series of architectural designs published in the German review "Moderne Bauformen",[21] and a vast quantity of furniture, decorative objects, stencilled ornament, bookbinding, art metalwork of all kinds - which epitomizes the distinctive traits of French interpretation of Art Nouveau. The furniture reflected a taste for delicate carving which, in Europe, was the particular faculty of French cabinet-making (still able to rely upon a highly skilled craftsmanship which was already disapearing in other countries), as well as the integration of the various decorative elements and the close link between decoration and structure in the pursuit of clarity of construction. Over and above its rich idiom, Sauvage's philosophy found its intrinsic coherence in his predominantly rationalist attitude, which also asserted itself in some of his architectural work carried out during the first decade of the century.

From the turn of the century, Sauvage, with his partner Charles Sarazin,[22] operated on two fronts: flats, shops and assembly rooms for the well-to-do middle class on the one hand, and low-cost working-class dwellings on the other. In the latter field, in which economic restrictions abounded, Sauvage and Sarazin achieved exemplary results in the rationalization of building methods. Among others mention should be made of the block built for the Société Anonyme des Logements Hygiéniques à Bon Marché, in the Rue Trétaigne in Montmartre.[23] At that time low-cost housing was a central interest of numerous private companies, for which reformism appeared as a new weapon to fight the spreading of Marxist socialism. A policy of low-cost housing was one of the priorities in the programme of this political reformism. The private companies also concealed their speculative aims beneath a show of philanthropy and ensured anonymity for important financial groups. However, a particular concept of the return on capital investment distinguished this form of enterprise. The concept of maximum short-term yield, calculated on the low-cost construction of dwellings liable to rapid obsolescence, was replaced by that of investment subject to long-term depreciation, but offering the prospect of a longer-lasting return. This approach implied that savings could result from rationalizing the

site-work rather than from using materials of inferior quality. Moreover, the new architectural complexes must not entail heavy expenses in maintenance. The hygienic low-cost block in the Rue Trétaigne (c. 1903) illustrates this policy by its rationalized construction (reinforced concrete frame and brick infill), the meticulous selection of the materials used and close attention to finishes.

The façade was characterized by an exposed concrete structure and simple brick infills. During the construction work, and for reasons of economy, brick infills replaced the textured surfaces of brick and glazed tile which had been originally planned in the design and were more Art Nouveau in style. The building was remarkable for its honesty of construction and innovative idiom, more so than Perret's building at 25 bis Rue Franklin, which was executed at almost the same time. The latter featured a ceramic cladding, in which a graphic treatment of surfaces revealed the structure, and the result seemed less timeless.[24]

Edmond Uhry noted that the block in the Rue Trétaigne "underwent especially detailed study in order to satisfy every requirement of modern hygiene: the abolition of all nooks and corners difficult to clean, an unquestionable source of epidemics; the best possible ventilation, and the active encouragement of tenants to maintain, of their own volition, the greatest cleanliness of their homes and persons; no gaps between floorboards to harbour dust; everywhere porphyrolite . . . an agglomerate of wood and manganese cement.... On the walls this mastic coating is applied to a height of three inches (ten centimetres) to round off the angles and make cleaning easier. The walls themselves are not papered and carry no hangings that might be

248 *H. Sauvage and Ch. Sarazin. Bathroom.*
Ceramics from Bigot. (C. 1902).

soiled or stained. Washable Ripolin paint is used everywhere. A rail or bead is fixed all round every room, allowing tenants to hang their pictures without damaging the paintwork. There are no cornices. Instead, a groove runs along the top of the wall making a flush joint with the ceiling, in which dust cannot collect. The kitchens. .. are very airy and light."[25]

The care for details, under the pretext of hygienic considerations, therefore ensured easy maintenance and long life for the building. The pursuit of profit might from now include, among those with a wider vision than that of English jerrybuilders, a concern for quality: "It was essential to distinguish this building from a sanatorium and strike . .. a modest note of domestic artistry, avoiding the excessive coldness of bare walls."[26] It was also possible to channel idiom of Art Nouveau to give an air of prosperity to low-cost architecture, which in this case did not neglect social activities (on the ground floor a peoples' "University" with library and lecture-room, equipped for plays, a "hygienic" restaurant, a co-operative supply store and shower-bath facilities for the tenants) and tried to reconcile mass-production and the quality inherent in the "one-off" job. The polychrome panes of the main door, the mural

paintings of the staircase with their floral motifs and the staircase itself were the last echoes of Art Nouveau and contributed to giving the superficial appearance of luxury apartments to an "inexpensive" architecture - as did the roof converted into a hanging garden, which has now been replaced by a Mansard roof containing additional rooms.

Low-cost architecture provided for Sauvage and Sarazin their largest field of activity, and the most stimulating, and this experience prompted them to extend their study of new techniques and novel materials, and to experiment with the rationalization of site-work, laying the foundations of further

249-250. H. Sauvage. Low-cost dwelling, 7 Rue Trétaigne, Paris 18ᵉ. (1904). Façade and detail of the entrance.

research which was to be undertaken in succeeding years. However, their work in the field of apartment blocks should also be recalled. Their early attempts in this sphere (such as the flats at 17 Rue Damrémont and at 22 and 22a Rue Laugier) were of a compe-

tent professional standard, but they did not escape the usual criticisms levelled at this type of building, nor did they present any particular architectural merits. The apartment block at 111 Avenue Victor-Hugo, also known as "Cité Argentine", is much more interesting. The request for the building permit was submitted on 7 November 1904.[27]

This building, in one of the roads converging on the Place de l'Etoile, shows a very clear discontinuity in the sequence of frontages, by a deliberate, even provocative shift away from the historically inspired architectural standards of the neighbouring structures.

251. H. Sauvage. Gabled house, 26 Rue Vavin, Paris 6⁶. General view.

Another such block, however, built at 26 Rue Vavin (1912-14) and characterized by its stepped plan, was to bring Sauvage international fame. In the block of the Rue Vavin - more than in the offices built around the same time in the Rue deProvence - Sauvage exemplified a rationalism now confident of its technical resources, which marked the culmination of one series of experiments and initiated another. His approach does not seem to have progressed in a straight line, but to have advanced in cycles, in which different phases of research alternated, which were of a similar kind but incomplete in themselves, and were to be developed in later stages. While the dominating theme of the his first phase of activity may be defined as the winning back of technology for art, the use of new materials as vehicles for a new vocabulary, in the succeeding phases - represented by his work in the field of low-cost housing - technical experiments tended to be confined to the verification of his own data, leaving incidental idiomatic problems subordinate to the needs of architectural standardization and rationalization. Following this experimental period, his technical expertise was directed towards the invention of a particular urban building-type, which opened up new opportunities for architectural research.

It seems that the first studies in which Sauvage and Sarazin proposed the stepped-building type, such as that of the block in the Rue Vavin, go back to

1907-08. The only drawing bearing a date, however, is one of 1909, for a street of stepped working- class houses, with terraced gardens.[28] The characteristics of the site, with its long and narrow rectangular shape, did not permit the clearly articulated plan around interior courts which is customary in Parisian architecture; the narrowness of the Rue Vavin suggested to Sauvage a solution suitable for application on a larger scale, consisting in the arrangement of the flats in a stepped formation, the floor above in each case set farther back than the one below, leaving spacious terraces on each storey of the façade. The loss of serviceable floor space caused by the terraces, to which the flower-boxes gave an air of hanging gardens, was balanced by the reduced size of the interior court. This building-type, which presented the advantage of a light and airy street, entailed the existence of an unbuilt space inside the building, which diminished progressively from the bottom to the top and formed a void of triangular section.

This implied a series of overhangs brought about by the use of reinforced concrete construction. There were obvious analogies here with the designs of Antonio Sant'Elia for his "Città Futurista": the two salient parts (containing the sitting-rooms of the flats) which break the horizontal effect of the terraces, and the basic concept of the stepped plan, had their equivalent in the stepped skyscraper of the Italian architect, linked by foot-bridges to the projecting features housing the staircases and lifts. In addition, even the Futurist movement which chauvinistically sought to place Sant'Elia at the head of the archaeological axis of modern architecture, did mention the Rue Vavin building as evidence of the influence exercised on Europe by the architect from Como, but it failed to indicate that Sauvage's work predated that of Sant'Elia. The building in the Rue Vavin had precedents in nineteenth-century designs by French architects Hector Horeau and Jules Borie, as well as in American designs - not widely known at the time - of the last decade of the nineteenth century (for example, a design for stepped skyscraper by Louis Sullivan, published in 1891)[29] and in sanatoria built at the turn of the century in Germany.

The developments which followed the Rue Vavin building are sufficient proof that Sauvage regarded it as a model for metropolitan architecture. Besides the low-cost flats of the Rues des Amiraux and Hermann-Lachapelle

(1923-25), which feature two stepped buildings fronting two parallel streets and including, in the space between, a public swimming-bath, he proposed this building-type in a series of designs, such as the stepped-streets (1920 and around 1922), the "Giant Hotel" (1927), a stepped building with a garage for 4,000 cars, fronting the Seine (1928), and the design submitted in a competition for the redevelopment of the Porte Maillot.[30] It is quite likely that these studies were known to Adolf Loos, an occasional member of Parisian artistic circles, who, in 1923 (one year after a long visit to the French capital), signed the plans for two groups of low-cost stepped dwellings and the Hotel Babylon, which brings to mind Sauvage's Giant Hotel designed a few years later, in 1927.

254. H. Sauvage. Low-cost dwelling, 1 Rue de Chine, Paris 20ᵉ. (1908). Overall view.

255. H. Sauvage. Worker's house, 13 Rue Hippolyte-Maindron, Paris 14ᵉ. (1905-06).

A brief analysis of Sauvage's early production pinpoints the complexity of his personality and the interest of his work; it also makes it impossible to evaluate his contribution to the modern movement without taking into account the work of his youth which bore the seeds of the achievements that brought him fame in the 1920s. The link between his pre-war work and that of this later period should be sought in the Rue Vavin building, but also in the low-cost blocks which enabled him to tackle the problems of standardization and rationalization in architecture. This preoccupation was to culminate in the brilliant feat of his standardized house, in which he used pipes of asbestos cement as weather-resistant and insulating elements, and the two-storey villa, with metal frame and interior partitions in "Solomite" and exterior walls in "Celotex", erected in the record time of forty-two days.

NOTES

1 This building was destroyed by bombing during the Second World War.

2 P. ROCHE, "Un Artiste décorateur – La Loïe Fuller", in *L'Art Décoratif*, X (2nd half-year 1908), pp. 167-174.

3 Anatole France, *Préface* to Loïe Fuller, *Quinze ans de ma vie*, Paris 1908, p. 6.

4 "The art of Loïe Fuller", Van de Velde wrote, "contains the most beautiful thoughts of our day and the finest materials in the world. The divine instrument of rhythm consecrates their union and we take part in a celebration of everything we love, in the way in which we love it – light, gold, life – life in the light and life in the shade. She clothes one and the other with a myriad of sparks, which spring up, evolve and disappear, making way for other lights and other shades" (quoted in A.M. Hammracher, *Le Monde de Henry van de Velde*, Fonds Mercator, Antwerp, 1976, P. 62.

5 Roger MARX, *Loïe Fuller*, in «Arts de la Viè, II (1905), 17, pp. 167, 169.

6 Roger Marx, "Loïe Fuller", in *Arts de la Vie*, II (1905), 18, p. 354.

7 *Ibid.*, pp. 352-353.

8 P. Roche described the techniques used on stage by Loïe Fuller (*op. cit.*, p. 171).

9 Roger Marx, "Loïe Fuller", in *Arts dans la Vie*, II (1905), 18, pp. 355-356. On the subject of Loïe Fuller as an inspiration for artists at the beginning of the twentieth century, see *Loïe Fuller: Magician of Light*, exhibition catalogue, Margaret Haile HARRIS, ed., The Virginia Museum of Fine Arts, Richmond; M.H. Harris, "Loïe Fuller". *The Myth, the Woman, the Artist*, in *Arts in Virginia*, XX (1979-1980), 1, pp. 16-29.

10 Roger Marx, *La Décoration et les industries d'art à l'Exposition universelle de 1900*, Paris, n.d., p. 20.

11 *Ibid.*, p. 22.

12 Frantz Jourdain, "L'Architecture à l'Exposition – Promenades à bâtons rompus, in *Revue des Arts décoratifs*, XX (1900), p. 345.

13 Two designs by Sauvage are known to have been made for Loïe Fuller's theatre before the one that was built. They were published in *Henri Sauvage 1873-1932*, exhibition catalogue, Brussels 1976, pp. 118-119.

14 Frantz Jourdain, "L'Architecture aux Salons de 1902", in *Art et Décoration*, XI (1902), p. 191.

15 *Ibid.*, p. 192.

16 Frantz Jourdain, "La Villa Majorelle à Nancy", in *L'Art Décoratif*, IV (1902), 47, p. 205.

17 *Ibid.*, pp. 206-207.

18 Although it was well preserved, the villa Majorelle has undergone some alterations to the interior and the north elevation: A veranda has replaced the flight of steps which linked the garden and the salon; the openings under the balcony, which used to comprise two large windows separated by two little ones in the middle, have been transformed into one uniform double window.

19 J.M. Jacques, "Deux salons de restaurant par M.H. Sauvage, in *L'Art Décoratif*, II (1900), 18, p. 247.

20 "Intérieurs", in *L'Art Décoratif*, V (1903), 54, p. 150.

21 "Moderne Bauformen", I (1902), pl. 72, 86; II (1903), pl. 28, 40, 64, 73, 94.

22 Charles Sarazin (Bourges, 1873 - Le Canadel, 1950) studied at the Ecole des Beaux-Arts, in Paris, where he met Sauvage. He was to work with Sauvage until 1912. After his break with Sauvage, Sarazin lived and worked in Mexico, where he built a hotel in Mexico City and luxury houses in Tempico. After he returned to France, he built the industrial slaughterhouse in Toulouse, some one-family houses and working-class blocks for the mining company in the Lille region. In 1929, he settled in Paris, where he became the architect of the Folies-Bergères. Later he moved to the south of France, where he worked with the architect Rena Darde from Sainte-Maxime. Together they designed several buildings in Toulon, a cinema house in Bastia and the Grand Hotel in Beauvallon.

23 Sauvage was not the only Art Nouveau architect to have been concerned with low-cost housing. Charles Plumet and Jules Lavirotte were also involved in this field and designed, among other things, two working-class cottages, which were built for the Exposition de l'Habitation in Paris in 1903.

24 B. Brace Taylor has written the – to this day – most thorough study on Sauvage: *Sauvage et l'habitat hygiénique ou la révolution de la propreté à Paris*, in *Henri Sauvage 1873-1932*, *op. cit.*, pp. 71-77.

25 E. Uhry, "Logements hygiénique à bon marché et maison de rapport", in *L'Art Décoratif*, VI (2nd half-year 1904), pp. 131-132.

26 *Ibid.*, p. 132.

27 See *Le XVIème arrondissement mécène de l'Art Nouveau 1895-1914*, exhibition catalogue, G. Vigne, ed., Paris, Beauvais, Brussels 1984, p. 72.

28 See Luciana Miotto-Muret, "Les œuvres de la maturité 1912-1932", in *Henri Sauvage 1873-1932*, *op. cit.*, pp. 80, 147-154.

29 On the subject of the stepped buildings in the work of Antonio Sant'Elia and Henri Sauvage, see R. Jullian, "Sauvage et Sant'Elia: Le problème des maisons à gradins, in *Bulletin de la Société de l'Histoire de l'art français*, 1979, pp. 291-298; E. Godoli, *Guide all'architettura moderna. Il Futurismo*, Bari, Laterza 1983, pp. 126-128.

30 For these designs, see *Henri Sauvage 1873-1932*, *op. cit.*, pp. 146, 155, 171, 194-201.

256-257. J. Lavirotte. Apartment block, 3 Square Rapp, Paris 7ᵉ. (1899-1900). General view and detail of the entrance.

VIII

JULES LAVIROTTE:
THE
HEDONISTIC FACTOR

Like Guimard, Jules Lavirotte was born at Lyons. He was regarded as the "second grand master" of Art Nouveau architecture in France. Comparing these two personalities, Michel Desbr[è]res wrote: "Lavirotte will be to Guimard what French rocaille is to Italian baroque".[1] The distinctive traits of these talented architects are to be sought, however, not only in decorative exuberance. Guimard did not benefit from circumstances which would have enabled him to found a school, but Lavirotte never had the "sweep" of the "master". His architecture was missing Guimard's continuity and coherence, his rational - albeit uninhibited - control of a combination of formal invention and technological experiment, his art of enhancing the expressive potential of various materials and his imaginative handling of space. Lavirottés work oscillated between Louis XV, a belated Gothic, a neo-classicism inspired by the Renaissance (extension of a town house, 46 Rue de la Faisanderie), neo-Moorish (villa and chateau at Chaouat, near Tunis) and features deriving from Swiss chalets (project for a villa in the Parc Beau Séjour and for a weighing-pavilion for the Compiègne races administration), betraying a lack of

continuity, and an uncritical approach to eclecticism which excluded any firm view of architectural preference.

He did not fail, however, to arouse the interest of his contemporaries, even if his influence on Art Nouveau architecture in Paris was limited. More particularly, his characteristic use of glazed earthenware on a large scale won him the unanimous favour of the technical press and two of the three prizes which he gained at the annual competition for the treatment of façades organized from 1898 by the Municipal Council of the City of Paris.[2] The report of the judges who, in 1901, awarded a prize

to the apartment block of the Avenue Rapp credited Lavirotte with an experiment of primary significance: "... It is the first instance of the application of ceramics to contemporary building . .. and on such a large scale. .. The lintels of casement windows, arches, mullions of bow-windows, the voussoirs, stair-heads, balustrades, eaves, tiles, etc., are in glazed earthenware of strong brilliant colour in striking contrast to the background tones of the stonework of the ground floor and mezzanine and the brick of the other storeys.... It is unlikely that we shall see very many buildings of this kind in Paris; but Monsieur Lavirotte's enterprise shows that which will be feasible in countless circumstances with the use of glazed earthenware..."[3]

The judges' report which, in 1905, made an award for a townhouse (the present Céramic Hotel) in the Avenue Wagram, expressed a similar view, but he made a distinction between the architectural idiom and the structural technique. "The main interest of this house lies in the use of brick and glazed earthenware which clad the construction from bottom to top. The architect. .. reveals to the passer-by an effect of harmonious colour, but the structural frame, which is less agreeable, seems to clash deliberately with aesthetic freedom. The judges, in awarding a prize to the architect of the façade ... have certainly taken their stand on the side of liberty; but their decision should not be judged as an encouragement to imitate the actual forms of the architecture. Majolica decoration may provide felicitous effects, without any need to resort to usages which have little in common with the genius of our French art, the finest examples of which rely on simplicity and sound logic".[4]

In the interval between these two realizations by Lavirotte, experiments in the application of glazed earthenware as a facing material for buildings had become common. This material had occasioned considerable interest from the time of the Exposition Universelle of 1900, where it had found an appropriate purpose in low reliefs and decorative friezes (Porte Binet) and the construction of such small-scale works as the fountain of the Cours-la-Reine, a kiosk by Plumet, a small pavilion by Henri Provensal and a few large vases. Its wide diffusion was closely linked, as Charles Saunier noted,[5] with the increasing use of iron and reinforced concrete of which it seemed to be "the indispensable auxiliary" capable of supplying the aesthetic quality which they lacked. Despite its relatively high cost, glazed earthenware offered appreciable advantages: It was waterproof, resistant to variations in temperature and strong. It also needed little maintenance and was well adapted to mass-production without requiring an expensive specialized labour force.

There are three most common techniques for glazed earthenware cladding: (1) a discontiguous cladding, obtained by applying "small ceramic pieces to the uncured cement which formed a kind of grey mount", and tried out by Anatole de Baudot (Saint-Jean de Montmartre, 1897-1905), the Perret brothers (apartment block in the Rue Franklin, 1903), Joachim Richard (house in the Rue Boileau, 1908) and Paul Guadet (house for Doctor Carnot, Avenue Elisée Reclus, 1907);
(2) imperfectly contiguous cladding, obtained by juxtaposing a series of discs which form between them little curvilinear triangles filled in with cement rendering or ceramic fragments; this process was applied to the façade of the block in the Avenue Perrichont by Joachim Richard (1907) and in the Quai d'Orsay apartments by Richard Bouwens van der Boijen;
(3) perfectly contiguous cladding, obtained by the precise alignment of geometrically regular mass-produced slabs, to which Emile Arfvidson resorted for the decoration of the block of studios in the Rue Campagne-Première (1912).

The favour enjoyed by glazed earthenware originated mainly in the technical perfection attained by such studios as those of Emile Müller at Ivry and Alexandre Bigot at Mers. The contribution of these two ceramists has not been closely studied yet. We owe them that, even during Art Nouveau's twilight, features borrowed from that idiom remained in Parisian architecture. Suffice it to recall that reputed

architects, among them Anatole de Baudot, the Perret brothers, Paul Guadet, Frantz Jourdain, Henri Sauvage, Charles Genuys, Edmond Autant, Adolphe Bocage, Albert Ballu, Théo Petit, André Arfvidson, Edmond Navarre, René Simonet, Lucien Woog and Jean-Camille Formigé, sought the collaboration of Alexandre Bigot.[6]

Bigot was the owner of the apartment block in the Avenue Rapp, designed by Lavirotte, which he obviously wished to be a kind of exhibition for his products. Thus Lavirotte was offered an opportunity without precedent in scope and variety for exploiting the uses of glazed ceramics. This apartment block was to be his most striking contribution to Art Nouveau in Paris, by which he opened the way for Edmond Autant, the designer of a house in the Rue d'Abbeville, and Charles Klein who faced the flats of the Rue Claude-Chahu with earthenware produced by Emile Müller's factory.

Jules Lavirotte began his studies in Lyons under the direction of Antoine-Georges Louvier. In 1894 he obtained his architect's diploma at the Ecole des Beaux-Arts in Paris, where he was a student of Paul Blondel. Before Lavirotte established himself professionally with the apartment block in the Avenue Rapp, he already attracted the attention of the critics in 1899 with a town house in the Rue Sedillot (the present Italian Lycée "Leonardo da Vinci») and, in the following year, the apartments of the Square Rapp. The town house mingled reminiscences of Louis XV and Louis XVI styles with Art Nouveau affinities, the latter particularly evident in the decoration of the main door and the elegant ironwork by Dondelinger. Aspects of the architect's taste came to the fore in the sculptural decoration of the salient window, in a tangle of plants and zoomorphic elements, mostly fantastic reptiles. Lavirotte conformed to a convention generally accepted in the Parisian architectural typology, which provided for a certain respectful rationalism and Louis XVI order in creating the building as a whole, but allowing a wider freedom of expression in the design of attics, principal entrances and prominent windows. Art Nouveau became to a certain extent acceptable to the general public as a decorative formula, filtering through memories of Louis XV, and manifest in the treatment of cartouches, tympana and even in the distribution of decoration.

While Lavirotte's tendency for pastiche remained latent in the Rue Sedillot house, it stood out, with a wealth of cultural allusions, in the apartments of the Square Rapp which, as Desbruères noted, "testifies more to a taste for decoration than to architectural genius".[7] The singularity of this work lies in its reference to a historical mannerist and baroque tradition, especially noticeable in the turret which counteracts the difficulty created by the blind wall of the "square"»; the latter discloses through the spatial illusion, suggested by the wooden trellises, obvious allusions to baroque scenography. The usual association between late Gothic and Art Nouveau is broken here and replaced by a different alliance: that between Art Nouveau and Renaissance, the sources of which are to be found in the early eclecticism of Philibert de l'Ormé's treatise, exemplifying the coexistence of the Gothic tradition and elements of Italian importation. The rusticated stone facing with voussoirs in emphatic chiaroscuro avoids, as does the use of multi-coloured bricks, the customary Gothic allusions detailed and lavishly illustrated by Viollet-le-Duc, so as to stress the topical relevance of older sources of the French tradition.

258. J. Lavirotte. Town house (now the Italian Lycée Leonard de Vinci), 12 Rue Sédillot, Paris 7ᵉ. (1899). Overall view.

"There is," Louis-Charles Boileau wrote, "a touch of the Gothic spirit here, in the deliberate accumulation of picturesque arrangements, and a fairly strong dose of early Renaissance genius at its zenith, when the sons of fifteenth-century craftsmen, enthusiastic about Italian discoveries, embroidered and embellished with an identical aim, competing in the invention of plastic motifs of enchanting vivacity, and marvelling all the time at their sudden capacity to evolve such an array of unexpected forms and their ability to apply them. .. Recollections of the Ecole, historical details, features of fantastic novelty, new-fangled flowers, delicate reliefs or crazy excrescences, corbels, volutes, crooks, consoles and unusual keystones, he takes everything, uses everything. He draws, moulds, models, blends, twists, loosens or knots, spreads on his palette brilliant enamels next to pale terracottas, white stone or black iron, combines,

entangles or straightens, and serves hot - to quote the final recommendation in French cookery manuals.... None of this can be appreciated without seeing it, the delight of a cat exhilarated by the smell of carp cooked in a cream sauce..."[8] Boileau stressed the "edible" characteristic in Lavirottés imaginative vocabulary of forms, thus heralding a theme which Salvador Dali was to develop fully in a subtle apologia of the "terrifying beauty of Art Nouveau architecture",[9] interpreted as "movement which. .. had above all the purpose of rousing a kind of great òriginal hunger", an "ideal architecture. .. which would embody the most tangible and delirious aspiration of hypermaterialism. .. not only because it denounces the violent materialist tedium of immediate needs ... but still more because. .. it alludes without euphemism to the nutritive, comestible character of these houses, which are, simply, the first edible houses, the first and only erotic buildings, the existence of which is proof of that urgent function", so necessary to the amorous imagination: the power actually to eat the object of one's desire".

Lavirotte's desire to shock the establishment and the eroticism in his architecture reached an unbridled, licentious, climax in the apartment block at 29 Avenue Rapp. The exhibitionist and publicist character of this building, which was stipulated by the owner, gave a free rein to the architect. It allowed him to indulge in erotic symbolism which, in spite of undisguised allusions and the obvious naturalism of certain motifs, was expressed in a superfluity of elements generating an near confusion heightened by the polychromy and exuberant decoration.

The design of the door inevitably

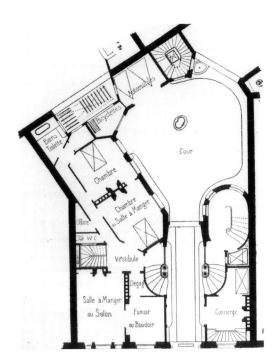

260-261. J. Lavirotte. Apartment block, 29 Avenue Rapp, Paris 7ᵉ. (1900-1901). Plan of the ground floor and façade (after a photograph of the time).

suggests the male organ, the upper part representing the testicles, the lower the penis. The handle is simply a lizard, French parlance for the penis. The ground floor plan also follows this phallic theme, in the connection of the entrance-hall and the two stairwells on the one hand, and in the entrance hall and court on the other. It is similarly developed in the façade with a segmental arch above the balcony of the third storey featuring a Dondelinger ironwork, and the small salient oval window. The impression of asymmetry, which is already created by the entrance placed off-centre, is enhanced by the tripartite window of the ground floor and the design of the casement-window fastening of the concierges'lodge, probably inspired by the architecture of Plumet. The female sex is symbolized by the keystones of the lintels of the ground floor windows and, more explicitly, on the frontal of the consoles supporting the balcony of the second storey, which is reached through French windows, the architraves of which are decorated with stylized scarabs, an obvious allusion to sexual penetration. The sculpture representing two nude adolescents emerging from the decoration round the entrance takes up in more frivolous and self-conscious terms the theme of the origin of life, common in German Jugendstil, notably in the entrances of the Ernst-Ludwig- Haus at Darmstadt (Josef Maria Olbrich) and the house of Ernst Osthaus at Hagen (Henry van de Velde).

This version of the apartment block - which might easily be confused with a brothel - witnessed the dying echoes of the erotic symbolism of an illuminist "architecture parlante" (Ledoux's Oikema springs to mind) dissolving into ingenuous forms, an evocative display of Vaudeville vulgarity. Certainly, the presence of erotic symbols

in Art Nouveau architecture was not unusual, as can be seen from some designs by the Italian Adolfo Coppedé or the students of Otto Wagner). But never had they appeared as ostentatiously as in the apartment block in the Avenue Rapp, which seemed to express in a parabolical manner that which Salvador Dali identified as the essential "values" of Art Nouveau architecture: "Deep disparagement of intellectual systems ... Positive lyrical imbecility - Total aesthetic unawareness - No lyrical-religious coaction; on the contrary: escapism, liberty, development of unconscious mechanisms - Ornamental automatism ... - Neologism - A great infantile neurosis, refuge in an ideal world, hatred of reality, etc - Folie des grandeurs, a perverse megalomania, objective megalomania ' - A need and feeling for the marvellous and for a hyperaesthetic originality - Utterly shameless vanity, frenetic exhibitionism ... - No sense of restraint - Realization of fossilized desires — A majestic blossoming of unconscious erotic-irrational tendencies ... Invention of hysterical sculpture - Unending erotic ecstasy ... Ornamental confusion and exacerbation associated with pathological infections; dementia praecox - Close links with dreams, day-dreams, reveries ... - Flowering of a sadistic anal complex - Flagrant coprophagous ornamentalism - Very gradual onanism, exhausting and accompanied by an enormous sense of guilt."[10]

This piece of bravura had no future. It was not long before Lavirotte's work showed the first signs of a decline in formal invention and the disappearance of the last connections with the figurative culture of Art Nouveau. In the flats at 134 Rue de Grenelle he used a restrained vocabulary not seen before. The only references to Art Nouveau consisted in a few details

262. *J. Lavirotte. Apartment block,*
29 Avenue Rapp. Façade detail.

263. *J. Lavirotte. Apartment block,*
29 Avenue Rapp. Entrance.

264-265. *J. Lavirotte. Apartment block,*
29 Avenue Rapp. Façade details.

carved by Dubost, the wrought-iron entrance-door by the firm of Dondelinger and the ceramic front of the pharmacy, now destroyed, which occupied the corner of the Rues de Bourgogne and de Grenelle. In the course of the same year, 1903, Lavirotte was invited, as were Léon Benouville, Eugène Bliault, Gustave Umbdenstock and Charles Plumet, to design two workers' dwellings for the Exposition de l'Habitation, inaugurated in Paris at the Grand Palais.

These two low-cost cottages marked a

266. *J. Lavirotte. Apartment block, Rue de Grenelle and Rue de Bourgogne, Paris 7ᵉ.*

267. *J. Lavirotte. Apartment block, 151 Rue de Grenelle, Paris 7ᵉ.*

change in direction of the architect's interest to the field of working-class construction. It led to the erection of a few housing units at Juvisy, Seine-et-Oise, and, in 1906, a low-rental block in the Boulevard Lefèbvre. In the latter building his taste for polychromy was mingled with "a certain rusticity", due to the use of exposed timbering and undressed stone and brick for the ground floor which, with ceramic friezes (of different designs), completed the decoration of the façade. The latter was organized according to a skilful arrangement of the bays, helped by the

268. *J. Lavirotte. Town house (now Ceramic Hôtel). 33 Avenue de Wagram, Paris 8ᵉ. Detail of a balcony.*

simultaneous development of a symmetrical theme centred on the vertical axis of the entrance, and asymmetries and variations of light on the bays which displayed, apart from the decorative treatment, a cultivated command of architectural idiom. Before his early conversion (c. 1906) to a "discreet conformism" and conse- quently to a more secure professional career, Lavirotte built a town house at 33 Rue de Wagram in 1904, in which he made a final attempt to return to a type of exercise which suited him particularly well: the use of glazed earthenware as a cladding for large surfaces, employing once again for this purpose the services of A. Bigot.

269-270. J. Lavirotte. Town house, (now Ceramic Hotel), (1904). General view and detail of the entrance.

The general arrangement restated the characteristics of the tower-house - more common in Flemish architecture - with a complicated superposition of storeys and attics, made feasible by a kind of structural arrangement combining ceramics with brick, the former mostly in the lower floors and the latter predominant in the upper storeys. Because of its intrinsic properties, the brick cladding did not allow for plastic treatment of features adopted for angles and projections, but the greater plasticity of the ceramic material made good this deficiency. The earthenware slabs presented, by way of an elaborate sequence of single pieces, vegetal motifs which branched out from the amphorae of the ground floor like climbing plants clinging to the projections of bow-windows and balconies. A marked preference for the convex and the round created an effect of pottery on an architectural scale.

Two years later, in 1906, Lavirotte built a block of flats and a town house on two adjacent plots, at nᵒˢ6 and 23, respectively, of the Avenue de Messine, for the same owner, a music publisher. The block of flats followed a generally conformist pattern, but distinguished itself by the extension of the customary bow-window feature to

271. J. Lavirotte. Tenement house, 169 Boulevard Lefebvre, Paris 15ᵉ. (1906). Façade plan.

the full width of the façade, so as to form an original covered loggia; the town house revealed in the clearest manner the architect's facility in architectural design. Its plan brilliantly answered the double requirement of privacy on the one hand and publicity on the other in a publisher's house which included on the ground floor a shop with access to the avenue, and on the first floor a large room which could be let for social occasions or auditions, without compromising the character of the building as a private

house. We meet here, beside the classic nature of the plan, the exterior display of interior spatial arrangement and its functions which is one of the recurrent principles of the rationalism of "bourgeois" architecture, to which Art Nouveau brought a striking contribution. In 1907, the judges of the Concours de Façades de la Ville de Paris awarded for the third time a prize to Lavirotte and praised this town house for "a judicious and felicitous trend which ought to be encouraged: the stone is simpler and the ironwork is more composed".[11]

This recall to order marked the architect's final return to a professional routine which allowed no departure from the dignified anonymity of his profession. Apart from some technical articles in contemporary reviews, Lavirotte´s critical success has been limited to a mention in works offering a panoramic view of Art Nouveau. They do not recognize, however, the significance of his contribution as he gave an artistic expression to an optimistic, irreverent attitude of mind and showed no restraint - verging on indelicacy - in a calligraphic exhibitionism and diversions which carried symbolist narcissism to caricature, in a retrogressive phase of Art Nouveau.

NOTES

1 M. Desbrueres, "Maisons 1900 de Paris, in *Bizarre,* 27 (1963), p. 25.
2 The most significant passages in the programme for the competition were: "(1) From 1 January 1893 a competition will take place each year for the architects and owners of houses built during that year in Paris. (2) The owners of six houses which are judged worthy of an award will be exempted from half the road charges applicable to new buildings. (3) A sum of 1000 francs will be set aside to allocate to the architect of the prize-winning house a gold medal, and to the contractor for each of the said houses a bronze medal.... Art. 3. The jury empowered to judge the competition will be composed of: (1) Five members of the Municipal Council; (2) the Director of the Bureau of Architecture of the City of Paris; (3) the Chief Architect-Surveyor or his deputy; (4) two architects chosen by the participants" (in *Les Concours de façades de la Ville de Paris. 1893-1905,* Paris n.d., vol. I, p. 6).
3 *Les Concours de façades..., op. cit.,* p. 15.
4 *Ibid.,* p. 22.
5 Charles Saunier, "Nouvelles applications du grès flammé au revêtement des façades, in *L'Architecte,* November 1908, pp. 83-87; December 1908, pp. 81-94.
6 On the growing use of ceramics in the architecture in Paris, see B. Marrey, "L'Age d'or de la céramique, in *Architecture intérieure Cree,* 1980, 175, pp. 63-68, and G. Dietrich, "Kunst und Kommerz, Werbung als kunsthistorische Quelle: die Keramiker Alexandre Bigot und Louis d'Emile Müller", in *Keramos,* 1977, 77, pp. 33-46.
7 M. Desbrueres, *op. cit.,* p. 22.
8 M-C. Boileau, "Causerie", in *L'Architecte, 17, 27 April 1901, pp. 142-143.*
9 *Salvador Dali,* "De la beauté terrifiante et comestible de l'architecture Modern Style", in *Minotaure,* 3-4 (1933), pp. 69-76.
10 *Ibid.,* p. 71.
11 *Les Concours de façades de la Ville de Paris, op. cit.,* vol. II, p. 7.

197

272-273. X. Schœllkopf. Apartment block, 29 Boulevard de Courcelles, Paris 8ᵉ. (1902).
Details of the façade.

IX

FROM HISTORICISM
TO ART NOUVEAU

CHARLES PLUMET
AND TONY SELMERSHEIM

Charles Plumet enjoyed a popularity greater even than Guimard's, which has little in common with the modest attention he is now given by recent historians of Art Nouveau architecture. Such ephemeral success was as much the result of the architect's undeniable sense of publicity as it was a demonstration of the limitations and contradictions of Art Nouveau culture in France. In 1900, Gustave Soulier noted in "Art et Décoration" that "Monsieur Plumet is one of the first representative figures, whether abroad or in France, of the contemporary phase in our arts of architecture and furniture. .. Monsieur Plumet has constantly endeavoured to recapture the tradition and fundamental principles of our national arts, as they have always manifested themselves in the golden days of artistic achievement, and to continue their natural evolution. .. We cannot introduce English practices or some extreme principles coming from Belgium in our architecture and industry. .. without diminishing the integrity of our character and art. .. And if we wished to take advantage of certain ideas which have found

successful application in arts and crafts abroad, a measure of adaptation would always be needed to include the results into the legitimate practice of our art. Such views have clearly guided Monsieur Plumet in his work; moreover, he has set his heart on spreading those views, being conscious of the urgent need, at a time when industry must be encouraged and made aware of its role, to prevent it from pursuing erroneous paths, which are as dangerous for the future of our art as the torpor from which it is being shaken."[1]

This opinion came perceptibly close to that expressed by G. M. Jacques in

"L'Art Décoratif": "In any case the honour redounds to Monsieur Plumet. .. of guiding French taste towards the future along the road of logic and reason, while remaining within the national tradition."[2] Camille Gardelle declared in the same review: "The perfect balance of his mind kept him from the crazy effusions of so-called innovators, who under the pretext of modern art have lost their way in extravagant fantasies, their insanity scaring the public instead of improving its taste... Plumet simply thought that architecture must be the reflection of an age and that the architect's role in expressing the main characteristics of the time through his work. He adhered to the mediaeval principles of rationalism, which were determined with such clarity that their application remains just as valid with the new methods at our disposal today. .. While incoherences constantly undermine reason, Plumet has guided modern thinking and steered our architecture back to the purest sources of its regeneration. He has restored the conditions, too long neglected, without which true beauty cannot exist: sincerity in the programme to be followed; adoption of a general structural plan which is a frank expression of the programme; perfect knowledge of materials and their correct use in accordance with their properties and function; selection of a discreet, composed and well-balanced scheme of decoration which complements and enriches the work without overloading it, lends character to the building elements without distorting their nature, adds unity to the whole and contributes to its perfect harmony.... Plumet's art is very French, for it is the product of clarity and logic."[3]

Moderation in innovation, continuity in the authentic tradition of national architecture (anti-classical and inspired by the Middle Ages), rejection of all recessions to the decorative exuberance which characterized Art Nouveau abroad, respect for the nature and expressive quality of materials, structural sincerity, such were the virtues of Plumet's work, which made critics regard him as the leading figure in the architectural renewal of the 1900s.

This opinion found an echo in reviews closely linked with the academic environment of the Ecole des Beaux-Arts (such as "L'Architecture") or even reviews openly opposed to Art Nouveau in the name of a constructive rationalism of classical or mediaeval inspiration (such as "La Construction Moderne"); it was shared also by influential publications which contributed in very wide measure to the establishment of Art Nouveau in France: the reviews "Art et Décoration" and "Art Décoratif" (which was initially conceived as a translation of "Dekorative Kunst" but was soon to stand on its own feet). This showed to what extent chauvinism irreparably hindered the acceptance of the international character of the Art Nouveau phenomenon, even for its partisans. Even the less conservative publications

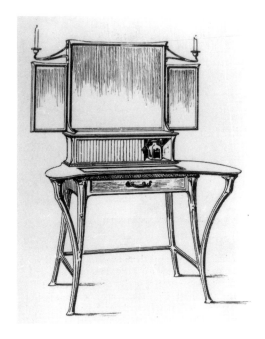

274. Ch. Plumet and T. Selmersheim. Dressing table. (C. 1900).

were very reluctant to accept the extension of such experiments to architecture, which the same reviews encouraged in the more ephemeral spheres of urban amenities, exhibition design and interior decoration. In practice, the historic compromise founded on the national tradition was judged in France inseparable from architecture, even by those reviews particularly well informed on the experimental work carried out in this field elsewhere in Europe. Between 1898 and 1902 "Art Décoratif" published articles on Van de Velde, Bruno Möhring, Hermann Obrist, Richard Riemerschmid, Mackay Hugh Baillie Scott, George Walton and Victor Horta. Similarly, we find in "Art et Décoration" the names of Josef Armas

Lindgren, Herman Gesellius, Eliel Saarinen, Charles Rennie Mackintosh, etc.

Plumet seized the occasion to establish himself as the sympathetic interpreter of this curious cultural climate by confronting the more daring European experiments with a French vision of Art Nouveau. In one of his articles of 1904, Plumet made his anti-classicism apparent in his choice of the great achievements in French architecture, unveiling the cultural soources which inspired him, and he confirmed the conscious adherence of his rationalism to the evolutionary line of Viollet-le-Duc's mediaevalism.

"The art of architecture was, in all the great periods, the expression of the individual's needs in society, that is to say the most important of the Àrts of Lifé'. .. The architect's mission is therefore to record the story of his times in lasting materials; this was. .. the characteristic of French art up to the end of the fifteenth century. .. Why has it been that from that time the inventive national qualities, compounded of wit, clarity, truth and logic, gave place to a gift for instant assimilation based on the copying of motifs created by other peoples in other ages? Why was this admirable tradition, which had determined the technique and aesthetic standards of French art, throughout almost five centuries of wonderful evolution equalled in the history of art only by the development of the Greeks until the days of Pericles, why was this tradition, so sure and so sound, abandoned? It was because the architects of this period had just dug up some remains of Greek and Roman art ... and at the same time the literary hacks were resuscitating the principles of Vitruvius. This art of life thus became an art of death. .. The copyists of these dead styles therefore lost for a

275-277. *Ch. Plumet and T. Selmersheim. Dining-room shown at the International Exhibition of 1900 (above); angle of a dining-room, about 1902 (centre); table and arm-chair, in Art et Décoration, January 1900 (below).*

long time a sense of society's needs ... Faith in logic, reason and truth, were alone capable of restoring sufficient vigour to the artist to enable him to express the genius of a people conscious of its ideals ... From the sixteenth century, French genius has simply turned away from its evolution ... Since then neither monuments nor dwellings have been built; we have simply put up façades" ... If, after studying the sound principles on which the art of building rested from the twelfth to the sixteenth centuries, we examine, by way of comparison, the buildings erected between those days and ours, we see that in place of those sound and clearly expressed truths there is nothing but pride, the vanity of display - in a word, the false façade, the mask behind which there lurks a shadowy, expressionless life which seeks to keep itself apart ... To many this conclusion may well appear extravagant. Nonetheless it has enabled us to establish that all modern teaching of the fine arts and especially of architecture is based on a lie and ...it should strengthen us today in the absolute conviction that every work of art has always and only been an expression of truth!"[4]

Plumet's work is relatively abundant, but on the whole it tends towards uniformity because of its unwearying repetition - with few variations - of certain themes. Up to the eve of the First World War he clearly found his sources of inspiration in the Middle Ages or the early French Renaissance.

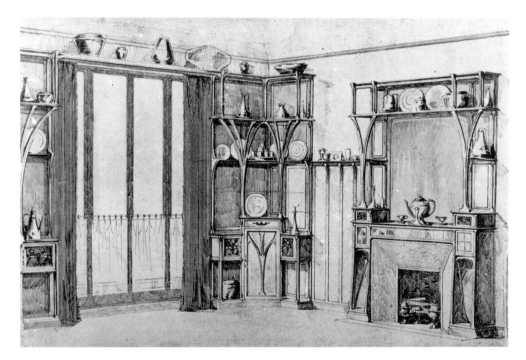

The dominance of the historical factor over concessions to the Art Nouveau vocabulary (non-existent or limited to such rare exceptions as Tony Selmersheim's ironwork, sculptural reliefs, the flooring of entrance halls, etc.) leads to question Plumet's contribution to Art Nouveau architecture. It is similarly appropriate to inquire into his real role in the initial phase of modern French architecture. More than a creator of new forms of expression and building, more than an experimenter, Plumet was the last and talented descendant of the great tradition of rationalism of mediaeval inspiration. It is important, however, not to minimize his influence on French architecture at the turn of the century, and not to delete him from the history of Art Nouveau in France. Plumet's name undoubtedly deserves to be mentioned in the latter context, less for the buildings he designed than for a number of interior designs and his considerable production of furniture in which the remnants of his historicism were dissipated by his adherence to the new idiom.

Plumet was a protagonist of the "Groupe des Six", which was to become "L'Art dans Tout", thus revealing a dichotomy found in a fair number of this contemporaries: adherence to Art Nouveau for the arts and crafts and furniture, unquestionable predominance of historicism in architecture. It is difficult to decide to what extent this partial confluence towards Art Nouveau was facilitated by Plumet's collaboration with Tony Selmersheim, who was responsible for the decoration of several works designed by Plumet.

The fitting of various shops, and the creation of many furnishing designs, among them the dining-room shown at the Exposition Universelle of 1900,

278. Ch. Plumet et T. Selmersheim. Decorated space under a stairwell. (C. 1900).

bore the signature of two architects, whose respective contributions it is impossible to identify. It may be inferred that the inspiration for such schemes of furniture and decoration came from Tony Selmersheim, who had a wider experience in the craft and a more extensive knowledge of woodwork. Selmersheim had attended the Ecole Guérin which, in spite of its conformist teaching, provided those students intending to devote themselves to the arts and crafts with an indispensable technical grounding. With some reservations, it may be said, with Henry F. Lenning, that "by 1900, the most important Art Nouveau firm in Paris was that of Charles Plumet and Tony Selmersheim, the former an architect, the latter an interior decorator. These two men are particularly interesting in that they founded a business partnership based

on complementary interests within the combined fields of architecture and decoration. .. Plumet and Selmersheim's goal was to integrate the new elements in British and Belgian designs and sharpen them by French piquancy and elegance."[5]

In order to present an objective picture of Plumet's contribution to the acceptance of Art Nouveau in France, it should be recalled that he was a supporter of Art Nouveau during the years 1903-1905 when he assumed the post of secretary of the architectural section of the "Salon d'Automne", the vice-president of which he was to become in 1906.

Plumet was not trained at the Ecole des Beaux-Arts. He attended the Ecole des Arts Décoratifs, where he was a student of Eugène Train, professor of industrial design and architect of the Collège Chaptal (1863-1879), in which Romanesque motifs mingled with elements inspired by the early Renaissance, and Eugène Bruneau, a friend of A. de Baudot at the Labrouste studio, who successfully carried out the restoration of the Château de Loches. In Camille Gardelle´s view, "Plumet completed his education as an architect with the 'Dictionnaire' of Viollet-le- Duc and the admirable Èntretiens", which are the best possible course in building. At the same time, he took an interest in all aspects of modern art, and was as loyal to the performances of the Théâtre Libre and Théâtre de l'Oeuvre as he was eager to respond to the appeal from the founders of the architectural section of the Société Nationale des Beaux-Arts, in which he found a distinguished position. A lover of literature, he greatly admired Baudelaire and Poe, Flaubert and the Goncourt brothers ... On all occasions he has shown himself to be a doughty fighter for the avant-garde."[6]

279. Ch. Plumet and T. Selmersheim.
Cadolle shop. (C. 1900). Demolished.

Of all Plumet's works, the apartment block built in 1895 at 67 Avenue Malakoff (since renamed Avenue Poincaré) perfectly illustrated the cultural theme and the formal characteristics of his early productions. The means of expression employed were minimal. The decoration of the façade, from which emerged simply two sequences of projecting side-windows and the loggia of the fourth storey, which were among the best plastic achievements of the architect, was dominated by a vigorous symmetry. "As a general principle for the decoration of this façade"; Plumet noted; "I looked for a marked contrast of values between the large, restful, brick surface and the motifs of the verandas, devoting all my efforts to the decoration of the latter. ... I should like to draw your attention to the treatment of the stonework which is a feature of the verandas, and to the decoration, based entirely on variations on the theme of the sunflower, depending upon wether

it stands out as a single element placed upright on the balconies, or is incorporated in the mouldings of the entrance-door, or indeed applied to the corbels and consoles."[7] As in the more modest houses at 151 Rue Legendre (1891), 33 Rue Truffaut (1893), and 37 Rue Levis (1893), the extreme sobriety of the façade was balanced by a skilful polychromy, suggested by the example of Auguste Vaudremer and achieved

through different materials including brick in various shades: "I have. ... attempted", Plumet continued, "a practical application of the principle of decoration used on the brick walls of Darius's palace. A large motif of sunflowers was outlined on a large clay surface, cut in accordance with the dimensions of ordinary bricks, so that the polychrome low-relief forms an integral part of the construction. Each brick, bearing its decorative element, is laid during construction by the bricklayer working to a drawing on which all the bricks are numbered, like a children's puzzle."[8] The building was also characterized by partition walls between the principal and service staircases in blown-glass bricks (Falconnier system) which form a transparent screen. Plumet was among the first to adapt this type of material to residential buildings.

Erected two years later, the apartment block at 36 Rue de Tocqueville marked an improvement in the quality of Plumet's work. L.-C. Boileau saw in it indications of historical inspiration: "Our colleague... chooses the final fling of the French Gothic style rather than the early version, although the latter is more respected, but it abolishes in its fifteenth century all the flourishes which are the joy of the tomb-makers of Père Lachaise. It retains only the rounded angles, the subdued mouldings which fade into them, the walls which continually

curve, the corbels which merge into the walls, the columns without capitals into which the arches are sunk; and he succeeds, by studying his construction with extreme care, with small and ingenious details, in creating distinguished architecture of a new pattern."[9]

In the Rue de Tocqueville, Plumet tackled a considerable difficulty arising from the combination of the customary vertical series of windows (whether fitted with a balcony or not, and slightly enlivened by the column of

204

projecting windows) with the balcony and loggia of the fourth storey. He resolved the problem with an approach to composition which commanded the approval of his contemporaries. He also contrived to break the succession of dormers by a pagoda-like shape which crowned the group of projecting windows, the V-shaped supports of which should be noted since they preclude the problem of intersection with the pitch of the roof.

Plumet liked simple straight cornices and showed discernment in the arrangement of the corbelling and more particularly the consoles, relying on purely visual effect. Thus a large console (last of a series supporting the loggia) anticipated by its conspicuously strengthened design the feeling of unbalance which comparison with the supports of the bow-windows would create; although they all carried the same static load.

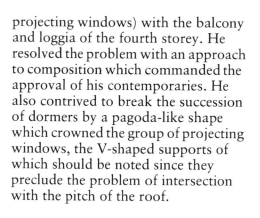

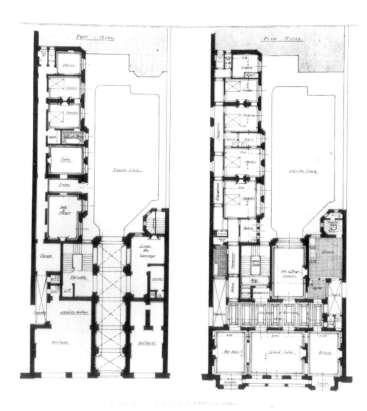

283-284. Ch. Plumet. Apartment block, 50 Avenue Victor-Hugo, Paris 16ᵉ. (1900-1901). Plan and façade overall view.

The gallery-loggia, dear to Plumet, reappeared in the block of flats at 50 Avenue Victor Hugo. Here it was inserted into the strict symmetry of the two sequences of bow-windows. This symmetrical layout, the only exception to which was the position of the main entrance, was dictated by the need to compensate for the lop-sided placing of the apartments by carefully balanced elevations.

Each apartment comprised a small and larger sitting-room, and a billiard-room, all three facing the street. The dining-room next to the kitchen and the bedrooms, which were lit by a small court, suffered from the unsatisfactory plan imposed by the shape of the site, three times greater in length than in width. Plumet built a town house on an unoccupied plot at the back of the court, and exploited every resource of cottage architecture, in the hope of alleviating its indifferent location, while making no concession to a vernacular idiom: a porch, jutting windows, large glazed doors, loggias, quadrigeminal windows. Nothing, however, could make up for the presence on both sides of the court of buildings of five storeys and a mansard-attic. But Plumet did no more than conform to the policy of making the fullest use of available ground which, at a time when the standards of architecture were appreciably higher than they are today, was the key to reputation and success for an artist who accepted urban conditions governed by the logic of maximizing profit.

Following the enormous real estate operations of Baron Haussmann and in view of the progressive saturation of the centre, which prevented large-scale speculation, the ability to get round urban regulations by clever expedients and to exploit to the limit the possibilities of sites still available in the heart of quarters occupied by the privileged classes, without abandoning a certain level of architectural quality, constituted an asset for middle-class professionalism, of which Plumet was one of the representatives. Moreover, Parisian architecture at the turn of the century offered a wide choice of original typological solutions which reflected their speculative origins.

The façade of the apartment block at 50 Avenue Victor Hugo became a sort of prototype which Plumet reproduced more or less faithfully thereafter. Erected between 1912 and 1913, the apartments at N°. 39 in the same street were an exact replica of it, except for the two rows of windows on the outside of the columns of bow-windows. Plumet returned to the same model, however enlarged, for the houses sited at Nᵒˢ. 15 and 21 Boulevard de Lannes, their façades measuring respectively 84 feet by 168 feet (25 by 50 metres) and 111 feet by 168 feet (33 metres by 50 metres). Although a balcony-gallery was substituted for the loggia, the two series of projecting windows remained as a kind of leitmotiv to emphasize the symmetry of a design in which the varying shapes of the bays and the decorative sculptures by Camille Lefèvre, lost in such a vast expanse, could not dissipate an "overall effect of the greatest monotony" for which L.-C. Boileau criticized Plumet. [10] It may be that Plumet did repeat himself, but, bearing in mind the ephemeral nature of professional success, it is fair perhaps to interpret this as the result of a kind of lassitude in creative inspiration, or indeed as a consequence of the demands of his clients.

Plumet owed his success with the critics and his professional status to the many blocks of flats which bear his signature, but also to a number of private houses. He remained loyal to his personal interpretation of the motifs of French fifteenth-century architecture - which, round about 1900, was the guiding impulse of his endeavours - in the residence, now demolished, which he built in 1898 at the corner of the Avenue Malakoff and the Avenue du Bois de Boulogne. It featured a vast main building and separate service premises, connected by a glass-house, or rather a two-storey glazed passage, "in which iron and ceramic materials were widely used". Within the framework of his early production, this work represented an exhaustive anthology of the particular traits of his idiom; for the same reasons as the apartment block in the Rue de Tocqueville, it represented a model of interpretation of the historic heritage, which was to be regarded by many precursors of the modern movement as a necessary stage in the quest for new modes of expression. The cultural attitude which led Plumet into a gradual detachment from historicism offers a possibly significant analogy with the philosophy of Hendrik Petrus Berlage, whose work created reverberations of a different sort throughout Europe - albeit through its more complex implications. Both artists designed works reflecting the continuity of a national tradition in the adaptation of Renaissance models in which mediaeval features persist and predominate. This preference expressed

itself in a strong opposition mediaeval inspiration in Art Nouveau which defined late Gothic as the source of inspiration of a new union between structural austerity and exuberant use of decorative attributes. Thus the same distance separating Berlage from the mediaevalism of some representatives of the Nieuwe Kunst in the Netherlands or from Art Nouveau in Belgium also distinguished Plumet from such Parisian architects as Charles Letrosne or from some protagonists of the School of Nancy: both were totally out of sympathy with the modernist interpretation of late Gothic, which aimed in the main to translate its decorative possibilities into a new vocabulary. They preferred the example of Renaissance civil architecture - while still reflecting mediaeval features - which was particularly susceptible to further formal refinement because of the essential character of its idiom, in which they particularly appreciated the organic correspondence between the organiza-

tion of interior space and mass. Their aspiration was demonstrated in the manner in which they reduced their means of expression to a skilful use of the chromatic effects produced by a combination of different materials, which also contributed to an analytical display of the various structural functions of the elements of construction. Berlage and Plumet's rationalism, however, was not limited to an honesty of construction; it also sought the

interrelation of volumes and surfaces most satisfactory the functional nature of the rooms inside.

This tendency was already apparent in the town house in the Avenue Malakoff, where sculptural decoration was restricted to sunflowers, which adorned the balcony console of the first floor. Plumet restricted himself to a restrained polychromy - combining the grey stone, the yellow ceramic balusters and the various shades of the terracotta and glazed brick of Emile Müller - for the design of the structural elements, whether overhanging or not, and to the changing articulation of volumes which defined externally the different functions of interior space.

This treatment produced its best results in the town house in the Rue Paul Valéry and still more in the houses of the Rues Feuillet and Marbeau - shown in 1908 at the Salon of the Société des Beaux-Arts. In the latter two cases, the theme - tackled

with obviously limited resources - was the same: an artist's house with studio. The two sites, much longer than they were wide, were of approximately similar shape. Except for the ground floor, the interior arrangement was identical for both houses. The first floor featured a hall, a large and a small sitting-room and a dining-room; the second contained the bedrooms with lavatories and bathroom, while the third consisted of a studio, a guest-room and a box-room.

The interior layout was indicated on the façade by the arrangement of the

286. Ch. Plumet. Hotel Péneau, 3 Rue Marbeau, Paris 16ᵉ. (1907). Demolished. Plan of the façade.

287. Ch. Plumet. Hotel Borchaert, 21 rue Octave-Feuillet, Paris 16ᵉ. (1907). Overall view. The building on the corner is by Maurice Du Bois d'Auberville.

bays which varied according to the purpose of the rooms which they revealed. The three-light window of the Rue Marbeau house and the large window with segmental arch of the building in the Rue Octave Feuillet were the only exceptions to this symmetrical arrangemeent.

In order to preserve unity in the treatment of surfaces, Plumet tried to incorporate any salient feature in the strict, unified, plastic concept. The house in the Rue Marbeau conforms to this idea: It shows a single balcony extending the terrace, partly covered

288-290. *Ch. Plumet and T. Selmersheim.*
Shop of the hatter, tailor, shirtmaker Roddy,
Boulevard des Italiens, Paris 9ᵉ. (C. 1898).
Demolished.

*291-292. Ch. Plumet and T. Selmersheim.
Roddy shop. Inside views.*

by two roofs; it is created by the recessing of the studio wall and crowns the loggia; a bedroom and the cloakrooms open on the loggia. This arrangement was handled with exceptional skill in the house of the artist Félix Borchaert in the Rue Octave Feuillet: The only projection is formed by an undulation in the surface (which allowed for a small divan to be installed in the studio), a kind of outgrowth which does not disturb the unity of the elevation. A critic's views on the subject of the Rue Marbeau house, published in "La Construction Moderne", could equally apply to that of the Rue Octave Feuillet: "This is purely rational architecture, in which the construction itself furnishes the decorative elements.... [Plumet] is able to keep well clear of that which one of our harsher critics. .. describes as an old trollop whose name is Stick-in-the-mud", and of the rascally and arrogant innovations of the modern style'. It could not be said either that he conceals or disfigures the materials which he uses; on the contrary, he finds in them the actual elements of his decoration."[11]

While, architecturally speaking, Plumet's work was scarcely receptive and was even, one might say, impervious to Art Nouveau, his adherence to it appears unrestrained in a series of shops built between 1898 and 1900 in collaboration with Tony Selmersheim. An incomplete record of these buildings, now demolished, has survived in reviews of the period. Exceptionally simple in design, the Colinval shopfront exploited the resources of expression offered by wood of various kinds and different colours, mostly imported from the colonies. Light-coloured panels, their surface treated in relief similar to that offered by superposing several layers of priming, were decorated with stalk-like bars of reddish

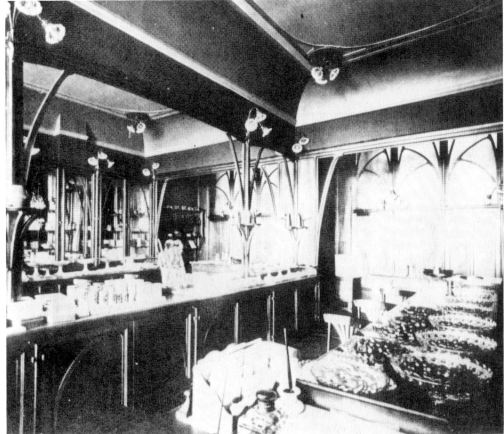

wood. Inside, the woodwork disclosed Plumet's interest in the framing of showcases decorated with borders of inlaid roses.

In the shop for Kohler chocolates, in the Boulevard de la Madeleine, curvilinear wooden frames in dark tones surrounded the display window and panels in cloisonné enamel carried floral motifs, in which yellow and green predominated. The art of Plumet and Selmersheim, consisting in creating multi-purpose furniture in which various components (sideboards and shelves, mirrors, display cases and lighting fixtures, etc.) were combined in a single piece, was seen at its best in interior decoration. It showed none of the irritating accumulation of elements of varying functions which impaired similar creations of other Art Nouveau artists, sometimes even of Guimard.

The Edouard Auvray restaurant, in the Place Boïeldieu, and the shop of the tailor/shirtmaker/hatter Roddy, at the corner of the Boulevard des Italiens

and the Rue Drouot, echoed the design of the shop front of Kohler chocolates, in which decorative panels with floral motifs abounded. The panels on the pillars and the background of the Roddy sign, worked in enamel by Clément Heaton, attracted attention by their unusual scale and an original technique of execution, the main peculiarity being that "the cloisons form a single piece with the background; the relief is obtained by embossing the copper". The theme of the iris, developed on the panels, was repeated on the outer door in fretted copper, and in bronze on the lower ends of the uprights of the display windows and protective screens. "The front in varnished ash", Frantz Jourdain observed, "is decorated with simple carving, enlivened by embossed motifs of impeccable design, standing on a base of polished marble of admirable vein, indicating an undeniable propensity for luxury. But what discretion and taste in this luxury! Not a trace of vulgarity or eagerness to amaze the passer-by! Its distinction lies in the choice of materials and in the perfection of execution, which one hardly expects to find in jobs of this kind.... This subtle richness is perfectly in tune with the type of merchandise handled in this shop and the elegant custom which it attracts; it is neither displeasing nor exceptional: no overtones of the flashy emporium, the raucous decoration of which, tarted up to sell the Choubersky stove on hire-purchase, would ruin a Rothschild and

295. Ch. Plumet and T. Selmersheim. Grand Hôtel du Havre, Rue d'Amsterdam, Paris 9e. (C. 1900). The entrance.

eclipse the foyer de la danse at the Opéra".[12]

The decoration of the Auvray restaurant revealed a greater economy of means; simple painted panels with a holly hock motif framed the windows of the mezzanine on which window-boxes were traced in shallow floral relief in verdigrised bronze. In view of the predominant graphic element, such frontage treatment owed more to draughtsmanship than to architecture. While admiring "the elegance, restraint and suitability" and praising "the absence of those scrolls describing senseless baroque curves in all directions across display windows and doors" - a strange device to which Belgian architects turned for the sake of novelty - a chronicler of "L'Art Décoratif" did not fail to note that "a décor in which the floral element was

less dominant might have seemed more suitable".[13]

Much of the furniture exhibited by Plumet and Selmersheim at the salons of the Société des Beaux-Arts and the Artistes Décorateurs, and at the "Salon d'Automne", and lavishly reproduced in reviews like "Art et Décoration" and "L'Art Décoratif", derived from a different attitude. Referring to the furniture of Sauvage and Benouville and, in particular, of Plumet and Selmersheim, Roger de Felice defined correctly the distinctive characteristic of these works as "architectural sense in furniture". "If the exterior appearance and character of a piece of furniture", de Felice noted, "have to be in strict accord with their practical purpose, they must also depend on the part played by construction. We need to know at the first glance 'how it is made', what is the intention behind the piece as a whole, what are its chief components and the most important points of support and strength. As a rule, the architect who knows his job devotes all his efforts to the satisfaction of this instinctive need; he knows that the role of ornament, especially the carving, is precisely to express this combined contribution, by subordinating itself to it, instead of concealing it by monopolizing all attention, as it does too often. The emphasis of the decoration must also coincide with that of the construction; this is as true of a sideboard as it is of a house, and here we are touching upon one of the

principal reasons why a good architect who learns the technique of woodwork and makes furniture makes it so well. In such an architect's furniture - Messrs Plumet's and Selmersheim's, for example - the carving, which is always very restrained and consists only in little more than a heightening of detail on mouldings, does not attract the eye, but draws attention nonetheless to the principal points: the legs, the lower and upper ends of vertical members, bracket- heads.... An architect's furniture is from the single point of view . .. of line and mass, well designed furniture. It is an organic whole with harmonious proportions, in which the solids and voids are precisely distributed, the volumes well balanced, and there is even a hint of asymmetry; in short, it has rhythm, as everything beautiful.... A greater concern for unity in decoration is perhaps the only undeniable progress we made in public taste in a decade".[14]

These characteristics appeared essentially in multi-purpose furniture of complex design in which the structure was heightened by a framework furrowed with delicately executed mouldings and linked together the various elements in a tightly interdependent whole. Plumet and Selmersheim succeeded where other similar works, which today enjoy much greater success, remain unconvincing. They avoided that specious facility which tends to fragment the general effect by attracting attention to details and

distinguished themselves by a perfect mastery in the design of structures of complicated arrangement, which enabled them to fit together the elements of furniture of different functions without gaps in continuity or mechanical assembly. This was the reason why their art was expressed most readily in the design of interiors: "Every interior design features two principal parts; the furniture proper, arranged throughout the room, and the mural decoration.... An interior installation, whatever it may be, conveys a particular impression and, so to say, a personality; it must assume a certain unity, establish a clear bond between its disparate elements. Messrs Plumet and Selmersheim have given a great deal of thought to this, and they are always seen to be greatly concerned with establishing a close relationship between furniture and wall decoration.

And first of all, if the necessary air of unity is to be preserved, it must be understood that restraint is the first rule to follow in furniture and ornamentation. .. Messrs Plumet and Selmersheim achieve this successfully by incorporating, as it were, the decoration of the walls in the concept for the furniture or, if you prefer, by making the furniture part of the mural decoration. .. It would not be true to say simply that the essential pieces of furniture are arranged against the wall, as would be usual. There is a bit more to this close association and interpenetration between the wall-cladding and the main pieces of furniture. The sideboards and chimneypiece. .. follow each other round the room and appear to be extended and linked together by shelves forming a border, above the verticals of the wainscot tracing on the wall, instead of complete panelling, longitudinal zones. .. the whole room is really like a continuous piece of furniture."[15] The interiors were thus planned in their entirety, leaving no nook or corner unused. "Let there be no mistake", Frantz Jourdain noted, "this desire to concentrate everything, to group everything, to arrange everything in a practical way is an admirable response to unspecifiable but potentially tyrannous needs. The hot-house life that we lead demands sordid economies in the allocation of our time; to lose an hour, a minute, seems an anomaly or a calamity. To open a door, cross a room, look for a book, rummage through a box perched on a high piece of furniture, frightens and vexes us. The busy man will therefore be infinitely grateful to the artist who guesses the requirements which sometimes do not occur to him, and who brings together, and within easy reach, the books most frequently consulted, the indispensable reference documents and papers, and also a few familiar objects of art to bring a little joy to everyday toil and struggle."[16]

While the decorative work of Plumet and Selmersheim was dominated by a constant quest for "decorative coherence", emphasized by closely coordinated furniture of varied function, a number of individual pieces of furniture are imbued with a constructive rationalism without concession to superfluous detail. A "large part of their interest comes from the construction of the legs and feet, splayed out to give the piece a firmer stance, bunched together to connect with a shelf or table-top that they support; the connections are therefore themselves reinforced; the individuality of the pieces' appearance comes directly from a supreme exactitude in appreciating the effect sought. Similarly in the various models of low armchairs, the novelty of the construction comes from the designers' concern to separate the stresses, by distributing the supporting points for the back and arms".[17]

In spite of certain contradictions, common also, as we have seen, to the militant critics who made Art Nouveau their battle-cry, Plumet deserves to occupy a special place in the history of Art Nouveau in France for his furniture and interiors. He deserves it not only by virtue of works of exceptional quality, but also because he played such a significant role in the revival of the arts and crafts from 1897, the date which marked the beginning of his participation in the "Société des Cinq", with Tony Selmersheim, Jean Dampt, Alexandre Charpentier and Félix Aubert.

MEDIAEVALIST TRENDS AT THE BEGINNING OF THE TWENTIETH CENTURY

Most of the works in a mediaeval style which were built in Paris at the beginning of the twentieth century belong to either of two trends: on the one hand a rationalist school, which had its masters in Charles Plumet and Léon Benouville and was characterized by an honesty of construction and little inclination for the imaginary forms of Art Nouveau; and on the other a school reaching to the French Late Gothic, reinterpreting its ornamentation in a modern key to create forms that were very close to the works of the architects in Nancy, and to that of Emile André in particular. One of the most representative buildings of that second group was the Hôtel Pauilhac (1910) at 59 Avenue Malakoff (today Avenue Raymond Poincarré), which was designed by Charles Letrosne.[18] He called upon the sculptor Camille Garnier, who created an exuberant decoration based on the motif of the pine cone.

Léon Benouville was probably the most responsible for a wind of renewal in the medievalist tradition. Because of his untimely death in 1903, however, at the age of forty-four, he did not leave more of a mark on French architecture at the turn of the century. He was born in an art-loving family – his father was the painter Achille Benouville, a friend of Camille Corot. In 1888, he joined the architectural firm of his brother Pierre. Under the benevolent direction of Anatole de Baudot, he set on a brilliant career as an architect of the Monuments Historiques. In 1891, he ranked first in the competition for diocesan buildings and, in 1894, first in the competition for historic monuments. He received important public commissions and worked on many restorations (mostly in the dioceses of Perpignan). He studied the monuments of the Middle Ages, as can be seen from a series of tracings from religious buildings which were shown at the exhibition organized at the Musée Galliera after his death. Finally, he was very active as a private architect.

In a commemorative article, Charles Knight correctly assessed the sense of Benouvilles research in design and his place in turn-of-the-century French architecture: "His was a lofty ideal, which he never ceased to pursue.'Truth in art', his whole work could be summarized in these words. He was of the opinion that beauty could be born only from truth: No beauty without truth. He was a sworn enemy of ornamentation for the sake of ornamentation and he tried to produce effects solely through harmonious and simple lines. He regarded ornamentation as a result of construction, to which it had to be entirely subordinate... He was also influenced by his own thorough study of Gothic art, and of

one marvel in particular, the cathedral at Beauvais. Strangely, this study of the Gothic brought about the most original element in his life, namely his devotion to Art Nouveau. Looking at Gothic masterpieces, he came to analyze, dissect if you will, this very logical art, in which nothing is left to chance and everything is deeply reasoned and judiciously calculated. Such study led him to conceive of a new art, not just any art that would seek novelty through the bizarre, but a new classical art based on the rational use of materials. He created and championed such art".[19]

This line of research found its most mature expression in several apartment blocks which Benouville designed around the end of the nineteenth century: a block of rental flats at 34 Rue de Tocqueville (1897), where the rational floor-plan and honesty of construction combined to emphasize the expressive possibilities of the

297. L. Benouville. Apartment block, 46 Rue Spontini, Paris 16ᵉ. (1899-1901).

materials and articulations and limit the decorative additions of sculptures; the building of the Count de Cherisay (1899-1901) at 46 Rue Spontini, the austerity of which – almost that of a mediaeval fort – was unusual for an apartment block in the sixteenth arrondissement. It was barely softened by the sinuous design of ironwork on the balconies and windows, the careful distribution of decorative sculptures and Bigot's ceramics in the vestibule.

Like Plumet, Benouville combined Art Nouveau interior decoration and furniture with an architecture drawn from a rationalism inspired by the Middle Ages. His furniture was characterized by a search for economy through the use of machine-produced parts and such less-expensive ornamentation as pyrography, in order to conquer the large middle-class market. The result of Benouville's efforts to rationalize and mechanize the production of furniture was not always well received by the critics. While Frantz Jourdain paid tribute to the goal and method pursued by Benouville and appreciated his simplicity of forms[20], others criticized "the great coldness of his furniture.... with its impoverished shapes and excessive elementary geometry".[21] This was, however, the idiom which Benouville knew to master. It was the very symbol of his artistic personality, which had attracted the attention of modernist critics when he had designed the installation for the Cuirs et Peaux at the Exhibition of 1900 in Paris. At the same exhibition, he had also built the complex of the Vieux Paris, one of this historic reconstitutions of a village which was to be a constant feature of such large-scale events. The design for the Cuirs et Peaux made the most of the natural qualities of the materials and used Art Nouveau curves in moderation for the boiseries. Simple moldings in unpainted mahogany outlined surfaces, in which he used "different types of leather, placing them according to the leather's degree of resistance; he reserved the fragile lamb skins for the friezes, covering the panels with cowhide, the benches and chairs with pig or goat skin". "Flowers, landscapes, seascapes were embossed, carved, incised, pyrographed.... by Félix Aubert to decorate panels of leather covering horizontal or inclined showcases".[22]

When he strayed from his usual line of expressive simplicity, Benouville was in danger of making a bad move which proved his most severe critics right. Gustave Soulier's remarks about some furniture exhibited at the Salon de la Société nationale des Beaux-Arts in 1902 were not without grounds: "It seems that this year Mr Benouville wanted to present furniture that was a little less simple than usual. In spite of the simple and economic machine construction, ornamental details add more rich touches. This preoccupation has led him to such an overly complicated construction as in his small table and his revolving bookcase, the uprights of which tend to get into a tangle.[23]

A significant episode in Benouville's work was in the field of workers' housing. He built small housing estates at Brogny-Braux, Beauvais and Epinal.

He chose as a dwelling type a free-standing one-family house with an open space for a garden or for raising animals, suggesting a patriarchal way of life tied to the traditions of a peasant world. The idea of a large room, also used for cooking, as the centre of the family's life referred to a rural architecture. Benouville's housing estates were marked by a social reformism grounded in Catholicism, which put forward – not without ingenuity – the celebration of the values of family life as opposed to the spending of one's free time in the political activities of workers' associations.

Among the types of low-cost houses studied by Benouville, mention should be made of that which he presented at the Exposition de l'Habitation at the Grand Palais in Paris, in 1903. This prototype of a house made in sections featured an exposed timber framing, the infills of which could be made of a regional material. The thin outer walls were made of two leaves separated by a cavity creating an air cushion 29 1/2 inches wide 75 centimètres; the cavity ensured the thermal isolation of the whole house as well as space for the closets, bathroom and toilet. Benouville exhibited also at the same Salon the furniture he had designed for the house, which was criticized for its price beyond the reach of the working class.

Benouville's interest for the machine production of modern furniture was shared by Louis Sorel, another mediaevalist architect influenced by Plumet's rationalism. His installation for the Papeterie at the Exhibition of 1900 in Paris had been noticed by critics and favorably commented on by Roger Marx.[24] The following year, Sorel revived the attention of the architectural reviews with a dining-room exhibited at the Salon de la Société nationale des Beaux-Arts. It presented a singular mixture of Gothic-like ogival shapes and elements drawn from Art Nouveau, revealing something contrived in the intricate forms resulting from an excessive number of shelves. Plumet's influence is particularly visible in the apartment blocks Sorel built at 9 Rue de la Tasse in Paris (1904-05) and in the Avenue de Neuilly in Neuilly-sur-Seine (around 1911). The design of two columns of oriels, placed on either side of the building and merging with the covered loggia running across the whole façade, was derived directly from Plumet's blocks of flats. Plumet's models were imitated by many architects in Paris, among whom Charles Rouillard – who designed the Miroudot building at 125 Avenue Mozart (1907) – and Constant Lemaire – whose Royal Palace Hotel in particular, at 8 Rue de Richelieu (1908), revealed how much he owed to Plumet.

Among the different mediaevalist trends in the architecture in turn-of-the-century Paris, one can be singled out as referring to such early works by Guimard as the Roszé house and the Jassedé house. This trend is characterized by a preference for rustic masonry, a polychromy created by different materials – brick, stone, wood, iron beams – and a quest for the picturesque in the openings, the various shapes of

which were connected with their function. Charles Blanche's Nozal house (1911) at 21 Quai Louis-Blériot is a good illustration of this style.

299. G. Chédanne. Mercédès Hotel, 9 Rue de Presbourg and avenue Kléber, Paris 16ᵉ. (1902-04). General view.

NEO BAROQUE
IN AN ART NOUVEAU CLOAK

Aside from the works proposing to renovate the mediaevalist tradition, there were many works in which a Baroque classicism of an academic nature tried to hide itself behind a rich ornamentation in a modern style. The pavilions of the Exhibition of 1900 in Paris were a celebration of such transformation, which could already be felt earlier, in such building erected in preparation for the exhibition as Victor Laloux's Gare d'Orsay.

Georges Chédanne, who had been awarded the Grand Prix de Rome, was among the first and most talented interpreters of this return to the Baroque in an Art Nouveau key. His Watel-Dehaynin house (1897) at 2 Rue de la Faisanderie – which was demolished in 1974[24] – established Chédanne as the leader of a Baroque trend within Art Nouveau, which was to prove very attractive to rich middle-class clients from the XVIth arrondissement. In this extension work of a building fronting the Avenue Foch, Chédanne was able to call upon a full team of artists, among whom there were such prestigious names as Luc-Olivier Merson, Adolphe-Paul Giraldon and the sculptors Paul Gasq, François-Léon

Sicard, Georges Gardet, Emile Derré, Edgar-Henri Boutry, Henri-Edouard Lombard and Charles-Raoul Lombard. These associates – Merson and Giraldon especially – were chosen for their affinity with Chédanne's artistic personality, which was open to figurative Art Nouveau without betraying the classic roots of his academic education. Together, they created a total work of art (*Gesamtkunstwerk*) in the Watel-Dehaynin house, presenting an exemplary combination of Baroque classicism and Art Nouveau. According to Victor Champier, Chédanne did not limit himself to indicating the iconographic programme to the artists

and he studied and designed many of the decorative elements himself.[25] He was commended for coordinating the works of so many artists without falling into an ostentatious opulence of form.

He did not display the same control, however, in the Elysée Palace Hotel (1899) at 103 Avenue des Champs-Elysées, which was built in preparation for the Exhibition of 1900 and is now the headquarters of the Crédit Commercial de France. Pascal Forthuny commented sternly that "Chédanne was forced, pushed to give a theatrical treatment to the façade of this Palace Hotel, which was the first in a series of hotels-caravanserais on the Champs-Elysées.... On the fifth floor, he designed a motif of columns and set-backs, which does not make one forget the lavishness of the whole.[26] Aside from the "theatrical" aspect, inspired by the element of publicity in such a hotel, Chédanne did not show here the same felicitous taste and consistency in the choice of a large number of associates, among whom there were Gasq, Boutry and Sicard (who had been praised before for their work with him), the sculptors Hipplolyte Lefèvre, Emile Peynot, Félix Soulès, Louis A. Baralis and the glass master Jacques Galland.

The arrangement of the wealth of sculptures was not always the most appropriate to enhance each artist's contribution. Moreover, they featured too many mannerist motifs, with excessive references to the neo-Renaissance, its putti, garlands, masks,

cul-de-lampes, bucranes and finials. The most successful examples of Chédanne's compromise between tradition and innovation were the Hotel Mercédès (1902) at 9 Rue de Presbourg and the French Embassy in Vienna (1901-1909). For the Hotel Mercédès, Chédanne was both architect and owner. It was meant for foreigners who would stay for a fairly long period of time and it was made, therefore, of small apartments. It was the equivalent of modern *Residences*, and its exterior resembled more that of a block of apartments than that of an ordinary hotel. Here, Chédanne's sensitivity to the sculptural element – which had expressed itself earlier in the lavish arrangement of sculptures – was applied directly to the building's outer shell, to which he gave a sinuous shape. "For Mr Chédanne, Roger Marx observed correctly, "the eleva-

300-301. V. Laloux. Project for a railway station on the Quai d'Orsay, Paris 7ᵉ.

tions of a building are like planes of the human body under the sculptor's eye. Anyone who is so passionately interested in masses, rippling shapes, plays of light, the distribution of voids and solid surfaces, the quality of a shape and an outline is entitled to a sculptural sense. Mr Chédanne shapes the facade with the care shown by a sculptor creating a face.... Stones soften and become as malleable as clay.... Walls hang in festoons like a soft curtain in the breeze...".[28] The decorative sculptures were based on the theme of the motor-car as a sport. They were not overpowering and were used to "emphasize the structure in the construction"[28], such as in the keystones of the large bays on the ground floor. Here again, Chédanne called upon the sculptors Gasq, Sicard and Boutry, who ensured the high quality of the decorative details. Elegant

302. *G. Chédanne. French Embassy, Schwarzenbergplatz, Vienna. (1901-09). Overall view.*

ironwork was a worthy accompaniment to the sculptures, especially the refined awning above the main entrance.

This masterful sculptural treatment of a building's outer shell was the most significant aspect of Chédanne's teaching. His influence can be detected in many apartment blocks and town houses in Paris, the Baroque feeling of which is not the result of an excessive ornamentation, but that of the elegant shaping of the façade itself.

XAVIER SCHOELLKOPF

Xavier Schoellkopf was generally seen as the principal representative of those claiming a kinship with the rococo tradition. His professional success lay in an able combination of historical continuity and features borrowed from Art Nouveau.

With reference to Schoellkopf's apartment block in the Boulevard de Courcelles, Gustave Soulier noted in "Art

Décoratif" that "the architect has quite rightly understood that, however modern a house is intended to be, a tenant cannot be expected to modernize all his furniture before he is entitled to move in. .. While Louis XV and Louis XVI furniture is not exactly adapted to our way of life and our present-day outlook, it is a fundamental part of our idiosyncratic national character and ought not to find itself out of its element because we still give it house- room. The concern for adapting the more traditional periods of our national art to our latter-day attitudes, equally traditional in point

of fact, is constantly reflected in interior decoration and organization, just as it is on the façades".[29]

Therefore Schoellkopf was able to make his mark for the same reasons that made Plumet's work successful. He did not, however, interpret the carrying of an indigenous tradition in the spirit of a revival; it was the fruit of an original mind which rejected stylistic imitation in order to delve deep into the heart of historical modes of expression, and adapt them.

This characteristic of Schoellkopf's way of thinking was clearly set out in an article published in "L'Art Décoratif": "The artist moulds masses instead of drawing lines. And it is here that architectural modernism assumes - without the least formal analogy - the Gothic tradition interrupted by the Renaissance.... In short, it gives the impression of a mass cast in a single mould with its irregularities, excrescences and cavities. .. With the principle of the moulded mass". ... architecture rediscovers the source of its natural processes. .. Additional components are born as if from a growth in the principal mass.... Everything is rounded, melted, softened, without emasculation or affectation. .. The consoles appear as if molten, without any sharp edges, and their shape is an indication of the manner in which they are born, while the balconies seem to grow out of the walls. The moulding of the bays, in which the artist seems to be trying to substitute the undefined for the defined, so to speak, are also characteristic features of this work."[30]

In fact, Schoellkopf did not really follow the Gothic tradition, as the anonymous author of this article asserted, but was far closer to the rococo. The resemblance, however, was restricted only to the sculptural handling of surfaces in which the various elements of the composition were fused into a continuous mass.

Schoellkopf laid down a precise definition of this characteristic feature of his architectural idiom: "Like everyone else, I began with classicism, the Renaissance, Louis XV. I soon realized that it is absurd to depend upon Greek or Roman architecture, the climate, the materials and modern needs having no connection with them; I therefore looked for something more practical. In classical architecture, no account is taken of materials, the same mouldings are made in stone. .. wood, etc. .. I considered at first the properties of stone. It is a material that lends itself to all forms, but on a grand scale; above all it has to preserve a sense of strength. Often, when looking at a building in the raw before finishing, I have found it full of character, which it loses when finished. I have therefore tried to get close to the unfinished look. Another consideration which has guided me is that we admire old monuments in ruins, on which the action of time has broken lines, blunted sharp edges and altered the whole mass. Nature behaves quite differently from architects. The branches of a tree are not connec-

303. X. Schœllkopf and E. George. Town house, 4 Avenue d'Iéna, Paris 8ᵉ. (1897). Altered. Perspective view.

ted to the trunk by a line, but by an enfolding form; the branch is one with the tree. In the human face there is no connecting line with the nose, and this makes the nose indispensable (in its effect) to the face as a whole. The eyes and the mouth, which may be compared with windows pierced in a façade, are not punched holes, but softened by rounded or gently inclined forms. Hence there is a whole wide road to be followed for every architect according to his taste and ideas, but always leading back to such considerations. To my mind, a style is less needed than a personal 'genre' for each architect, which would even vary according to the building-type on which he is working."[31] In fact, Schoellkopf's architectural work must be interpreted as a continuous and coherent illustra-

tion of the method which he expounded here.

Xavier Schoellkopf was born in Moscow. He settled in Paris and undertook classical studies at the Collège Saint-Barbe. Admitted to the Ecole des Beaux-Arts, he became the pupil of Julien Guadet and Gustave Raulin. After gaining two medals in the second class, he was promoted to the first in 1892; in the course of the same year he was awarded another medal at the Salon des Artistes Français, where he continued to exhibit. His long and close association with this most conservative of Salons is a sufficient indication of the success which he enjoyed even in academic circles.

The private residence built about 1898 at 4 Avenue d'Iéna marked the beginning of Schoellkopf's brilliant and rapid professional career. The site of the building, which opened on to two streets at different levels, inspired him to create a hanging garden on the Avenue d'Iéna frontage. Placed underneath this garden, the stables were accessible from the Rue Fresnel, situated lower down. The house was intended to accommodate a large family and comprised three storeys and an attic, where the linen-room and servants' quarters were installed. The ground floor contained a spacious hall, the kitchen, a billiard-room and a games-room for the children. The first storey featured a large salon leading to the hanging garden, the dining-room, the library, another sitting-room and a winter-garden. The second storey contained five bedrooms with bathroom and a small sitting-room.

The main storeys were organized around central landings served by a staircase and lift, while the upper floors were pierced by an elliptical well lit by a glazed cupola. Schoellkopf did

221

not yield to the temptation to extol opulent living implied by a theme involving questions of status. He designed a decoration which was to prove one of his finest achievements and demonstrated in concrete form a certain restraint in the means of expression employed.

Thus the façade was not simply conceived as surface decoration or even as a display of mannerist expertise, but as the sculptural shaping of the whole building envelope which reduced the succession of projections and recesses by smoothing away the breaks in continuity. Through the plastic character of the façades, Schoellkopf conceived of sculptural decoration as "closely linked to the methods employed in obtaining this effect of the insolubility of the whole".[32] In this work, as in his later realizations, adherence to the criteria of Art Nouveau was expressed in some elements of detail: the canopy over the main entrance and still more, inside the building, the decoration of the fireplaces, the bedrooms, the games-room and the billiard- room.

The dominant traits of Schoellkopf's idiom reached their most complete expression in 1900 with the town house (now demolished) of the singer and diseuse Yvette Guilbert in the Boulevard Berthier. "An inventive mind discriminating enough to discover originality without indulging in eccentricity",[33] the architect tried to temper his concessions to his famous client's craving for publicity. A certain humorous perception prevented him from descending into the most trivial "kitsch". In delicate compliment, "the impish face of the mistress of the house, framed in a Louis XV cartouche", surmounted the main entrance "on an overhang, the salience of which supports the arched windows". This detail excepted - which illustrates the

305-306. X. Schœllkopf. Apartment block, 29 Boulevard de Courcelles, Paris 8ᵉ. (1902). General view (photograph of the time) and detail of the façade.

extent to which Parisian Art Nouveau architects continued to give way to the self-promotion of their clients, even when the themes which they were tackling by no means justified such liberties - there is no doubt that Schoellkopf's stylistic formula embraced all the qualities needed to introduce into a home an air of social status, characteristic of a well-heeled middle class. While historical continuity was a factor in bestowing upon the work the hallmark of gentility, the repetition of this eclectic gamut achieved a unity which often looked like an absence of personality and individuality, indeed like a rejection of the new trends. Art Nouveau architects were obliged to contrive a clever combination of conformity and daring, to adapt the historical heritage to contemporary taste by giving a new response to the crisis of the eclectic culture of the nineteenth century.

Their art was also expected to reflect

the personality of their client, through the use of symbolic shapes. The floral motifs of the façade (the rose, the peony, the sunflower) and the interior decoration of Yvette Guilbert's house, including the work of the sculptor Marcel Roullière, sounded a resonant fanfare to acclaim the taste of its mistress. Mention of these flowers occurred frequently in her songs. Their presence fulfilled the prophecy of Van de Velde, according to whom "the art of the future will be more personal than that existing until now. At no other period has the desire to know oneself been so strong in man, and the house is the place where man can best develop and broaden his personality, the house which every one will build to his heart's pleasure and satisfaction".[34]

Yvette Guilbert's house also exploited admirably Schoellkopf's plastic mastery. He demonstrated his capacity to create "a whole the soft lines of which and logical saliences accentuate the relief rather than the silhouette".[35] The treatment of the façade revealed the interior layout of the building through the arrangement and interrelation of the bays on the various floors. The triaxial theme was repeated from the ground floor to the top storey and developed into one of coupled bays complemented by balconies and a concave cornice, which suggested two recessed loggias corresponding to the owner's bedroom and boudoir. The measured effect of light and shade from the corbelling and plastic features balanced the excessive emphasis of the blank wall which, sited between the two loggias, surmounted the empty space created by the large tripartite window. Designed to light the dining-room and drawing-room, the window was framed by four half-columns, their shape and proportion drawn from a humble vegetable, the leek. To its left the fenestration of the promi-

307-308. X. Schœllkopf. Apartment block.
Boulevard de Courcelles. Detail of the
stairwell and light brackets.

309. O. Raquin. Maison des Arums, Rue du ▷
Champ-de-Mars, Paris 7ᵉ.

nent bay disclosed the reception-room which, placed three steps higher than the dining-room, could also serve as a setting for private conversation.

Generally speaking, the apartment block in the Boulevard de Courcelles, built in 1902, followed the stylistic principle devised by Schoellkopf for Yvette Guilbert's residence. However, the handling of various components was appreciably modified because of the different requirements of the brief. While Schoellkopf used plastic effects rather than decoration in the town house, he adopted the opposite attitude for the apartment building. Gustave Soulier observed rightly that "when we consider an elevation by Monsieur Schoellkopf, we are immediately struck by his aim to describe, as far as possible, supple contours in the stone-work, to raise shallow reliefs on the surface of the wall. These reliefs are gently absorbed into the background and help in the interpenetration of the various planes, creating a closer organic relationship between the surface as a whole and such projections as the balconies, the reliefs of which provide the connecting link. This careful interest in the play of gentle contours fading in and out and avoiding angles and sharp ridges on the façade, places Monsieur Schoellkopf close to Monsieur Plumet.... The façade ... incorporates a few features of discerning and interesting decoration, for example, the clusters of sunflowers featured between the windows of the second storey and those of the first storey, which support the balcony above. Bunches of iris replace the capitals of the columns of the fourth storey and,

like the sunflowers, they are treated in a very free manner, gradually merging into the background. In addition, shells appear and cling to the base of the balconies, an echo of the eighteenth-century tradition and themes drawn from nature. This association with the past is felicitous enough, but the form it assumes is here too sharply defined. As a result, it seems rather too self-conscious. The reliefs would have gained by greater restraint at a few particular points".[36]

The concern for a rigorous continuity of smooth, flat or undulating surfaces emphasized the floral decoration resembling a crystalline efflorescence (prudently preferred to the representation of plants with more pronounced stems) delicately creeping across or invading the surfaces it occupied. Schoellkopf offers a coherent illustration of this theme the façade, but still more in the decoration of the interior, the ceiling of the carriage entrance and the stairwell. The ingenious association between the wall-surfaces and the intrados of the stairs permitted the

repetition of lavishly decorated elements capping the stucco plant motifs with appliquéd features, sometimes of branches of wrought iron, sometimes of glass objects decorated with foliage. Schoellkopf totally rejected any element that could not be integrated with the surface. The theme of continuity was confidently adapted to different functions and to materials such as stucco, iron and glass. Continuity was a connecting thread, a biological constant of nature transposed into a work of architecture.

These two brilliant performances by Schoellkopf enjoyed only a short-lived success. He was mentioned occasionally in the technical press as a contributor to the Salons of the Société des Artistes Français of 1906 and 1907, in which he exhibited a small house built at Montbéliard and a restoration plan, but he sank into oblivion. His untimely death in 1911 passed almost unnoticed. Only the review "L'Architecture" made a laconic reference to it. His example found some echoes, as can be seen from the building Les Arums in the Rue du Champ-de-Mars by Octave Raquin and the apartment block at 38 Rue Fabert by Hodanger, who had won first prize at the Concours de Façades in 1902. In the former, Schoellkopf's influence is visible in the shaping of the façade ensuring the continuity between the projecting parts – balconies and series of windows – and the flat surfaces. The sculptural ornamentation contributed to this shaping and concealed the articulations which were the most difficult to resolve.

1 G. Soulier, Charles Plumet et Tony Selmersheim", in *Art et Décoration*, VII (1900), 1, pp. 11-12.

2 G.M. Jacques, "Du compliqué au simple", in *L'Art Décoratif*, II (1899), 14, p. 56.

3 C. Gardelle, "Charles Plumet, architecte", in *L'Art Décoratif*, I (1899), 5, pp. 202-203.

4 Charles Plumet, "Le Mensonge de l'architecture contemporaine", in *Les Arts de la Vie*, I (1904), 1, pp. 36-38.

5 H.F. Lenning, The Art Nouveau, The Hague 1951.

6 C. Gardelle, *op. cit.*, pp. 201-202.

7 Quoted in L.-C. Boileau, "Causerie", in *L'Architecture*, IX (1896), 52, p. 398.

8 *Ibid.* 9. L.C. Boileau, "Causerie", in *L'Architecture*, XX (1907), 3, pp.2018-19.

10 *Ibid.*, p. 19.

11 D.A., "Hôtel privé, rue Marbeau à Paris", in *Construction Moderne*, 3rd series, II (1907-1908), p. 509.

12 Frantz Jourdain, "Tony Selmersheim", in *Art et Décoration*, XVI (1904), 12, pp. 194-195.

13 J., "Nos Illustrations", in *L'Art Décoratif*, II (1899), 14, p. 89.

14 R. De Felice, "Le Sentiment architectural dans l'ameublement", in *L'Art Décoratif*, VI (2nd half-year 1904), pp. 194, 197.

15 G. Soulier, "Croquis d'intérieurs", in *L'Art Décoratif*, IV (1902), 41, pp. 192-194.

16 Frantz Jourdain, *op. cit.*, p. 197.

17 G. SOULIER, *op. cit.*, p. 195.

18 Charles Letrosne was born in Paris in 1868, the son of the architect Paul-Ernest Letrosne (1827-1902). He attended the Ecole des Beaux-arts between 1886 and 1894, where he was the student of Gustave Laurent Raulin. After his graduation, he distinguished himself by winning several prizes in different competitions: first prize and execution at the competition for the monument to the soldiers of 1870 at Fontenay-le-Comte; first prize for a theatre at Noyon in 1896; second prize for the pavilion of the Republic of Argentina at the Exhibition of 1900 in Paris, in 1898; second prize for a school at Saint-Mandé in 1899; third prize for the municipal building at Ivry in 1901; third prize for the municipal building at Brunoy; third prize for a kindergarten at Ivry, etc. He designed several apartment blocks in Paris, among which that at 60 Avenue Kléber (1911-12). After the First World War, Letrosne established himself as a member of the Art Déco movement. He designed the installation of the Grand Palais for the Exposition des Arts décoratifs et industriels modernes in 1925.

19 Charles Knight, "Notice sur la vie et l'œuvre de Léon Bénouville", in *L'Architecture*, XVII (1904), 11, pp. 98-99.

20 See Frantz Jourdain, "Les Meubles et les tentures murales aux Salons de 1901", in *Revue des Arts Décoratifs*, 1901, p. 206.

21 Ch. Genuys, "L'Ameublement aux Salons", in *Arts Décoratifs*, IX (1901), 6, p. 199.

22 R. Marx, *La décoration et les industries d'art à l'Exposition Universelle de 1900*, Paris s.d., p. 44.

23 G. Soulier, «Le mobilier aux salons», in *L'Art Décoratif*, IV (1902, n° 46), p. 169.

24 R. Marx, *op. cit.*, p. 42.

25 See V. Champier, «L'art moderne dans les habitations parisiennes - L'Hôtel de M. Dehaynin», in *Revue des Arts Décoratifs*, XXI (1901), p. 383.

26. P. Forthuny, «Dix années d'architecture», in *Gazette des Beaux-Arts*, LI (1910, n° 633), p. 196.

27 R. Marx, «A propos d'une construction récente de M. Chédanne», in *Art et Décoration*, VXI (1904, II semestre), pp. 157-158.

28 Ibid., p. 158.

29 G. Soulier, «Une maison de rapport», in *L'Art Décoratif*, IV (1950, n° 50), pp. 324-325.

30 J., «Le modernisme dans l'architecture», in *L'Art Décoratif*, I (1899, n° 8), p. 47.

31 Ibid., p. 47.

32 Ibid., p. 48.

33 Ch. Saunier, «L'Hôtel de Mme Yvette Guilbert», in *L'Art Décoratif*, III (1901, n° 29), p. 190.

34 H. Van de Velde, *Aperçus en vue d'une synthèse d'art»*, Brussels 1895, p. 31.

35 Ch. Saunier, op. cit., p. 190.

36 G. Soulier, «*Une maison de rapport»*, cit., pp. 323-324.

X

THE DIFFUSION OF AN IDIOM

310-311. *P. Auscher. Maison Potin,*
140 Rue de Rennes, Paris 6ᵉ. (1902-04).

THE TRIUMPHANT PASTICHE

The Triumphant Pastiche As Bernard Champigneulle noted, "It is rather surprising that, even at a time of prosperity when Paris was building a great deal, examples of Art Nouveau architecture are, in fact, remarkably few."[1] There are mostly examples of conventional buildings based on nineteenth-century housing typology, to which some Art Nouveau details bring a contemporary note by giving in to a preference for superfluous decoration among the well-heeled middle class. With his usual zest, Frantz Jourdain expressed the "De Profundis" of this production, which demonstrated an unresolved symbiosis of historicism and Art Nouveau: "Just as in riots, in which people of questionable principles from the seedier districts pile into the fray not from political conviction, but in the hope of theft, pillage, spoliation, profitable windfalls and nameless infamies, every artistic movement sees a mingling of the genuine and the intelligent with wretched hangers-on of no ideas or beliefs who try to disguise their complete lack of talent and personality underneath a ludicrous brashness and contrivance. Art Nouveau has not escaped the common fate, and a number of failures commit indescribable obscenities in the name of the Art Nouveau.... Talent is a rare jewel possessed by a selected few, and - let us be frank - principles, even of the highest order, do not endow with genius those who lack it. In any case, those guilty of such insanities would have done no better if they had copied the most impeccable specimens of the art of antiquity."[2]

In relation to the work of the graduates of the Ecole des Beaux-Arts (whose professional supremacy had been denounced by Frantz Jourdain in "L'Atelier Chantorel") and that of the protagonists of a rationalism which claimed kinship with the teachings of Viollet-le-Duc or Julien Guadet, Art Nouveau architecture made little impact on the French capital. It received only lukewarm support from reviews such as "L'Art Décoratif" or "Art et Décoration" which, of the many architectural trends apparent in Paris around 1900, did not conceal their preference for Plumet's mediaevalism and the Schoellkopf version of rocaille. Confined to the 16th, 17th and 18th arrondissements, it found only relatively ephemeral expression in the centre of the city, in theatres and the embellishment of shops and restaurants. The competition for the group of façades in the Rue de Réaumur is another proof of this, in spite of the fact that Georges Chedanné's design for the building of "Le Parisien Libéré" had been approved - a surprisingly liberal decision considering the conservative standards of the commission in charge of the issue of building permits. Only one façade avoided the academic eclecticism of its neighbours: that of Nº. 118, a prize-winning design by Charles De Montarnal; however, this award caused much misgiving about the possible encouragement of similar works.

"The façade", the judges report read, "breaks with precedent in the characteristic boldness of the design. It is no more, so to speak, than an immense

312. *Ch. de Montarnal. Commercial building, 118 Rue Réaumur, Paris 3ᵉ. (1900).*

313. *F. Dufat. Display-window of the shop L'argentier moderne. (C. 1900).* ▷

open bay in a stone frame, with a metal infill except for the ground floor.... At first sight, this arrangement of the façade creates some surprise, a surprise not unmixed with a tinge of anxiety, but it must be recognized that the architect, who was determined to avoid banality, has emerged with much credit. The motif is certainly original".[3] The "originality", however, is limited to a bold display of materials (iron and glass) worked in accordance with a conventional procedure, and an eclectic bias; there is no sign of any attempt to use the technological possibilities of these materials in order to achieve a greater freedom of expression. De Montarnal's façade[4] tellingly illustrates the limits to formal experimentation which were tolerated in the centre of Paris by the urban authorities. Only impermanent street decoration and shop-fronts were treated less strictly, but this attitude did not extend to the granting of a building permit for Guimard's design of a Métro station at the Opéra.

ART NOUVEAU IN SHOP FRONTS

Architects and also influential Art Nouveau artists - such as Alphonse Mucha, who put his name to the front of Fouquet, the jewellers in the Rue Royale, on which a dainty figure drawn from his posters stood out - chanced their hand in this field. Mucha, however, confined himself to introducing Art Nouveau elements of an essentially graphic, eye-catching character into a conventionally treated

314. *E. Petit. Shop window, 21 Boulevard de Reuilly, Paris 12ᵉ.*

315. *H. Senet. Window of the Restaurant Les Fleurs, 275 Rue St- Honoré, Paris 8ᵉ.*

shop-front, and this was true of most Art Nouveau shop-decoration in Paris around 1900.... Even the ablest architects were no exception to the rule. Indeed, the contemporary press was unanimous in regarding this as the only feasible course, and a good number of reputable architects and critics shared this view.

Gustave Soulier wrote: "It is undeniable that if a shop-front is to fit into the fashionable scene, it must charm the eye - the most effective of all advertising ploys: The façade must play to advantage the role of the poster."[5] Other architects expressed a similar view in the "Revue des Arts Décoratifs". "The necessary steps to give a modern shop-front a physiognomy acceptable to contemporary taste and aesthetic attitudes? But there are none to be taken", Frantz Jourdain claimed, "except to let everybody follow his instincts and defer to the demands of the particular enterprise. The moment a design attracts the curious, delights the eye, provides an adequate setting for the merchandise shown, it is perfect. For heaven's sake, let us have no rules and no attempts to create a shop-front type!"[6] And Louis Bonnier added: "The shop-front is above all a 'display- case' fashioned to attract the eye of the passer-by and, usually, to present the goods in the best possible manner."[7]

Only Léon Benouville disagreed, "A really modern front . .. is very simple: The front must be so constructed that the windows are easy to clean, and to open should ventilation be needed, and so that the shop-blinds and their mechanism stay securely in position; if it is necessary to have one, the night-lock must be easily affixed.... My feeling is that a true artist must never concern himself with aesthetic theories

231

new or old; he does so instinctively by going straight ahead, building as best he can according to his brief, using the newest and most practical techniques, and decorating as well as he can. Surely there are aesthetic satisfactions to be found in easily movable frames containing good ice-creams, for a café.... Above all, nothing impractical: The modern shop-front contains already a pretty enough confusion of mechanisms and, by limiting ourselves to decorating a few elements, we can avoid the dazzle and complication which are the sorry attributes of some so-called modern shop-fronts, and which are merely freakish."[8]

This tendency, criticized by Benouville, to give pride of place to the graphic and decorative rather than to the structural elements, and to transform the fronts of shops into enormous posters, typified the diffusion of Art Nouveau into the decoration of Parisian shops. In many cases the desired graphic effect was obtained from to the woodwork, the plant-like shapes of which framed the shop-fronts. Its curving lines often revealed a taste for orientalizing shapes, which was also apparent in the choice of geminate shapes evoking hearts or the leaves of water-lilies. These decorative elements became almost a cliché in many windows of stores and restaurants - most of which are now demolished - such as Lebègue' s window for the "Modern Style" boutique at 338 Rue Saint-Honoré, that by Henri Senet for the restaurant "Les Fleurs" at 275 Rue Saint-Honoré, or that by Eugène Petit for the brasserie at 21 Boulevard de Reuilly. The latter showed a wish for the exotic effect even in the choice of typeface in the sign.[9]

When Art Nouveau was used for more modest stores, surfaces were often clad with ceramic tiles, the stylized natura-

316. *Julien and Galopin. Café Au vrai Saumur, 116 Avenue Ledru-Rollin, Paris 11ᵉ. (1902).*

listic motifs of which were drawn from the many manuals on decoration which had been published. These tiled surfaces were framed by floral cornices made in stucco or carved in stone, according to the owner's means. One of the last existing examples of this type of decor on the street is to be found in the Landier bakery at 11 Rue Gustave Flaubert, designed by Gustave Lauzanne, who availed himself of the collaboration of the ceramists Janin and Guérineau.[10]

ART NOUVEAU
IN THE TEMPLES OF FASHION

Even more than in the decoration of the street, Art Nouveau left a definite mark in the interior decoration of various temples of Parisian fashionable life, restaurants and brasseries for the choice clientele belonging to the world of music-hall. The spread of Art Nouveau to this field of interior architecture was such as to fulfill the prophecy which had been made by Comte de Laborde in 1851. In his "Rapport sur

les Beaux-Arts", he gave such temples of fashionable life as hotels, restaurants and luxury cafés a role in the spreading of painting and sculpture which, in the past, had been that of rich patrons of the arts.

The "Café de Paris" - now demolished - by Majorelle and Sauvage was among the best designs in this field, along with the restaurants "Chez Maxim's" by Louis Marnez and Léon Sonnier (1899), "Konss" by the German architect Bruno Möhring[12] - whose German restaurant at the Exposition Universelle in 1900 had been well received by the French modernist critics - and "Lucas Carton", at Place de la Madeleine, by Majorelle. Mention should be made also of the "Café Voisin" by Louis Bigaux.[13] These interior designs expressed a refined elegance which was more architectural in the works of Sauvage, Majorelle and Möhring, while more painterly and decorative in that of Bigaux, Marnez and Sonnier. However, it did not find many talented imitators nor did it become popular.

The trend which became the most popular was that of a showy opulence through an excessive display of sculptures, paintings and decorations. The architect Edouard Niermans - Dutch by birth, but French by adoption - was the most representative of that trend, which found an expression in fashionable establishments built as neo-Baroque "total works of art" (Gesamtkunstwerk) at the turn of the century in Paris. He designed the renovation of the "Casino de Paris", the "Moulin Rouge", the "Olympia", as well as the façade of the "Parisian" concert hall, the "Théâtre de Marigny" and the "Théâtre des Capucines", the "Brasserie Mollard" in Rue Saint-Lazare, the extension of the "Taverne Pousset" in Boulevard des Italiens and the "Brasse-

317-319. *Restaurant «Chez Julien», 16 Rue*
du Faubourg Saint-Denis, Paris 10ᵉ. (1899).
Decoration by the painter F. Trezel.

rie Universelle" in Avenue de l'Opéra. Outside of Paris, Niermans was commisioned the rebuildings of the "Grand Hôtel du Palais" at Biarritz, and the construction of the "Casino Bellevue" at Biarritz, the casino at Trouville and the gambling rooms in the casino at Nice.[14]

Niermans's work was often limited by his concessions to ideas regarding a wealth of forms typical of the newly rich and his inconsistent choice of collaborators - who had been selected perhaps by his clients. This inconsistency was detrimental to the unity of the whole as it combined paintings, sculptures and stained-glass by Art Nouveau artists with pathetic attempts at modernist mimicry by academic artists.[15]

In the "Taverne de Paris" in Avenue de Clichy Jacques Hermant displayed a

subtle ability to coordinate the contributions of different artistic personalities, as well as a great skill for going round the difficulties presented by the plan of the establishments which he was supposed to renovate. His work was uneven in quality, but his professional ability was such that he mastered historic styles as well as Art Nouveau and could tackle remarkably complex works.[16] For the "Taverne de Paris" he could rely on the contribution of an elite of exceptional artists, Lucien Métivet, Alexandre Théophile Steinlen, Adolphe Wilette, Jules Chéret, Abel Faivre, Charles Léandre, Jules Alexandre Grün. They created a series of paintings on the theme of Paris having a good time, laughing, singing, dancing and strolling, in which they confirmed their talent as sharp observers of urban life.

The Brasserie Cadéac in Place du

322-323. *E. Niermans. Brasserie Universelle, 33 Avenue de l'Opéra, Paris 2ᵉ.*

324-326. E. Niermans. Brasserie Mollard,
rue Saint-Lazare, Paris 9ᵉ. Vues intérieures.

327-329. Bouvier. Restaurant Rougeot,
59 Boulevard Montparnasse, Now Bistrot de
la Gare, Paris 6ᵉ. (C. 1904).

330. L. Woog. Café-Concert «La Cigale», Boulevard Rochechouart, Paris 9e. (1905). Demolished.

331. E. Niermans. Concert Hall «Parisiana», 27 Boulevard Poissonnière, Paris 2e.

Châtelet is closer to the neo- Baroque style of Niermans. It was designed by Barbaud and Bauhain, who designed the "Grand Café" at Bordeaux with the same characteristic profusion of sculptures, paintings on the walls and ceilings, multi-coloured glass panels, stucco, ceramic panels, marble, skylights and mirrors.[17]

The renovation of the music-hall "La Cigale" in 1905 makes for one of the most representative examples of the spreading of Art Nouveau in a frivolous form befitting the theme of the commission. It was designed by Lucien Woog, an architect who had already distinguished himself in studies and renovation work for the bathing establishment and casino at Vichy, which were executed with Charles Lecœur between 1898 and 1903.[18] The attraction of the façade relied on a bright chromatic effect - the turquoise-blue ceramic facing by Bigot on the base of the building and the frame of the entrance, standing out against an the orange background - and a frieze on the coping featuring a serie of dancers with bright tambourins. The interior decoration of the casino, like that of other establishments with a similar function, displayed an illustrative trend combined with stylized naturalistic motifs.

In Paris, Art Nouveau was not limited

332. G. Guyon. Cabaret du Chat Vert, rue du Val d'Osne, Charenton.

only to restaurants for the elegant rich; it also developed in more modest establishments, such as "Rougeot", at 59 Boulevard Montparnasse, and "Vagenande", at 142 Boulevard Saint-Germain, both attributed to Bouvier and built about 1904, and the "Julien" (1899), in the Rue du Faubourg-Saint-Denis, which was the work of the painter Trézel. The many mirrors, the mass-produced faience with floral motifs, and the inferior woods - the staining of which failed to confer the natural chromatic quality of the choice woods prized by Majorelle and Sauvage - in the "Rougeot" and

the "Vagenande" revealed genuine savings. A leaning towards pastiche and a profusion of decorative elements verging on "kitsch" could not to conceal the absence of any authentic formal inspiration; they foreshadowed the spreading of a popular, ingenuous version of Art Nouveau, apparent in the use of modest materials. While the restaurant "Julien" responded to the same concern for economy and graphic effect, it distinguished itself by the quality of its panels, which made up for the absence of any architectural concept of the organization of space. For these panels, the painter Trézel mingled enamel and glass; the peacocks outlined against floral motifs and the female figures garlanded with flowers might have strayed from Mucha's posters.

Some examples of Art Nouveau decoration in working-class cafés are still extant, among which the "Café au Vrai Saumur" (to day "Le Carrefour"), on the ground floor of a building built by Julien and Galopin at 116 Avenue Ledru-Rollin in 1902. Elements of Art Nouveau are to be found in the design of the woodwork in the window and the canopy, and the interior ceramic panels with female figures. Georges Guyon's "Cabaret du Chat Vert" in Rue du Val d'Osne in Charenton is a curious example of Art Nouveau reaching to the remote

333. Barbaud and J.-P. Edouard Bauhain.   Syndicat de l'Epicerie Française, 12 Rue du Renard, Paris 4ᵉ. Sculptures by J. Rispal. (1901).

outskirts of Paris.[19] Its curved wood structure, left exposed, bring to mind the lessons of Guimard's chalets.

ART NOUVEAU AS A SCULPTURAL ORNAMENT

While Art Nouveau was lavishly used in the appointments of shops and restaurants, it found only limited architectural application. It was essentially a matter of isolated achievements by architects who, after a brief flirtation with Art Nouveau, were to sink into a professional routine which was not recorded in the reviews of the period. It is difficult to detect the slightest unity among these heterogeneous realizations. Frequently they were fragmentary works in which Art Nouveau was confined to details. Such was the case with the apartment block at 85 Rue La Fontaine, built in 1905-07 by Ernest Herscher,[20] in which the most striking characteristic was an exposed iron structure supporting a

334. E. Herscher. Apartment block, 85 Rue La Fontaine, Paris 16ᵉ. (1905-07). Détail de la façade.

335. Apartment block. Angle to Rue d'Abbeville and Faubourg Poissonnière. Paris 10ᵉ.

terrace-roof. Here once again was Guimard's theme of the "freed framework" - the external projection of the vertical loadbearing components. The theme of the metal braces, extending and curving in two planes, was brilliantly exploited by Herscher, despite a certain inclination towards form for form's sake, suggested by the excessive size of a structure in relation to its static function - for example, the support of a small balcony - and the unsuccessful integration of the iron elements in the wall decoration, which was heavy and inelegant.

There were many more common buildings in which the Art Nouveau element was restricted to sculptural ornament: caryatids inspired by the posters of Mucha, Grasset and Chéret, the decoration of doorways and the consoles of bow-windows, as on the block built at the corner of Rue d'Abbeville and Rue du Faubourg-Poissonnière, and luxuriant vegetation wreathed about corbels.

242

◁ 336. Torchet and M. Gridaine. Apartment block, 7 Rue Damrémont, Paris 18ᵉ.

337. M. Du Bois d'Auberville. Appartment block, 1-5 Avenue Mozart, Paris 16ᵉ. (1906).

338. M. Du Bois d'Auberville. Apartment block, 19 Rue Octave-Feuillet, Paris 16ᵉ. (1909).

Often the sculptural treatment of the main entrance was given particular care, and this may have been the main and only element of Art Nouveau in buildings with a conventional architecture. Among the most significant examples of Art Nouveau main entrances which are still extant, mention should be made of the ones in the apartment building by Torchet and Gridaine at 7 Rue Damrémont and in the apartment building by Emile Thomas at 30 Avenue Daumesnil.

The quality of these decorative carvings was often high. The repetitive production of untalented sculptors left aside - who simply reproduced models drawn from contemporary manuals - there emerged the more personal and creative works of sculptors, whose names were rightly engraved on the building's façade along with that of the architect. It even happened that the personality of the sculptor was such as to outshine that of the architect. This can be seen in the arrangement of the carved components on the façade: While logic would have the sculpture enhance the architecture, it seems meant instead to give prominence to the sculptor. The building of the

Syndicat de l'Epicerie Française at 12 Rue Renard, dated 1901, offers an example for such relationship between architecture and sculpture: Its architects Barbaud and J.P.-Edouard Bouhain worked with the sculptor Jules Rispal, who collaborated with them on other apartment buildings at 199 Avenue Victor Hugo (1903) and 5 Rue Lalo (1906), and with Auguste Bluysen on the apartment building at 40 Avenue du Président Wilson (1906).

Pierre Séguin, Léon Binet and Camille Garnier were among the sculptors who played a fundamental role in the development of a modernist surface in the housing architecture in Paris, which, in the end, marked the aspect of several arrondissements, especially the 16th. Séguin successfully worked with the architect Maurice du Bois d'Auberville, with such particularly felicitous results as the great apartment building at 1-3-5 Avenue Mozart (1906), the block of flats at 19 Rue Octave Feuillet, and, above all, the town house at 3 Rue Alfred-Dehodencq (1911). Séguin also worked with Louis-Pierre Marquet in the blocks of flats at 2 bis and 4 Avenue des Gobelins (respectively 1902 and ca 1902); Eugène Chifflot on the block of flats at 90 Boulevard Raspail (1907); Armand and P. Sibien on the apartment building at 77 Avenue Paul Doumer (1911). Léon Binet collaborated with, among others, Jules Lavirotte, Germain Roth, Louis-Henri Boileau Jr. and Hervé Tauzin on the Hotel Lutetia at 23 Rue de Sèvres and 45-47 Boulevard Raspail (1910).

Among the architects who made the best possible use of the floral ornamentation in Art Nouveau, Louis-Pierre Marquet - who won first prize in the Concours de Façades de la Ville de Paris in 1900 with the house at 14 Rue

341. *H. Tauzin. Lutetia Hotel, 23 Rue de Sèvres and 45 Boulevard Raspail, Paris 7ᵉ. (1910). Sculptures by Léon Binet.*

342. *C. Garnier. Sculptures of the Foyer Féminin, angle to Rue de Charonne and Faidherbe (1910). Architects: A. Labussière and Longerey.*

de la Pitié - showed uncommon ability in exploiting sites to the limits permitted by planning controls.[21] As Edmond Uhry noted, "While the new regulations of 1902 were more liberal than their predecessors, they were full of restrictions nevertheless. They enabled him to display his ingenuity in making interesting innovations which often derived from these same restrictions.

The T-shaped bow-window of the house in the Rue Truffaut was surely a consequence of the clause which allowed such projections to occupy only one third of the surface of the upper part of buildings. The progressive widening of the court limited the height of certain parts of the building, but it also made it possible for the main body opening on to the street to rise much higher, the height of the court side being linked to the surface of the court. By adroit contrivance, Marquet made the best possible use of a very narrow site".[22]

Often the Art Nouveau carved decoration was grafted on buildings combining elements of the early Renaissance with allusions to the Middle Ages. The house of the jeweller René Lalique comes to mind. Built at 40 Cours-de-la-Reine (since renamed Cours-Albert-Premier), it was designed in collaboration with the owner by Louis and Alfred Feine.[23] Three levels of the building - basement, ground floor and mezzanine - were allotted to the studios and the sales-space, the other four - including the attics - contained flats. The intensive use of the roof-space, in which no less than two floors of flats and servants' rooms were accomodated, cleverly circumvented the planning regulations which, in this area bordering the Seine, limited the height of the masonry frontage to 52 feet (15.54 metres). The Lalique house set a precedent for its neighbours, which

were also heightened by additional attic space.

Aside from the financial criteria, the Lalique house illustrates perfectly a combination of Art Nouveau decoration and a conventional architectural plan, which is found in most Art Nouveau buildings in Paris. "What is chiefly missing here", Tristan Destève wrote, "lies in the architectural lines themselves, the unity, I mean the cohesion between the various components, the balance between the different parts of the work.... Some details are very good, however: the corbelling of the large balconies, the slender grace and openwork design of the tall mansard windows, the cornices, and the handsome pircieng of five bays on the ground floor, which indicates so clearly the purpose of the interior".[24] The architects grafted a decoration based on different kinds of fir - from spruce to Norway pine - on this spare Louis XVI structure. Two pine trunks stand on either side of the main entrance, "their branches rising and spreading their deliucate shoots over the

345. C. Letrosne. Hotel Pauilhac, 59 **Avenue Raymond Poincaré (formerly avenue Malakoff). Plan of the façade. (1910).**

opening, right up to the wrought-iron balcony of the first floor".[25] The same decorative theme was repeated on the glazing of the door, in the diaphanous transparency of Lalique glass. Other trunks stand out as an echo of mediaeval decoration, like pinnacles against the dark surface of the roof.

The decorative Art Nouveau carvings were not limited to buildings for the well-to-do middle class. Some very good carvings could be found on low-cost housing for the working class. They were often the work of the same sculptors who made the carvings in the posher districts. This was the case, for instance, of Camille Garnier, who worked in the 16th arrondissement with architects Charles Letrosne (59 Avenue Raymond Poincaré, 1910, and 60 Avenue Kléber, 1911), Schroeder (28 Rue de Belles-Feuilles, 1911) and Moliné (43 Rue Emile-Menier, 1913). He also designed the sculptures decorating a group of working-class flats built by the architect Auguste Labussière at 124-126 Avenue Daumesnil (1907). It was probably Garnier

246

343-344. *S. Wagon. Apartment block, 24 Place Félix-Faure, Paris 15ᵉ. (1905). Overall view and detail of the entrance.*

346. *P. Auscher. Potin house, 140 Rue de Rennes, Paris 6ᵉ. (1902-04). After a photograph of the time.*

who also designed the sculptures decorating the Women's Hall of the Salvation Army (which was a low-cost hotel for single women) on the corner of Rue de Charonne and Rue Faidherbe (1910), built by Labussière and Longerey.

The concept of "edible" architecture, invented by Salvador Dali, can be applied to a number of works characteristic of Art Nouveau in Paris. The Potin house belongs to this group; it was designed by Paul Auscher[26] and built - in six months - in the Rue de Rennes, thanks to the use of reinforced concrete (Hennebique patent). Reinforced concrete gave a new impetus to the neo- Gothically inspired rationalism of A. de Baudot. The essential qualities of its structural continuity and the monolithic functioning of its skeleton frame stimulated exercises in rocaille of an architectural type which, precisely because of the rather amorphous continuity of the concrete, resulted in features which exhibit more than a hint of ice-cream or whipped cream in confectionery. This "wedding-cake architecture", which tried to be a hedonistic version of the monumental architecture of some on the Côte d'Azur, was well suited for the commercial character of this building intended to contain a grocery store. The Potin house marked the initiation of reinforced concrete into large stores and distinguished itself by a remarkable freedom in the connection between the various components in the design, notably between the little tower at the corner and the rest of the building. The block in the Place Félix Faure, by S. Wagon, displayed similar formal characteristics: Within the framework of a conformist typology, the expressive features extended to all corbelling and projections, and especially to the attic storey, while floral themes were rejected in favour of an abstraction that seems to recall something beyond the facile virtuosity of confectionery - perhaps memories of a popular baroque art like, for example, that of South America. Auscher and Wagon reintroduced into Art Nouveau that hedonism which assumed here a fabulous, carnival quality, in which entertainment can barely be separated from a disillusioned self-mockery, and while the same hedonism in Lavirottes work had evolved into a ribald exhibition of erotic symbols.

THE GOLDEN AGE OF CERAMIC IN ARCHITECTURE

A series of buildings followed Lavirottés pioneering experiment in the apartment block on the Avenue Rapp, in which he used glazed earthenware for the cladding of large surfaces. In the house built by Edouard Autant in 1901 at 14 Rue d'Abbeville, with a reinforced cement frame (Cottancin patent),[27] a series of bow-windows ending in a loggia were faced with glazed earthenware, produced by Alexandre Bigot, featuring a design of vegetal motifs which gave the appearance of a plant climbing along the stone- and brick-clad façade. In the same way, René Simonet[28] turned to collaboration with Bigot when he designed the apartment building at 62 Rue Boursault (1900-01). This work earned the praise of Frantz Jourdain. "J. Simonet (sic)", the architect of La Samaritaine wrote, "has produced a work of art with an aesthetic value much superior to those aggressive

348 J. Richard. Town house, 16 Rue de Montevideo, Paris 16ᵉ. Detail of the ceramic decoration.

slabs in which the builder fails to conceal his lack of taste and imagination under a tiresome extravagance of ornament and carving. .. Let me pause and refer to the contribution of the structural system adopted for the façade, which is closely linked with the decoration. We see here the application of a matter of fundamental importance, which I consider to be the very essence of architecture. To split the concept of a building in two, putting on one side the technical elements and, on the other, the artistic features, is to commit a heresy, a monstrous crime which ruins an art based on sincerity, logic and carefully considered balance between imagination and practical reality. .. The house which concerns us is not like this. The façade is partly in sections of exposed iron to form salient windows and increase the dimensions of the rooms on the streetside. .. The bulge of the windows is supported by extending the floor-joists as an overhang which rests on iron bands aligned to the street frontage. ..

These metal bands are carried, on the one hand, on a strong central stanchion completely undisguised at the entresol and first floor and, elsewhere, on the party walls. This practical solution is not hidden under any deceptive plaster, reinforcement or architectural device or moulding. .. On the contrary, the architect has emphasized his intention by incorporating robust consoles of ordinary commercial iron, shaped at the smithy, unburdened and uninsulted by foolish cast-iron ornament. These consoles appeal to the mind and the eye, because we recognize their function, because we sense that they are genuine supports and that they play an indispensable part in the design as a whole. And, from this metal upon which the hand of man has left its imprint, from this metal in which we see the contest

349-350. R. Simonet. Apartment block, 62 Rue Boursault, Paris 17ᵉ. (1901). Detail of the ceramics.

between brain and brawn and fire, from this metal which proclaims the triumph of mind over matter, there emanates a beauty never to be attained by the clumsy, impersonal florescence of cast-iron".[29]

Adolphe Bocage's office block at 6 Rue de Hanovre satisfied the same criteria as Simonet's apartment block: the exposed metal frame of the façade was faced with ceramics by Bigot, which

351-353. *A. Bocage. Apartment block,*
6 Rue de Hanovre, Paris 2ᵉ. (1908).
Ceramics of Alexandre Bigot.

were decorated with shells and motifs inspired by deep-sea vegetation.[30]

Following the apartment block by Lavirotte in the Avenue Rapp, the building which attracted the attention of contemporaries because of its entirely ceramic cladding was the block of apartments in the Rue Claude Chahu, erected in 1903 by Charles Klein[31] and an award-winner in the Concours de Façades de la Ville de Paris. Provided with a reinforced concrete structure (Hennebique patent), the building demonstrated a pioneering construction technique which was summarized in "La Construction Moderne": "The first phase was the construction of a reinforced concrete frame, in pits.... The second phase comprised the construction of partition walls and infilling. In the third phase, the façade was built, consisting of two skins. One of the skins is a thin wall of stock bricks, to which is fixed the other, formed of thick outsize bricks of Müller earthenware. Between the two an air-cushion provides insulation against cold and heat. The ceramic skin is fitted into a system of vertical metal sections, which are linked by metal horizontals to the brick wall".[32] On the uniform background of pale green ware a single motif, inspired by the leaves and flowers of the thistle, stands out and "frames the doorway, runs the length of the first storey, blossoms above the windows of the second floor, reappears higher up on the voussoirs and springers of openings to bloom once again on the finials at the top".[33] The only exception was the decoration of the mouldings of the windows of the entresol and the second storey, which took its theme from geranium leaves. As Charles Saunier noted, the great merit of this work lay in the execution of a vast decorative design which required neither the budget, nor the skills, of a team of specialized craftsmen: "There can be no doubt. .. that, on the façade of a building of the importance of this one, this decorative design, however discreet, would be very expensive if it had to be carved in stone. But here the motifs repeated and diversified by the providential kiln are reduced to a few models".[34]

The introduction of earthenware made it possible for other social classes to satisfy their aspirations for a standard of decoration hitherto the prerogative of the well-to-do few. The mass-production of decorative elements appeared henceforth the only alternative to the gradual disappearance of skilled craftsmen in stone and the increase in costs resulting inevitably from this circumstance.

For this reason also, earthenware enjoyed, from Art Nouveau to Art Déco, a remarkable vogue in Parisian architecture.

1. B. Champigneulle, *L'Art Nouveau* Paris 1972, p. 210.
2. F. Jourdain, "Une petite maison à loyer", in *Art et Décoration* VI (1902), 11, p. 124.
3. *Les Concours de façades de la Ville de Paris,* n.d., I, p. 24.
4. E.-Charles-J. Guirard de Montarnal was born at Moilins, Allier, in 1867. He was admitted at the Ecole des Beaux-Arts in Paris, where he studied with Marie-Alexandre-Georges Guicestre and Paul-René-Léon Ginain. In Paris he designed commercial buildings at 91 and 130 Rue Réaumur (respectively in 1897 and 1898), as well as the department store "100.000 Chemises" at 26 Rue Louis-Blanc (1906). He executed several pavilions in international exhibitions (Amsterdam 1895, Brussels 1897, Glasgow 1901, Hanoï 1902, Saint-Louis 1904, Liège 1905, Milan 1906 and Brussels 1910). He was awarded a gold medal at the Exposition Universelle in Paris in 1900, and a first prize at the exhibitions in Saint-Louis and Liège. He also designed the Institut Orthopédique and a few small hotels at Berck-Plage, a sanatorium at Roscoff, the Château Montaigu, the Famars development at Valenciennes and blocks of working-class housing at Levallois-Perret.
5. G. Soulier, "Les Aménagements de magasins" in *Art et Décoration*" VII (1900), 2, pp. 34-35.
6. Quoted in P. Forthuny, "La Rue pittoresque - Devantures et boutiques" in *Revue des Arts Décoratifs* XIX (1899), 11, p. 240.
7. *Ibid.* p. 242.
8. *Ibid.* pp. 240-242.
9. An illustrated documentation of these shop-fronts can be found in *L'Architecture au XXème siècle* vol. I, edited by Henry Guedy, Paris, n.d. (ca 1904), pl. 55, 57; for Lebègués store, "L'Esthétique de la rue" in *Art et Décoration* VIII (1904), 10, p. 144; for the restaurant "Les Fleurs", "Façade de restaurant à Paris" in *La Construction Moderne,* 2nd series, VII (1901-02), p. 281.
10. See "Boutique de boulanger à Paris", in *La Construction Moderne,* 2nd series, VIII (1902-03), p. 139, pl. 28, and L'Architecture au XXème siècle, op. cit., pl. 55.
11. Regarding this work, see R. Bouyer, "La Décoration d'un restaurant", in *Art et Décoration* IV (1899), pp. 151-155.
12. Regarding this work, see G.M. Jacques, "Un Restaurant allemand à Paris", in *L'Art Décoratif* IV (1901-02), 1st semestre, pp. 54-60.
13. Regarding this work, see R. Bouyer, *op. cit.,* pp. 86-92.
14. Edouard Jean Niermans was born on 30 May 1859 at Enschede, the son of the architect and engineer Doorward Niermans. He studied at the Institute of Technology at Delft. He first worked in the field of railways and military engineering. In 1883, he settled in Paris, where he made prints, watercolors and designs for jewellry and decorative pieces. In 1889, he designed several pavilions for the Exposition Universelle in Paris - that of the Netherlands, the Dutch West Indies, the Diamonds, Bols and Van Houtem - as well as the Javanese village and the Brasserie Heineken. He became a French citizen in 1893. Mention should be made of his pavilion for the Manufacture des Verreries et Glaces de Saint-Gobain at the Paris exhibition in 1900, the Koelher & Co. store in Moscow and the Protestant Chapel in Rue Blanche in Paris. He made his most significant contribution to Art Nouveau with some houses at Mers, Somme, the balconies of which display a wooden structure reminiscent of some chalets built by Guimard for a seaside resort.
15. In his review of the "Brasserie Mollard", Frantz Jourdain rightly points to this weakness in Niermans's interior architecture; see F. Jourdain, "La Décoration d'une brasserie", in *Art et Décoration* IV (1898), pp. 154-160.
16. Jacques-René Hermant was born in Paris in 1855, the son of the architect Achille Hermant (1823-1903). In 1874 he was admitted at the Ecole des Beaux-Arts in Paris, where he studied with J.-A.-E. Vaudremer and G. Raulin. In 1888 he ranked second for the Grand Prix de Rome. One of his first important commissions was that of designer for the French section in several international exhibitions: Paris in 1889 and 1900; Chicago in 1893; Brussels in 1897. He made his most significant contribution to Art Nouveau with his arrangement of the Section of Musical Instruments at the Paris exhibition in 1900 - where he also designed the centennial museums - and the Luc house at 25 Rue de Malzéville in Nancy. A remarkable eclecticism marked his work, which often achieves an unusual combination of historicism and building experiments. Thus the barracks "Des Célestins" (1893-95) at 12 Boulevard Henri IV is a complex designed in a Louis XIII style, but it includes a riding-school, the steel structure of which is reminiscent of the Galerie des Machines. In the same vein, the Gaveau concert hall at 45-47 Rue de la Boétie was designed in the Louis XVI style but built with a structure in reinforced concrete, with a success unprecedented in Parisian halls for the performing arts. The quality of his work often attracted notice; in 1900, he received a prize at the Concours de Façades de la Ville de Paris for his store "Magasin des Nouveautés" at 85 Rue du Faubourg Saint-Martin; in 1901, a prize for his commercial building at 132 Rue Réaumur. Among his most significant works, mention should be made of the commercial building at 19 Rue Yves-Tondic (1900), the blocks of flats at 10 Rue Legendre (1904) and 4 Avenue Alphand (1904), the Société Générale building at 29 Boulevard Haussmann (1906-11), the block of flats at 5-7 Rue Legendre (1910-11) and 212 bis Boulevard Pereire.
17. Regarding the "Grand Café" in Bordeaux, see *L'Architecture au XXème siècle, op. cit.,* pl. 87-88.
18. Lucien-Léon Woog was born at Saint-Gilles, Belgium, in 1865, of French parents. In 1886 he was admitted at the Ecole des Beaux-Arts, where he studied with J.-A.-E. Vaudremer and Ch.-L. Genuys. Among his works, mention should be made of the church at Cesson, the municipal theatre at Niort (1911) and the Pavilion of Célestin Spring at Vichy. In the latter two works, he came closer to neo-Baroque.
19. Georges Guyon was very active as an architect in Paris and its outskirts. His contribution to Art Nouveau deserves further study. However, his work was not overloooked in several popular repertories of architecture published at the turn of the century: *L'Architecture au XXème siècle*, vol. I, *op. cit.,* pl. 46; *L'Architecture au XXème siècle,* 2nd series, Paris, n.d. (ca 1907); E. Rivoalen, *Maisons moder-*

nes de rapport et de commerce (ensemble et détail) publiés d'après les plans, devis et règlements communiqués par les architectes, Paris, n.d. (1907), pp. 161-168; E. Rivoalen, *Petites maisons modernes de ville et de campagne récemment construites...*, Paris, n.d. (1903), pl. CX- CXIV, CLIX; Th. Lambert, *Répertoire de l'habitation. Maisons de ville et de campagne, chalets, cottages, habitations à bon marché, mairies, hôpitaux, écoles, communs, garages, etc.*, Paris, n.d. (1909), pl. 45-46. Guyon's designs for the headquarters of church guild in Rue Vigée-Le Brun, in Paris, was illustrated in these repertories, as well as three blocks of flats in Rue de Paris and at 4 and 15 Rue Gabrielle in Charenton, a small hotel in Saint-Maurice, Seine, a villa in Rue Rouget-de-l'Isle in Maisons-Alfort, Seine, two neighbouring hotels at 28-30 Rue Decorse in Saint-Meurice, Seine, seaside houses at Mers, Somme, a hen- and pigeon-house at 10 Rue de Sully in Charenton.

20. Ernest-Marie Herscher was born in Paris in 1870. He graduated from the Ecole des Beaux-Arts, where he studied with Jean-Louis Pascal from 1891 to 1898. He worked both as an architect and printmaker. From 1906 he took part regularly in the Salon d'Automne, where he exhibited mostly etchings. He published a very successful book of etchings, Souvenirs du Paris d'hier (1911-12). Among his many architectural works, mention should be made of an apartment building at 39 Rue Scheffer (1911), the headquarters of the "Veritas" company, the design for a theatre in the Tuileries gardens (ca 1910), with L. Feine, and a town house at Cambrai

(see *La Construction Moderne* XXIX (1913-14), pl. 91-93).

21. Louis-Pierre Marquet was born in Paris in 1859. He studied with Jean-Louis Pascal at the Ecole des Beaux-Arts, where he graduated in 1890. He built many apartment buildings in Paris, among which the ones at 204 Rue de Grenelle (1898), 2 bis, 4 and 10 Rue des Gobelins (respectively 1902, ca 1902 and 1901), 4 Rue Hermel (1902), 53 Rue Truffaut (1903) and 14 Rue de la Pitié (1906).

22. E. Uhry, "Maison de rapport de L.P. Marquet à Paris", in *L'Art Décoratif* VI (1904, 2nd semestre), pp. 174, 176.

23. Louis-Eugène Feine was born in 1868, and Albert-Pierre Feine in 1872, both in Paris. Both studied with Jean-Louis Pascal at the Ecole des Beaux-Arts, where they graduated in 1895 and 1898 respectively.

24. T. Desteve, "La Maison de René Lalique", in *Art et Décoration* VI (1902), 12, p. 162.

25. *Ibid.*, p. 163.

26. Paul Auscher was born at Marseilles in 1866. He studied with Julien Guadet at the Ecole des Beaux-Arts in Paris. He designed commercial buildings at Reims, Le Mans and Lille, as well as the "Nouvelles Galeries" at Bordeaux.

27. Edouard Autant was born in Paris in 1877. In 1898 he was admitted at the Ecole des Beaux-Arts, where he studied with Paul Sédille, Honoré

Daumet, Charles-Louis Girault and Pierre-José Esquié, and he graduated in 1900. He built a bathing establishment and a casino at Enghien, with an Art Nouveau interior decoration.

28. René-Auguste Simonet was born at Boulogne-sur-Mer in 1865. He studied with Ch.-L. Genuys and Redon at the Ecole des Beaux-Arts.

29. F. Jourdain, *op. cit.*, pp. 125-126.

30. Adolphe Bocage was born in Paris in 1860. In 1878 he was admitted at the Ecole des Beaux-Arts, where he studied with Julien Guadet. He designed many apartment buildings in Paris, among which the ones at 133 Boulevard Ménilmontant (1902; awarded a prize in 1903 in the Concours des Façades de la Ville de Paris), 1-3 Rue Charles-Dickens (1908), 95 Avenue Gambetta (1908), 12 Rue des Eaux (1909), 15 Rue de Téhéran (1910), 4 Chaussée de la Muette (1910?); 6-8-10 Avenue Constant-Coquelin (1913), 5-7-9 Avenue Daniel Lesueur (1913).

31. Charles Klein was born in Paris in 1873. He studied with Julien Guadet at the Ecole des Beaux-Arts.

32. "Maison, rue Claude Chahu, à Paris" in *La Construction Moderne*, 2nd series, VIII (1902-03), p. 365. This piece seems to contradict a recent theory that Charles Klein limited himself to a "re-facing" of a building put up in 1897 (*Le XVIème arrondissement Mécène de l'Art Nouveau*, exhibition catalogue, Mairie du XVIème arrondissement, Paris; Musée départemental de l'Oise, Beauvais; Musée Horta, Brussels, 1984, p. 53).

33. Ch. Saunier, "Une nouvelle construction en grès", in *L'Art Décoratif* V (1903), 55, p. 173.

34. *Ibid.*, p. 174.

BIOGRAPHICAL NOTES

Léon BENOUVILLE

(Rome, 8.3.1860 - Paris, 11.10.1903)

1884	Obtained builder diploma at the Ecole Centrale des arts et manufactures in Paris and joined the Chemins de fer de l'Ouest.
1886-87	Worked in Charles Le Cœur's agency, architect appointed by the Government.
1888	Became a associate of his brother Pierre (Rome, 5.4.1852 - Paris, 15.4.1889).
1889	Obtained silver medal at the International Exhibition. After his brother Pierre's death, he managed the office on his own.
1891	Obtained a credit at the Salon de la Société Nationale des Beaux-Arts. Admitted to the Société Nationale des Architectes Français.
1894	Obtained first prize in competition for diocesan buildings. Exhibited a mantelpiece at the Salon de la Société Nationale des Beaux-Arts.
1895	Exhibited a billiard-room and a couch at the Salon de la Société Nationale des Beaux-Arts.
1896	Exhibited a scheme for new fittings of the Haarzwilen, castle, near Utrecht, at the Salon de la Société Nationale des Beaux-Arts.
1897	Apartment block, 36 Rue de Tocqueville, Paris 17ᵉ. Bibl.: 283; 490.
1898	Exhibited a hotel billiard-room in Neuilly-sur-Seine, a residence, 66 Rue Duplessis, Versailles and a low-cost house, Rue Nationale, Paris, at the Salon de la Société Nationale des Beaux-Arts.
c.1899	Entrance gate of a park, Bogny-sur-Meuse.
1899-1901	Apartment block, 46 Rue Spontini, Paris 16ᵉ. Bibl.: 82; 87; 109.
1900	Obtained gold medal and silver medal at the International Exhibition. Ancient Paris at the International Exhibition. Beer and cider factory at the International Exhibition. Fittings of stained-glass windows section at the International Exhibition. Fittings of chemical products section at the International Exhibition. Bibl.: 138. Fittings of leather and hides section at the International Exhibition. Bibl.: 127; 138; 169.1.
1901	Exhibition of a bedroom and a glass-works cabinet at the Salon de la Société Nationale des Beaux-Arts. Bibl.: 175.1; 178.
1902	Exhibition of small table, bookcase and study at the Société Nationale des Beaux-Arts. Bibl.: 183.
c.1902	Appointed as architect of diocesan buildings of Lyon.
1903	Exhibition of furniture for a worker's dining-room at the Salon de la Société Nationale des Beaux-Arts. Bibl.: 53; 184.1. Standard design of portable worker's house at the Exposition de l'Habitation, Grand Palais of Paris. Bibl.: 21; 92; 283.
n.d.	Day-nursery, Bogny-Braux. Château de Liez. Château de Villers-le-Bel. Worker's houses, Bogny-Braux (Ardennes). Bibl.: 92. Worker's houses of Ed. Laisné's Factory. Bibl.: 53; 92; 283. Apartment block, 17-19 Boulevard Pasteur, Paris 15ᵉ. Bibl.: Dekorative Kunst, II, n.9, 1899, p. 128.

René BINET

(Chaumont, Yonne, 1866 - Ouchy, Suisse, 19.7.1911)

1886	Admitted to the Ecole des Beaux-Arts, where he was a pupil of Victor Laloux.
1891	Obtained Chapelain Prize.
1893	Obtained Chaudesaignes and American Architects Prize.
1896	Obtained Rougevin Prize.
1898	Project for competition for the Grand Palais at the International Exhibition of 1900, (in collaboration with Deglane), second prize.
1900	Gateway to Cours-la-Reine at the International Exhibition. Bibl.: 14; 68; 135; 153; 158; 159; 160; 292. Dairy at the International Exhibition. Bibl.: 127; 135; 158. Fittings of Agriculture Section at the International Exhibition. 1900, 1902, 1903, 1906, 1907 Exhibition in Galerie Durand in Paris of a series of water-colours, brought back from his travelling studies in Italy, Sicily and Spain.
1901	Chevalier de la Légion d'Honneur. 1901, 1903, 1907 Three projects for rebuilding of the Pont Notre-Dame.
c.1903	Artist's resting home, Pont-aux-Dames. Bibl.: 285; 293.
1908	New fittings for a telephone room, rue Gutenberg, Paris 15ᵉ. Bibl.: 288.
c.1908	Post Office of La Madeleine, Paris.
1909	Post and Telegraph Office for Maison Dorée, Boulevard des Italiens, corner of Rue Laffitte, Paris. Bibl.: 289.
1910	Obtained a medal from the Société Centrale des Architectes, of which he became a member in 1911.
1910-11	Enlargement and transformation of the Magasins du Printemps, 58 Boulevard Haussmann, Paris 9ᵉ. Bibl.: 58; 64; 67; 69; 83; 286; 290; 291; 292; L'Architecte, VI (1911), pl. VII-XII.
1922	Exhibition of his works organized by the Salon d'Automne.

Louis Bernard BONNIER

(Templeuve, 14.6.1856 - Paris, 1946)

1877-86	A pupil of Louis Jules André and Constant Moyaux in the Ecole des Beaux-Arts. 1881, 1886 Exhibition of paintings in the Salon.
1889	Inspector of works for the International Exhibition.
1889-91	Restoration of a church, Toucy, Yonne.
1890	Architect for London Exhibition.
1890-92	"Les Sablons" House, Ambleteuse. Bibl.: 295; 296; 297. "Les Dunes" House, Ambleteuse. Bibl.: 295; 296. "Les Oyats" House, Ambleteuse. Bibl.: 295; 296; 297. "Les Algues" House, Ambleteuse. Bibl.: 295; 296.
1893	Projects for a competition for Issy-les-Moulineaux Townhall. First Prize. His project is carried out.
1893-94	George Flé house, Ambleteuse. Bibl.: 295; 296. Townhall, Templeuve. Bibl.: 295; 296.
1895	Arrangement of Bing's Art Nouveau shop, 22, rue de Provence, Paris IXᵉ. Demolished about 1925. Bibl.: 106; 112; 520; 624; 625; Dekorative Kunst vol. I (1898), pp.28-31.
1897	Restaurant "La Pointe à Z'Oies, between Ambleteuse and Wimmereux. Bibl.: 21; L'Art Décoratif, n.5, 1899, pp. 226-227.
1897-98	Project for the Globe Elisée Reclus, at the International Exhibition of 1900.

1898-99 The Sorbonne maritime zoology laboratory, Wimmereux. Bibl.: 296.
Project for a farm. Bibl.: *L'Art Décoratif" n.5, 1899, p. 226.*
Sketch for a garden gate. Bibl.: L'Art Décoratif, n.5, 1899, p. 227.

1900 Pavilion of Creusot factories at the International Exhibition. Bibl.: 138.
Pavilion of Administration and General Commission for the International Exhibition. Bibl.: 112; 520.
Pavilion Schneider, at the International Exhibition.

1901 Appointed as architect of Palais de l'Elysée.

1902 Villa "La Collinette", Essômes-sur-Marne. Aisne.

1902-04 Dispensaire antituberculeux (or Dispensaire Jouy-Rouve), 190 rue des Pyrénées. Paris 20ᵉ.

1904-05 House of André Gide, 38 avenue des Sycomores. Paris 16ᵉ.

1906 Exhibition of a scheme for low-cost house at the Salon de la Société des Artistes Français.

c.1907 Villa, Cagnes. Bibl.: 296.

c.1908 Country house in the neighbourhood of Château-Thierry. Bibl.: *L'Architecte*, IV (1909), pl. XIII-XIV.

1908-11 School complex, Rue Sextus-Michel, Rue du Dr Finlay, Rue Emeriau, Rue de Schutzenberger, Paris 15ᵉ. Bibl.: 62; 63; 64; 67; 83; 298; 299.

1920-24 Swimming pool of La Butte-aux-Cailles, 5 Place Paul- Verlaine, Paris 13ᵉ (in collaboration with François Hennebique).

n.d. Testelin monument.
Competition project for the Palais des Beaux-Arts in Lille.

Georges-Paul CHEDANNE

(Maromme, Seine Inférieure, 25.9.1861 - Paris, 1940)

A pupil of Julien Guadet at the Ecole des Beaux-Arts.

1887 Obtained the Grand Prix de Rome.

1888-93 Lived in Rome, where he was appointed for a restoration project of the Panthéon.

1891 Obtained a third-class medal at the Salon.

1892 Obtained a second-class medal at the Salon.

1893 Chevalier de la Légion d'Honneur for his studies of the Panthéon.

1894 Obtained Honour Medal at the Salon for his studies of the Panthéon.

1897 Dehaynin residence, Rue de la Faisanderie, corner of Avenue du Bois-de-Boulogne, Paris 16ᵉ, demolished. Bibl.: 109; 302.

1897-99 Riviera Palace Hotel, Montecarlo.

1898-99 Royal-Palace, Ostende.

1899 Elysée-Palace-Hotel, 103 Avenue des Champs-Elysées, Paris 8ᵉ. Bibl.: 77; 300.

1900 Grand Prix at the International Exhibition.

1901-09 French Embassy, Schwarzenbergplatz, Vienna. Bibl.: *Wiener Bauindustrie Zeitung*, XXVII (1909-10), pp.51-52, pl. 17-18.

1902-04 Mercedes-Residence, 9 Rue de Presbourg, Paris 16ᵉ. Bibl.: 67; 77; 109; 303; 304.

1903-04 Office block (Le Parisien Libéré), 124 Rue Réaumur, Paris 2ᵉ. Bibl.: 21; 47; 67; 68; 77; 106.

1906-08 Galeries Lafayette, Boulevard Haussmann, Paris 9ᵉ. Bibl.: 21; 22; 68.

n.d. Monuments commemorating the defence in 1871 of Rouen and Châteaudun.

Alms-house of Châteaudun.
Hôtel Terminus, Lyon.
French Legation, Pekin.
Archives of the Ministère des Affaires Etrangères.

Hector GUIMARD

(Lyon, 10.3.1867 - New York, 20.5.1942)

1867 Born at Lyon 10 March of Germain René Guimard and Marie Françoise Bailly.

1885 Obtained diploma at Ecole des Arts Décoratifs and in autumn admitted to Ecole des Beaux-Arts, where he became student of Gustave Raulin.
Project for a palace entrance.
Project for a monument to H. Rivière.

1886 Project for a monument to sergeant Blandan.
Project for a garden bridge.
Project for a café-concert in a public garden.

1887 Enlisted in 33ʳᵈ artillery regiment.
Project for the doorway of a village church.

1888 Project for an orangery.
Project for Calais town hall.
Café-restaurant "Au Grand Neptune", 148 Quai d'Auteuil (now Quai Louis Blériot), Paris 16ᵉ (demolished c.1909).

1889 Project for a monumental fountain.
Electricity pavilion at the Paris Universal Exhibition.

1891 Hôtel Roszé, 34 Rue Boileau, Paris 16ᵉ. Bibl.: 320; 322; 324; 327. Villa Toucy, Billancourt (demolished).

1892 Project for a monument to Christopher Columbus.
Tomb of Victor Rose, Batignolles cemetery, Paris 17ᵉ.

1893 Hôtel Jassedé, 14 Rue Chardon-Lagache, Paris 16ᵉ. Bibl.: 50; 109; 320; 322; 323; 324; 327; 336; 339.
House at 63 Avenue de Clamart (now Avenue Charles de Gaulle), Issy-les-Moulineaux. Bibl.: 323; 324.

1894 Exhibited many architectural drawings at the Salon de la Société Nationale des Beaux-Arts.
Visit to England.
Monument to the Devos Logie family, Gonards cemetery, Versailles.
Reconstruction of parts of the ruins of the old church of Auteuil in the courtyard of the presbytery of the new church, 4 Rue Corot, Paris 16ᵉ. Bibli.: 109.

1894-95 Private residence and studio of Madame Carpeaux at 39 Boulevard Exelmans, Paris 16ᵉ. Bibl.: 322; 324; 327. Hôtel Delfau, 1ᵗᵉʳ Rue Molitor, Paris 16ᵉ. Bibl.:67; 323; 324; 327.

1894-98 Castel Béranger, 14 Rue La Fontaine and Hameau Béranger, Paris 16ᵉ. Bibl.: 14; 18; 19; 21; 22; 38; 67; 70; 82; 83; 97; 109; 116; 117; 309; 319; 320; 322; 323; 324; 324.1; 324.2; 327; 328; 339; 343; 348; 350; 351; 352; 353; 354; 355; 356; 357; 358; 359; 360; 361; 362; 363.

1895 Exhibited at the Salon de la Société des Beaux-Arts a scheme of decoration for a room in a Parisian home, carried out in collaboration with E. Müller and T. Guérin.
Travelled in Belgium, where he met P. Hankar and V. Horta.
School of the Sacré-Cœur, 9 Avenue de la Frillère, Paris 16ᵉ. Bibl.: 67; 83; 106; 319; 320; 322; 323; 324; 336; 343; 345; 346.

c.1895 Monument of Rouchdy Bey Pacha, Gonards cemetery, Versailles.
Tomb of the Obry-Jassedé family, Issy-les-Moulineaux cemetery, Rue de l'Egalité, Issy-les-Moulineaux.

1896 Exhibited at the Salon de la Société Nationale des Beaux-Arts travel-sketches from England, Scotland, Belgium and Holland (Bibl.: 320; 322; 345; 346.); a scheme for the Universal Exhibition of 1900; drawings of the house in the Rue Molitor (Hôtel Delfau- see above) and painted fabrics.
Villa "La Hublotière" for Monsieur Noguès, 72 Avenue de Montesson, Le Vesinet. Bibl.: 324; 333.
Théâtre de la Bodinière and Melrose tea-room,18 Rue Saint-Lazare, Paris 9ᵉ (demolished c.1910).

1897 Exhibited interior scheme with library at the Salon de la Société Nationale des Beaux-Arts. Bibl.: 323. Coutollau shop, Boulevard de Saumur (now Boulevard du Maréchal Foch), Angers (demolished).
Porch for a large Parisian home in ceramic ware at the Exposition de la Céramique et de tous les Arts du feu, at the Palais des Beaux-Arts de Paris. Bibl.: 323.

1897 Hôtel Roy, 81 Boulevard Suchet, Paris 16ᵉ, demolished. Bibl.: 83; 109; 345.

1898 Private residences, 9 and 9 bis Impasse Racine, Hameau Boileau, Paris 16ᵉ, altered.

1898- House and shop of ceramist Coilliot, 14 Rue de Fleurus, Lille.
1900 Bibl.: 67; 83; 320; 322; 323; 324; 339; 345; 346; 369.

1897- Hubert de Romans concerthall, 60 Rue Saint-Didier,
1901 Paris 16ᵉ (demolished). Bibl.: 13; 14; 19; 21; 36; 55; 68; 70; 83; 109; 319; 320; 322; 323; 324; 328; 343; 348; 364; 365; 366; 367; 368.

1899 His father died 7 June, his mother 27 December.
Tomb of the Caillat family, Lachaise cemetery, Paris 20ᵉ. Bibl.: 320; 324.
House for Madame A. Canivet, Avenue du Parc-de-Beauveau-Craon (now 18 Rue Alphonse-de-Neuville, Garches (altered 1937-38). Bibl.: 320; 322; 348.
Villa "La Bluette"', Rue Pré-de-l'Isle, Hermanville, near Lions-sur-Mer (Calvados).

c.1899 Villa Barthélemy, 5-6, Rue Pré-de-l'Isle, Hermanville, near Lions-sur-Mer (Calvados). Bibl.: 333.

1899- Castel Henriette, Rue de Binelles, Sèvres (enlarged 1903;
1900 demolished March-April 1969). Bibl.: 70; 320; 322; 323; 326; 328; 336; 339; 343; 345; 370.

1900 Project for people's university of 15th arrondissement. Bibl.: 320; 322.

1900-01 Entrances and underground stations, Paris. Bibl.: 13; 18; 21; 22; 36; 38; 40; 67; 68; 83; 99; 106; 116; 117; 319; 320; 322; 323; 324; 327; 328; 333; 339; 343; 345; 371; 372; 373; 374; 375; 376; 377; 378; 379; 380; 381; 382; 383.
Porter's lodge, 10-12 Impasse Boileau, Paris 16ᵉ (demolished).

1902 Participated in foundation (22 May) of the Société du Nouveau Paris.
Dwellings and offices for the Nozal company, 132 Avenue de Paris (today Avenue du Président Wilson), Saint-Denis (demolished).

c. 1902 House at Versailles.

1902-03 Warehouses for Léon Nozal (demolished).
Castel Val, 4 Rue de Meulières, Chaponval (near Auvers-sur-Oise). Bibl.: 324; 333.

1903 One of founder-members of the Salon d'Automne, Paris.
Small House in garden at the Exposition de l'Habitation de Paris.
Artist's studio, 12 Avenue Perrichont prolongée, Paris 16ᵉ, demolished. Bibl.: 109.

c.1903 Chalet "La Surprise", 22 Avenue Aristide Briand, Cabourg. Bibl.: 327; 348.

Monument (demolished) to Paul Nozal (killed in car accident), near Barbezieux.

1903-05 Jassedé building, 142 Avenue de Versailles and 1 Rue Lancret, Paris 16ᵉ. Bibl.: 22; 67; 106; 319; 320; 322; 323; 324; 327; 332; 339; 343; 346.

1904 Exhibited furniture and a country house at the Salon d'Automne.
Hôtel Nozal, 52 Rue Ranelagh, Paris 16ᵉ; altered in 1937 and 1955, demolished in 1957. Bibl.: 21; 109; 320; 322; 323; 324; 328; 332; 333; 343.

1905 Castel Orgeval, 2 Avenue de la Mare-Tambour, Villemoisson. Bibl.: 83; 320; 322; 323; 324; 328; 346.

1904-07 Hôtel Deron Levent, 8, Villa de la Réunion, Paris 16ᵉ. Bibl.: 322; 323; 324; 327. 1906 Additional storey of tenement and building of pavilion, 25 Rue Erlanger, Paris 16ᵉ. Bibl.: 109.

c. 1906 Villa, Avenue de la Pépinière, Morsang-sur-Orge.
Villa "Clair de Lune"',18 Avenue du Muguet, Morsang-sur-Orge

c.1906-10 Model of standardized house. Bibl.: 345.

1907 Exhibited furniture, cast-ironwork, jewels, embroidery, carpets, wallpaper and fabrics at the Salon des Artistes Décorateurs.

c. 1907 Villa, 16 Rue Jean-Doyen, Eaubonne.

1908 Exhibited carved objets d'art at the Salon des Artistes Décorateurs

c. 1908 Chalet Blanc, 2 Rue du Lycée. Sceaux.

1909 Married 17 February the American painter Adeline Oppenheim 1909-10 Tremois building, 11 Rue François Millet, Paris 16ᵉ 1909-12 Hôtel Guimard, 122 Avenue Mozart, Paris 16ᵉ. Bibl.: 13; 21; 67; 68; 70; 109; 319; 320; 322; 324; 327; 328; 332; 338; 339; 345; 596.

1910 Exhibited a clock and embroidery at the Salon des Artistes Décorateurs, of which he became vice-president.
Project for the Grivellé Residence, 147 Avenue de Versailles, Paris 16ᵉ.

1910-11 Hôtel Mezzara, 60 Rue La Fontaine, Paris 16ᵉ. Bibl.: 21; 109; 319; 320; 322; 323; 324; 327; 339; 346; 386;

1909-11 Group of apartment blocks, 17-21 Rue La Fontaine; 43 Rue Gros; 8-10 Rue Agar, Paris 16ᵉ. Bibl.: 21; 109; 315; 320; 322; 323; 324; 327; 339; 346; 386; 387.

1912 Exhibited at the Salon des Artistes Décorateurs the flats in the Rues Agar and La Fontaine, and a gilded picture frame in carved wood.
Charles Deron-Levent tomb, Auteuil cemetery. Paris 1⁶e. Bibl.: 324.

1913 Exhibited a decorative marble wall-basin and the flats in the Rues Agar and La Fontaine, at the Salon des Artistes Décorateurs.
Villa Hemsy, 3 Rue de Crillon, Saint-Cloud.Bibl.: 324; 328.
Synagogue, 10 Rue Pavée, Paris 4ᵉ. Bibl.: 21; 67; 70; 320; 322; 323; 324; 327; 339; 388.

1914 Town house, Rue Pierre Ducreux, Paris 16ᵉ, demolished. Bibl.: 109.

1914-19 Office block, 10 Rue de Bretagne, Paris 3ᵉ. Bibl.: 67; 323; 324; 327.

1921-22 Town house, 3 Square Jasmin, Paris 16ᵉ. Bibl.: 322; 323; 324; 327; 328.

1922 Tomb of Albert Adès, Montparnasse cemetery, Paris 14ᵉ.

1925	Mairie of French village at the Exposition Internationale des Arts Décoratifs et Industriels, Paris. Bibl.: 327.
1926	Flats, l8 Rue Henri-Heine, Paris 16ᵉ. Bibl.: 67; 109; 322; 323; 324; 327.
1925-29	Flats, 36-38 Rue Greuze, Paris 16ᵉ. Bibl.: 67; 323; 324; 327; 339.
1929	Decorated with Legion of Honour.
1930	Competition entry for monument commemorating Battle of the Marne.
c. 1930	Villa "La Guimardière", Rue Lenôtre, Vaucresson (demolished 1969). Bibl.: 323; 333.
1938	Left for New York, where he arrived in September.
1942	Died in New York 20 May.

Frantz JOURDAIN
(Antwerp, 3.10.1847 - Paris, 1935)

1847	Born at Antwerp; his father a singer; his mother Mme Laure Jourdain, pœt of La Pléiade.
1861	After classical studies at the Lycées Napoléon, Henri IV and Stanislas, he obtained his baccalauréat.
1867	Admitted to Ecole des Beaux-Arts, where he attended Honoré Daumet's studio.
1870	Applied for French naturalization and enlisted in the army.
1871	Mentioned in dispatches 19 January for his part in retaking the redoubt of Montretout. Wounded, and decorated with the Military Medal.
1878	Admitted to the Architects'Central Society.
1882	Won a medal for a scheme for a billiard room at the Salon des Artistes Français.
c.1887	Published *Beaumignon*, a collection of short stories. Villa at Chelles. Bibl.: 447. Outbuildings for a residence in the Avenue du Bois de Boulogne, Paris 16ᵉ. Bibl.: 448.
1888	Published *Jean-Jean*, a patriotic tale. Factory in Pantin. Monument to La Fontaine, Square Ranelagh, Paris 16ᵉ (in collaboration with sculptor Dumilâtre). Bibl.: 444.
1889	Won a bronze medal at the International Exhibition, where he designed the Perfumery and Woven Fabrics sections.
1891	Project a new building for La Samaritaine, Rue Baillet, Paris 1ᵉʳ. Designed installations for the Panorama of the Crowning of the Czar at the World Exhibition, Moscow.
c.1893	Restoration of the Château de Verteuil. Printing-shop, Rue Cadet, Paris 9ᵉ.
1894	Officer of the Academy and Chevalier of the Legion of Honour. Member of Fine Arts Committee at the Chicago World Exhibition. Exhibited at the Salon of the Société Nationale des Beaux-Arts: a villa at Saint-Leu (Seine-et-Oise) and the library of the Château de Verteuil. House for the master-smith Schenck, 9 Rue Vergniaud, Paris 13ᵉ. Bibl.: 444. Design for entrance shelter of La Samaritaine, Rue du Pont-Neuf, Paris 1ᵉʳ. Bibl.: 450.
1895	Exhibited a small block of flats at Sèvres at the salon de la Société des Beaux-Arts .

	Design for a veranda and a bow window for La Samaritaine, Rue de la Monnaie, Paris 1ᵉʳ.
1896	Member of the Fine Arts Committee at Brussels World Exhibition.
1897	Exhibited a chapel for the Ursuline Sisters at Chelles, at the Salon de la Société Nationale des Beaux-Arts. Funeral monument for Alphonse Daudet, Père-Lachaise cemetery, Paris. Bibl.: 444.
1898	Supported Emile Zola's campaign for the rehabilitation of Dreyfus. His one-act play *Le Gage* is presented by Lugné Poe at the Théâtre de l'Oeuvre.
1899	Addition of two storeys to La Samaritaine, 75 Rue de Rivoli, Paris 1ᵉʳ.
1900	Officer of the Legion of Honour. Member of the Council of the Société Centrale des Architectes Modernes. Moët et Chandon pavilion and perfumery building at the International Exhibition. Bibl.: 444; 449. Perfumery buildings at the International Exhibition. Bibl.: 138; 147; 160; 444. Exhibited at the decennial Salon des Beaux-Arts, at the Grand Palais des Champs-Elysées, Paris: library for the Château de Verteuil, a villa at Bouffemont, the Panorama d'Iéna and perfumery building at the International Exhibition. Bibl.: 132; 444.
1902	Took part in foundation of the Société "Le Nouveau Paris", of which he became president. Tomb of Emile Zola, Montparnasse cemetery, Paris. Bibl.: 444.
1903	Founded the Salon d'Automne, of which he became president.
1904	"Le Nouveau Paris" protested against the rejection of Guimard's plans for the Opéra (Métro) station. Scheme for a timber warehouse for La Samaritaine at the corner of the Rue des Prêtres-Saint-Germain-l'Auxerrois and the Rue de la Monnaie, Paris 1ᵉʳ.
1905	President of the Syndicat de la Presse Artistique.
1905-07	Second shop La Samaritaine, Rue Baillet, Rue de l'Arbre-Sec, Rue de la Monnaie, Paris 1ᵉʳ (altered). Bibl.: 14; 67; 68; 69; 70; 82; 83; 106; 444; 451; 452; 453; 455; 460; 461; 493.
1906	Appointed President of the Association "L'Art pour Tous", a member oh the Society "l'Art à l'Ecole".
1909	New scheme for enlarging La Samaritaine, Rue Baillet, Rue de l'Arbre-Sec and Rue de la Monnaie, Paris 1xer.
1912	Building, l2 Rue du Louvre, Paris 1ᵉʳ. Bibl.: 67; 444. New face of building for "La Samaritaine", Rue de Rivoli, Paris 1ᵉʳ, demolished. Bibl.: 454; 461.
1914-17	La Samaritaine de luxe, 27 Boulevard des Capucines, Paris 2ᵉ (collaboration with G. Bourneuf). Bibl.: 69; 444; 456; 457; 461.
1922	President of the Groupe des Architectes Modernes.
1926-28	New buildings for La Samaritaine, Rue de la Monnaie, Paris 1ᵉʳ. Bibl.: 67; 69; 458; 459; 461.
n.d.	Restoration of the Château de la Roche-Guyon (Seine-et-Oise). Bibl.: 444. Restoration of the Château de Châteauneuf-sur-Sarthe (Maine-et-Loire). Bibl.: 444. Théâtre des Nouveautés, Paris. Théâtre des Variétés, Paris. Théâtre de Cluny Paris. Théâtre de l'Athenée, Paris: Théâtre Sarah-Bernhardt, Paris.

Jules LAVIROTTE

(Lyon, 25.3.1864 - 1928)

1892	After studies at the Ecole des Beaux-Arts de Lyon under the guidance of Louvier, he was admitted to the first class at the Ecole des Beaux-Arts de Paris, where he attended Paul Blondel's studio.
1894	Gained architect's diploma at the Ecole des Beaux-Arts, Paris.
1898	Apartment block, 151 Rue de Grenelle, Paris 7ᵉ. Bibl.: 55; 67; 93; 116.
1899	Private residence (now Italian Lycée Leonardo da Vinci), 12 Rue Sédillot, Paris 7ᵉ. Bibl.: 19; 55; 67; 117; 147.
1899-1900	Apartment block, 3 Square Rapp, Paris 7ᵉ. Bibl.: 55; 67; 79; 82; 83; 117; 147; 469; 470.
1900-01	Apartment block, 29 Avenue Rapp, Paris 7ᵉ. Bibl.: 14; 21; 22; 55; 67; 70; 77; 82; 83; 87; 97; 99; 116; 117; 454; 471; 472.
1903	Apartment block, 134 Rue de Grenelle, Paris 7ᵉ. Bibl.: 117; 468. Built two workers' cottages for Housing Exhibition at the Grand Palais, Paris. Bibl.: 92; 190.
1904	Became Officer of the Academy. Exhibited at the Salon de la Société des Artistes Français a design for a villa in the Parc Beauséjour, Avenue Marthe. Bibl.: 95; 480. Town house (now Céramic Hôtel), 34 Avenue de Wagram, Paris 7ᵉ (exhibited at the Salon d'Automne).
c. 1904	Château at Chaouat (Tunisia). Bibl.: 468. Villa at Chaouat (Tunisia). Restoration and decoration of church at Chaouat (Tunisia).
1906	Low-rental houses, 169 Boulevard Lefèbvre, Paris 15ᵉ. Bibl.: 77; 95; 474. Private residence. 23 Avenue de Messine, Paris 8ᵉ. Bibl.: 58; 97; 475; 477; 478; 479.
1907	Extension of a private residence 46 Rue de la Faisanderie, Paris 16ᵉ. Bibl.: 109.
c. 1907	Apartment block, 6 Rue de Messine, Paris 8ᵉ. Bibl.: 58; 476; 479.
1909	Exhibited a casino scheme at the Salon de la Société des Artistes Français.
c.1910	Medicinal water establishment (pump-room) of le Châtelet, Evian-les-Bains. Bibl.: 481.
1913	Exhibited design for a weighing-pavilion for the Société des Courses (Races) de Compiègne at the Salon de la Société des Artistes Français. Bibl.: 482.
n.d.	Group of artist's studios, Négrier development scheme, Rue de Grenelle, Paris. Château at Saint-Cyr-au-Mont-d'Or, near Lyon. Villa at Creusot. Workers' housing at Juvisy (Seine-et-Oise). Scheme for improving and decorating the medicinal-baths facilities at Aix-les-Bains, including proposed enlargement of town hall. Project for a monumental fountain with statue of Lamartine. Scheme for building stands at Flers (Orne).

Charles PLUMET

(Cirey-sur-Vezouze, Meurthe-et-Moselle, 17.5.1861 - Paris, 15.4.1928)
Apprentice of Anatole de Baudot and of Bruneau.

1891	House at 151 Rue Legendre, Paris 17ᵉ.
1893	House at 33 Rue Truffaut, Paris 17ᵉ.
	House at 37 Rue de Lévis, Paris 17ᵉ. House, 2bis Rue Léon Cosnard, Paris 17ᵉ.
1894	Exhibited the house in the Rue Legendre at the Salon de la Société Nationale des Beaux-Arts. Apartment block, 67 Avenue Malakoff (now Avenue Raymond Poincaré), Paris 16ᵉ, (in collaboration with Tony and Pierre Selmersheim; exhibited at the Salon of the Société Nationale des Beaux-Arts). Bibl.: 111; 500; 501; 505; 507; 509.
1895	Became associate of the Société Nationale des Beaux-Arts and exhibited at the Salon a scheme of ceramic decoration for an entrance hall.
1896	Exhibited a fireplace and furniture for a dining-room at the Salon de la Société des Beaux-Arts.
1897	One of founder members of the "Société des Cinq". Exhibited a dressing-room at the Salon de la Société Nationale des Beaux-Arts. Bibl.: 599. Rented flats, 36 Rue de Tocqueville, Paris 17ᵉ. Bibl.: 490; 500; 505; 509; 523; *Dekorative Kunst*, II, n.5, 1899, pp. 202-206.
c. 1897	Dining-room of M. Léon (in collaboration with T. Selmersheim). Bibl.: 500; 574.
1898	Town house, 112-114 Avenue Malakoff and 39 Avenue du Bois de Boulogne, Paris 16ᵉ, demolished. Bibl.: 64; 76; 87; 109; 502; 508; 509; 523.
c.1898	Restaurant Auvray, Place Boïeldieu, Paris 2ᵉ (in collaboration with T. Selmersheim), demolished. Bibl.: 112; 501; 520; 522; 524; *Dekorative Kunst*, II, n.5, 1899, p. 208. Shop Colinval, Paris (in collaboration with T. Selmersheim), demolished. Bibl.: 524. Shop for the hatter-tailor-shirtmaker Roddy, at the corner of Boulevard des Italiens and Rue Drouot, Paris 9ᵉ (in collaboration with T. Selmersheim), demolished. Bibl.: 21; 112; 501; 520; 522; 577; *Dekorative Kunst*, III, n. 7, 1900, p. 205.
1899	Exhibited a dining-room and living-room furniture (in collaboration with T. Selmersheim) at fourth exhibition of "L'Art dans Tout". Bibl.: 629. Exhibited a dining-room in oak (in collaboration with T. Selmersheim) at the Salon de la Société Nationale des Beaux-Arts.
c.1899	Kohler chocolate shop, Boulevard de la Madeleine, Paris (in collaboration with T. Selmersheim), demolished. Bibl.: 526.
1900	Chief-architect of the International Exhibition Installation of fixed decoration class at the International Exhibition. Bibl.: 138; 160. Decoration scheme for ceramic kiosk (executed by E. Muller). Bibl.: 158. Dining-room presented at the International Exhibition (in collaboration with T. Selmersheim). Bibl.: 151. Won a gold medal in class 66 (fixed decoration of public buildings and dwellings) and a bronze medal in class 10 (architecture) at the International Exhibition.
c.1900	Cadolle shop, Paris, demolished. Bibl.: 526.
1900-01	Apartment block, 50 Avenue Victor-Hugo, Paris 16ᵉ. Bibl.: 77; 82; 504; 505; 506; 510. Town house, 50 avenue Victor-Hugo, Paris 16ᵉ. Bibl.: 82; 505; 510; 510.1.
1901	Exhibited a dining-room (in collaboration with T. Selmersheim) at the Salon de la Société Nationale des Beaux-Arts. Exhibited a dining-room and a bed-room (in collaboration with T. Selmersheim) at the Salon "L'Art dans Tout".

Château of Chênemoireau (Loir-et-Cher), exhibited at the Salon de la Société Nationale des Beaux-Arts in 1902.

1902   Exhibited a bedroom in padouck wood (in collaboration with T. Selmersheim) at the Salon de la Société Nationale des Beaux-Arts. Bibl.: 183.
Exhibited a dining-room sideboard at the Exhibition of Modern Decorative and Industrial Arts at Turin and the apartment block, 50 Avenue Victor-Hugo at the Salon de la Société Nationale des Beaux-Arts.

1903   Worker's house at the Exposition de l'Habitation at the Grand Palais of Paris. Bibl.:92.
One of founder members of the "Salon d'Automne", of which he was secretary of the architecture section.
Exhibited a dining-room in waxed oak and a country house at the Salon d'Automne. Bibl.: 190.1.

1904   Decorated with Legion of Honour.
Private residence, 49 Avenue Victor-Hugo and Rue Villejust (now 24 Rue Paul-Valéry), Paris 16e. Bibl.: 109; 505; 511.

1905-06   Apartment blocks, 13-15 Boulevard de Lannes, Paris 16e. Bibl.: 56; 70; 93; 95; 505; 506.

1906   Vice-president of the Salon d'Automne.
Apartment block, 21 Boulevard de Lannes, Paris 16e. Design for a monument to Stendhal.

1907   Vice-president of the Salon d'Automne.
Town house, Rue Marbeau, Paris 16e.Bibl.: 225; 512.
Townhouse, 21 Rue Octave-Feuillet, Paris 16e.Bibl.: 77; 82; 109; 225: 229.

1908   Exhibited the above two residences at the Salon de la Société Nationale des Beaux-Arts.

c.1908   Project for competition of the Monument de la Réforme at Genève. Bibl.: *Schweizerische Bauzeitung*, LII (1908), p. 262.

c.1909   Transformation of a refectory, 40 Rue Manin, Paris 19e. Bibl.: 76.1.

1910   Exhibited an amateur's printroom at the Salon d'Automne. Bibl.: 249.

c.1910   Villa for the musician Gustave Kéfer, 45 bis Boulevard Richard Wallace, Neuilly-sur-Seine, demolished. Bibl.: 513; 514.

1911   Pavilion of French decorative art at Turin exhibition. Bibl.: 515; 516.
Villa, 81 Boulevard Montmorency, Paris 16e, demolished. Bibl.: 518; 519.

1912   Circular gallery for the Salon d'Automne. Bibl.: 517.
Apartment block, 1 Boulevard Montmorency, Paris 16e. Bibl.: 506.

1912-13   Apartment block, 39 Avenue Victor-Hugo, Paris 16e. Bibl.: 267; 270; 506.

1913-14   Office block, 33 Rue du Louvre and 10 Rue d'Aboukir, Paris 2e. Bibl.: 67; 506.

1925   Chief Architect for the Exposition des Arts Décoratifs et Industriels, Paris.
Four large regional towers and "cour des métiers" at the Exposition des Arts Décoratifs et Industriels, Paris.

1927   Commander of the Legion of Honour.
s.d. Private residence, 76 Rue Charles-Laffitte, Neuily-sur-Seine (in collaboration with Castex). Bibl.: 95.

Henri SAUVAGE
(Rouen, 10.5.1873 - Paris, 1932)

1890   Admitted to the Ecole des Beaux-Arts, where he attended Jean-Louis Pascal's studio.

1895   Left the Ecole des Beaux-Arts, after winning several medals.

1896   Projects of pieces of furniture, influenced by Serrurier-Bovy.

1897   Took part in competition for cover of *Art et Décoration* Magazine.

1898   Exhibition of draft for a flamed stone ware door and stencilled tapestries for the Salon de la Société Nationale des Beaux-Arts.

1898-   Villa Majorelle, 1 Rue Louis Majorelle, Nancy. Bibl.: 21; 55;
1901   67; 82; 83; 181.1; 545, 549; 550; 551.

1899   Decoration of two salons for the Café de Paris, 41 Avenue de l'Opéra, Paris 8e, demolished in 1955. Bibl.: 21; 22; 429; 545; 547; 548 Exhibition of tea-table and furniture for a musician at the Salon de la Société Nationale des Beaux-Arts. Bibl.: 173.1; 173.2.
Gained third prize in competition organized by the review *L'Art Décoratif* for a "desk and its arm-chair for the study of an apartment rented at 3000 francs".
Gained a prize of 1000 francs for a writing-table, chair, tea-table, door and window-furniture, and a painted muslin curtain in the second competition organized by the Union Centrale des Arts Décoratifs.

1900   Loïe Fuller theater at Exposition Universelle. Bibl.: 21; 70; 83; 132; 138; 158; 160; 163; 545. Grand Guignol at the International Exhibition. Bibl.: 545; 633.
Majorelle House Pavilion at the International Exhibition. Bibl.: 545.
Installation of printed materials at the International Exhibition. Bibl.: 127
Won a medal at Exposition Universelle.
Exhibition of a music-stand at fifth Exhibition of "L'Art dans Tout".

c. 1900   Premises of tapestry-dealer Jansen, 9 Rue Royale, Paris 8^e, destroyed. Bibl.: 21; 545; 552. Project for 120 bathing huts on the beach.
Project for a hotel by the seaside.
Project for a small country house for Mme Majorelle. Bibl.: 545; *Moderne Bauformen*, 1902.
Project for a villa by the seaside. Bibl.: 545.

1901   Exhibition of table and chair at the sixth Exhibition of "L'Art dans Tout". Bibl.: 636; 637.
Exhibition of dining-room, card-table and drawing-room chair at the Salon de la Société Nationale des Beaux-Arts.

c. 1901   Project for a small mountain chalet. Bibl.: 545.

1902   Exhibition of Majorelle villa in Nancy and scheme for premises of tapestry-dealer Jansen at the Salon de la Société Nationale des Beaux-Arts.
Second project for a country house for Mme Majorelle.

c. 1902   Apartment block, 17 Rue Damrémont, Paris 18e. Bibl.: 77; 533; 545.
Bathroom covered with flamed stoneware of Bigot, stained glass paste relief by Alexandre Charpentier. Bibl.: 545; *Moderne Bauformen*, II (1903), pl. 64.
Shop window and indoor fittings of premises of material manufacturer Coudyser. Bibl.: 545.
Design for a park gate. Bibl.: 545; *Moderne Bauformen*, II (1903), pl. 94.
Design for the façade of a building between partywalls. Bibl.: 545; *Moderne Bauformen*, II (1903), pl. 28.
Project for public bath on the coast of Alger. Bibl.: 21; 545; *Moderne Bauformen*, II (1903), pl. 73.
Project for a corner building. Bibl.: 545; *Moderne Bauformen*, II (1903), pl. 40.

1903   Hygienic low-cost housing, 7 Rue Trétaigne, Paris 18e. Bibl.: 61; 106; 533; 545; 553.
Hygienic low-cost housing, 1 Rue Fernand Flocon, Paris 18e. Bibl.: 545.
Villa Oceana for M. de Lestapis, Biarritz. Bibl.: 60; 218;

545; 554.
Exhibition of children's bedroom and sandstone mantelpiece at Salon de la Société Nationale des Beaux-Arts. Took part in a shop-sign competition organized by the magazine *L'Art Décoratif*.

1904 Apartment block, 22 Rue Laugier, Paris 17ᵉ. Bibl.: 545.
Galerie d'Argentine, 111 Avenue Victor Hugo, Paris 16ᵉ. Bibl.: 106; 545. "An actress's dressing-room" designed for Salon des Artistes Décorateurs. Bibl.: 14; 21; 199; 545.
Exhibition of Villa Oceana in Biarritz, apartment block and worker's house in Paris, large wardrobe at Salon de la Société Nationale des Beaux-Arts.

1905 Hygienic low-cost housing, 20 Rue Sévero, Paris 14ᵉ.
Bibl.: 545.

1906 Project for the lay-out of fortification spaces, for the account of the Association des Cités-Jardins de France; won a price at the Milan Exhibition.

1907 Project of travellers'hotel in Biarritz.
Villa Leubas, 110 Rue d'Espagne, Biarritz. Bibl.: 545.
Schoolroom designed for the Salon d'Automne (Bibl.: 76.1; 223; 435.1) where he exhibits a sketch of Château de M.E. at B.

1908 Villa Majorelle, Avenue Thiers, Compiègne. Bibl.: 225; 229; 535; 545.
Hygienic low-cost housing, 165 Boulevard de l'Hôpital, Paris 13ᵉ. Bibl.: 545.
Low-cost flats, 1 Rue de la Chine, Paris 20ᵉ. Bibl.: 545.
Secretary of the architecture section of the "Salon d'Automne". Exhibited a desk at Exposition Franco-Britannique. Bibl.: 235.

1909 Exhibition of office furniture at "Salon de la Société Nationale des Beaux-Arts".

c. 1909 Project for the Grand Hotel "Les Terrasses".
Projects of a gabled house. Bibl.: 545.

1911 Apartment block, 29 Rue de la Boétie, Paris 8ᵉ.

1912 Gabled house, 26 Rue Vavin, Paris 6ᵉ. Bibl.: 67; 82; 106; 535; 541; 557; 558.

1912-13 Shops and office blocks for Mr. Majorelle, 126 Rue de Provence, Paris 9ᵉ. Bibl.: 535; 545.

c. 1919 House for manager of S.E.C.B., Mimizan.

1920 Gambetta cinema, 4 Rue Belgrand, Paris 20ᵉ. Bibl.: 535; 545.
Project of a street with gabled houses. Bibl.: 535; 541; 545.

1921 Project for a theatre, Boulevard Raspail, Paris 6ᵉ.

1922 Sèvres cinema, 68 Rue de Sèvres, Paris 7ᵉ, demolished in 1976.
Project for small standard houses, cottage style. Bibl.: 545.
Project for small standard houses, villa style. Bibl.: 545.
Apartment block, 22 Rue Beaujon, Paris 8ᵉ. Bibl.: 545.

1922-25 Series of low-cost gabled house for the town of Paris, Rue des Amiraux, Paris 18ᵉ. Bibl.: 67; 535; 545.

1923 "Travellers'Hotel. American House. Apartment block: final constructions for accomodation of visitors of 1925 Exhibition"; project presented by a delegation of the group of Modern Architects including Guimard, Sauvage, Joachim Richard, Louis Brachet, Louis-Pierre Sézille et Georges Rœmrich.

1924 Apartment block, 50 Avenue Duquesne, Paris 7ᵉ. Bibl.: 535; 545.
Apartment block, 137 Boulevard Raspail, Paris 6ᵉ.

1924-25 Apartment block, 16 Boulevard Raspail, Paris 7ᵉ. Bibl.: 535.

1924-28 Apartment block, 19 Boulevard Raspail, Paris 7ᵉ. Bibl.: 535.

1925 Pavilion of Grands Magasins du Printemps, shopping gallery, electric transformer (in collaboration with Zette Sauvage), Souk Tunisien and Diorama of North Africa at Exposition des Arts Décoratifs et Industriels modernes de Paris. Bibl.: 535; 545.
Apartment block, 42 Rue de la Pompe, Paris 1⁶e.Bibl.: 535.
Apartment block, 6 Avenue Sully-Prudhomme, Paris 7ᵉ.

1926 Apartment block "Studio Building", 65 Rue La Fontaine, Paris 16ᵉ. Bibl.: 545.
Villa in Saint-Martin-La-Garenne for the architect's family. Bibl.: 541; 545.

1926-28 Garage, Rue Campagne-Première, Paris 14ᵉ. Bibl.: 541; 545.
Prefabricated cells, exhibited at first Salon des Appareils Ménagers, afterwards built in three days in Auteuil.

1926-28 New stores La Samaritaine, Rue du Pont Neuf, Paris 1ᵉʳ (in collaboration with Frantz Jourdain). Bibl.: 541; 545.

1927 Project for steel houses.
Project for "Giant Hotel". Bibl.: 535; 545.
Villa for the Manager of *Le Matin*, Mr. Bruno Varilla, Orsay (Seine-et-Oise).
"Institut du Syntol", Neuilly, demolished.

c. 1927 Private club house "Le Sphinx", Boulevard Edgar Quinet, Paris 14ᵉ.

1928 Project for a gabled house and garage facing the Seine.
Apartment block, 8 bis Boulevard Maillot, Paris 16ᵉ. Bibl.: 535. Apartment block, 27 Rue Legendre, Paris 17ᵉ. Bibl.: 535.
Project for pyramidal tower on Montparnasse Cemetery. Bibl.: 545.

1929 Town house, Neuilly-sur-Seine.
Prototype of house in "Eternit" tubing. Bibl.: 545.
Project of industrialized houses, type B, Monteils method.
Office blocks, 10 Rue Saint-Marc, Paris 7ᵉ.

1930 Competition project for a monument commemorating the victory of the Marne (in collaboration with Zette Sauvage). Bibl.: 545.
Competition design for the façade of the Galeries Lafayette.
Project for standard houses, T process, "Eternit" tubing. Bibl.: 545.
Project for villas, type B and C.

1931 Decré stores, Nantes (destroyed 23 september 1943). Bibl.: 69; 539; 541; 545.
Scheme for environmental and architectural replanning of Porte Maillot,Paris. Bibl.: 541; 545.
Scheme for replanning large town (in collaboration with André Ventre).

1932 Vert Galant building, 42 Quai des Orfèvres, Paris 1ᵉʳ.
All works between 1900 and beginning of First World War (except the pavilions of Exposition Universelle in 1900) were carried out in collaboration with Charles Sarazin.

Xavier SCHOELLKOPF

(Moscou, 18.8.1870 -? 1911)

1889 After classical studies at the Collège Sainte-Barbe, admitted to the Ecole des Beaux-Arts, where he attended the studios of Julien Guadet and Gustave Raulin. He won four medals in second class.

1892 Admitted to first class in the Ecole des Beaux-Arts.
Won a medal at the Salon de la Société des Artistes Français.

1895 Won a medal at the Salon de la Société des Artistes Français.

1897 Town house, 4 Avenue d'Iéna, Paris 16ᵉ (in collaboration with Edouard George), demolished. Bibl.: 77; 559; 560; 561; *Architektonische Monatshefte*, VII (1901), pl. 93.

1900 Yvette Guilbert's house, Boulevard Berthier, Paris 1ᵉ, demolished. Bibl.: 18; 21; 55; 70; 77; 563; 564; 565; *Architektonische Monatshefte*, VII (1901), pp. 45, 48, pl. 93.

1901	Apartment block, 29 Avenue de la République, Paris 11ᵉ. Bibl.: 55; 77; 562.
1902	Apartment block, 29 Boulevard de Courcelles, Paris 8ᵉ. Bibl.: 55; 566.
1906	Exhibited a small house (built at Montbéliard) at the Salon de la Société des Artistes Français. Bibl.: 211.
1907	Exhibited a restoration scheme at the Salon de la Société des Artistes Français. Bibl.: 220.
1909	Exhibited the "chalets" " Fief de la Thuillerie" at Dammartin and "L'Hermitage " " at Veneux-Nardon, at the Salon de la Société des Artistes Français. Bibl.: 236.

Tony SELMERSHEIM

(Saint-Germain-en-Laye, 2.6.1871 -?)

1895	Exhibited an architect's drawing-office and a library at the Salon de la Société Nationale des Beaux-Arts.
1896	Exhibited furniture for a bedroom and a studio for an art amateur at the Salon de la Société Nationale des Beaux-Arts.
1897	One of the founders of the "Société des Cinq". Exhibited furniture at the Salon de la Société Nationale des Beaux-Arts. Bibl.: 599.
c.1897	Mr. Léon's dining-room (in collaboration with Ch. Plumet). Bibl.: 500; 574.
1898	Electric light fittings for a private residence, 112-114 Avenue de Malakoff, Paris 16ᵉ of Charles Plumet.
c.1898	Restaurant Auvray, Place Boïeldieu, Paris 2ᵉ (in collaboration with Ch. Plumet), demolished. Bibl.: 112; 501; 520; 522; 524. Shop of the hatter-tailor-shirtmaker Roddy at the corner of the Boulevard des Italiens and the Rue Drouot, Paris 9ᵉ (in collaboration with Ch. Plumet), demolished. Bibl.: 21; 112; 501; 522; 577. Shop Colinval, Paris (in collaboration with Ch. Plumet), demolished. Bibl.: 524.
1898	Exhibited a dining-room made for Edouard Detaille (in collaboration with Ch. Plumet) and a hairdressing table in padouck at the Galerie des Artistes Modernes, 19 Rue Caumartin, Paris 9ᵉ. Bibl.: 575.
1899	Exhibited a dining-room (in collaboration with Ch. Plumet) at the Salon de la Société Nationale des Beaux-Arts. Bibl.: 173.1; 173.2. Exhibited a dining-room and lounge furniture (in collaboration with Ch. Plumet) at the Salon "L'Art dans Tout". Bibl.: 629; 631; 632.
c.1899	Kohler chocolate shop, Boulevard de la Madeleine, Paris (in collaboration with Ch. Plumet), demolished. Bibl.: 526. Dining-room shown at the International Exhibition of 1900 (in collaboration with Ch. Plumet). Bibl.: 151; *Innen Dekoration*, 1902, pp. 38-39.
1901	Exhibited a loungechair at the Salon de la Société Nationale des Beaux-Arts. Bibl.: 175.1. Exhibited a dining-room (in collaboration with Ch. Plumet), a dek, a bed and a glass cabinet at the sixth Salon of "L'Art dans Tout". Bibl.: 636; 637.
1902	Exhibited the petting for a drawing-room and a bed-room in rosewood and padouck (in collaboration with Ch. Plumet) at the Salon de la Société Nationale des Beaux-Arts.
1903	Exhibited a lady's desk in sycomore at the Salon d'Automne. Furnishing of a worker's house of Charles Plumet at the Exposition de l'Habitation at the Grand Palais at Paris.
c.1903	Furniture of apartment for Mr. Deniau. Bibl.: 578.
c.1905	Car for Mr. Dietrich. Bibl.: 579.

1908	Decoration of the Pommery residence at Reims (in collaboration with Ch. Plumet). Bibl.: 596.
c.1908	Entrance hall of the Rouché house, Rue d'Offémont, Paris (in collaboration with Pierre Selmersheim).
c.1910	Furnishing for the villa Kéfer at Neuilly-sur-Seine (in collaboration with Ch. Plumet).
1910	Exhibited a cupboard, chairs and a table at the Salon de la Société des Artistes Décorateurs.
1911	Exhibited a scheme including a dining-room, a boudoir and a bedroom at the Salon de la Société des Artistes Décorateurs.
1912	Won the 1ˢᵗ prize in the competition for the "Décoration du bureau du Président du Conseil municipal de la Ville de Paris". Bibl.: 581.
c.1912	Furnishing of a villa, 81 Boulevard Montmorency, Paris 16ᵉ (in collaboration with Ch. Plumet).
1913	Exhibited a small lady's desk, an arm-chair, a small wooden lounge table and a desk at the Salon de la Société des Artistes Décorateurs.
1919	Exhibited a ship's cabin at the Salon de la Société des Artistes Décorateurs.
1971	*Le Figaro* annouced a commemorative festival on June 3ᵈ on the occasion of the 100ᵗʰ anniversary of Selmersheim's birth.

Louis SOREL

(Grenoble, 25.6.1867 - Toulon, 10.3.1934)
A pupil of Auguste Vaudremer at the Ecole des Beaux-Arts.

1900	Fittings of Papeterie section at the International Exhibition. Bibl.: 138; 158; 160.
1901	Exhibition of a dining-room at the Salon de la Société Nationale des Beaux-Arts. Bibl.: 175.1; 178. Exhibition of a dining-room at the Salon "L'Art dans Tout". Bibl.: 636; 637.
1903-04	Town house, 65 Rue des Belles-Feuilles, Paris 16ᵉ. Bibl.: 56.
1904-05	Residence, 9 Rue Le Tasse, Paris 16ᵉ. Bibl.: 56; 77; 82; 93; 109.
1906	Exhibition of an apartment block at the Salon de la Société Nationale des Beaux-Arts. Bibl.: 210.
1907	Exhibition of a project for a villa at the Salon de la Société Nationale des Beaux-Arts. Bibl.: 216; 219; *Art et Décoration*, I semester, p. 160.
c.1909	Villa, Avenue de Ceinture, Enghien. Bibl.: *L'Architecte*, IV (1909), pl. LXIII, V (1910), pl. XXIV. Villa for a manager of champagne firm, Boulevard Vasnier, Reims. Bibl.: 64; 588; *L'Architecte*, V (1910), pl. LXI-LXVI. Keeper's cottage, Reims. Bibl.: *L'Architecte*, VI (1911), pl. LXVI.
1909-12	Sadla store building, 48 Boulevard Raspail, 29 Rue de Sèvres, Paris 16ᵉ. Bibl.: 63; 98; *L'Architecte*, IX (1914), pl. XXXVIII-LXI.
1910	Exhibition of project for the Paris Swedish Church (in collaboration with L. Brachet) at the Salon de la Société Nationale des Beaux-Arts. Bibl.: 244; 245.
c.1910	Apartment block, Rue Chauveau, Neuilly-sur-Seine. Bibl.: 93. Private residence, Boulevard du Château, Rue Chauveau, Neuilly-sur-Seine. Bibl.: 95.
c.1911	Residence, Avenue de Neuilly, Neuilly-sur-Seine. Bibl.: 252. Villa, Francport (Oise). Bibl.: 64; 252; *L'Architecte* VI (1911), pl. XIV-XV.
1916	Private pavilion at the Exposition de la Cité, rebuilt in Paris. Bibl.: *Gazette des Beaux-Arts*, 1914-16, II, p. 383.

BIBLIOGRAPHY

GENERAL

Books:

1. Nocq H., *Tendances nouvelles. Enquête sur l'évolution des industries d'art*, Paris 1896.

2. Bajot E., *L'Art Nouveau. Décoration et ameublement*, Paris 1898.

3. Fierens P. - Gevaert H., *Essai sur l'Art Contemporain*, Paris 1899.

4. Mourey G., *Les Arts de la vie et le règne de la laideur*, Paris s.d. (1899).

5. Lahor J., *L'Art Nouveau. Son histoire, l'Art Nouveau à l'Exposition, l'Art Nouveau au point de vue social*, Paris 1901.

6. Bayard E., *Le Style moderne*, Paris s.d. (1919).

7. Kielland Th. B., *L'Art Nouveau 1895-1925*, Oslo 1928.

8. Lenning H. F., *The Art Nouveau*, Den Haag 1951.

9. Seling H. (written by), *Jugendstil. Der Weg ins 20. Jahrhundert*, München 1950.

10. Tschudi Madsen S., *Sources of Art Nouveau*, New York 1956.

11. Bini V. - Trabuchelli V., *L'Art Nouveau*, Milano 1957.

12. Cassou J. - Langui E. - Pevsner N., *Les Sources du XXᵉ siècle*, Paris 1961.

13. Schmutzler R., *Art Nouveau*, Stuttgart 1962.

14. Cremona I., *Il tempo dell'Art Nouveau*, Firenze 1964.

15. Rheims M., *L'Objet 1900*, Paris 1964.

16. Guerrand R.H., *L'Art Nouveau en Europe*, Paris 1965.

17. Rheims M., *L'art 1900 ou le Style Jules Verne*, Paris 1965.

18. Amaja M., *Art Nouveau*, London 1966.

19. Tschudi Madsen S., *Art Nouveau*, Paris 1968.

20. Champigneulle B., *L'Art Nouveau*, Paris 1972.

21. Massobrio G. - Portoghesi P., *Album del Liberty*, Bari 1975.

22. Masini L.-V., *Art Nouveau*, Firenze 1976.

23. Bouillon J.-P., *Journal de l'Art Nouveau*, Genève 1985.

Articles:

24. "L'Art Nouveau", in *La Construction Moderne*, 2nd serie, II (1896-97), pp. 440-441.

25. Genuys Ch., "A propos de l'Art Nouveau - Soyons Français", in *Revue des Arts Décoratifs*, XVII (1897), pp. 1-6.

26. Grasset E., "L'Art Nouveau", in *Revue des Arts Décoratifs*, XVII (1897), pp. 182-200.

27. Rivoalen E., "Art Nouveau", in *La Construction Moderne*, 2nd serie, III (1897-98), pp. 289-290.

28. Planat P., "Actualités", in *La Construction Moderne*, 2nd serie, V (1899-1900), pp.589-591.

29. Grasset E., "L'Art Nouveau", in *La Plume*, special issue, 1900, pp. 1-63.

30. Planat P., "Actualités", in *La Construction Moderne*, 2nd serie, VI (1900-01), pp. 253-256.

31. Planat P., "Causerie", in *La Construction Moderne*, 2nd serie, VI (1900-01), pp. 277-279.

32. Planat P., "Actualités - Haute Esthétique - l'Art Public", in *La Construction Moderne*, 2nd serie, VII (1901-02), pp. 49-50.

33. P. (lanat) P., "L'Art Nouveau", in *La Construction Moderne*, 2nd serie, VII (1901-02), pp. 469-471.

34. Planat P., "Actualités. Architecture - Critique et Art Nouveau", in *La Construction Moderne*, 2nd serie, VII (1902-03), pp. 481-483.

35. "L'Art Nouveau", in *La Construction Moderne*, 2nd serie, VIII (1902-03), pp. 546-547.

36. Gelbert A., "Conférence sur l'architecture au XXᵉ siècle et l'Art Nouveau par M. Paul Gout, architecte", in *La Construction Moderne*, 2nd serie, IX (1903-04), pp. 148-149; pp.158-159.

37. P.(lanat) P., "Art Nouveau et Modern Style", in *La Construction Moderne*, 2nd serie, IX (1903-04), pp. 397-400.

38. Dali S., "De la beauté terrifiante et comestible de l'Architecture Modern'Style", in *Minotaure*, 3-4, s.d. (1933), pp. 69-76.

39. Chastel A., "Le Modern Style", in *L'Information d'Histoire de l'Art*, IX (3, 1964), pp. 118-124.

40. Waldberg P., "Modern Style", in *L'Oeil*, 71, 1960, pp. 48-61.

41. Bruand Y., "L'ambiguïté de l'Art Nouveau en architecture", in *L'Information d'Histoire de l'Art*, IX (3, 1964), pp. 118-124

42. Brunhammer Y., "1900 un style", in *La Maison Française*, November 1964, pp. 162-167 and p. 200.

43. Berthier-Lemaire M., "Le Style 1900", in *Pénéla*, 6, 1967, pp. 20-37.

44. Ragon M., "Hommage au Modern Style", in *Cimaise*, 1971, pp. 47-55.

45. Champigneulle B., "L'Art Nouveau", in *Médecine de France*, 1973, 239, pp. 25-42.

Biographical Dictionaries:

46. Curinier C.-E., *Dictionnaire national des contemporains*, Vol..4, Paris 1899-1906.

47. Delaire E., *Les Architectes élèves de l'Ecole des Beaux- Arts, 1793-1907*, Paris 1907.

48. Edouard J., *Dictionnaire biographique des artistes contemporains, 1910-1930*, Paris 1931.

49. Oudin B., *Dictionnaire des architectes*, Paris 1970.

MODERN ARCHITECTURE IN FRANCE

Books:

50. Champier V., *L'art décoratif moderne. Documents d'atelier*, 2 vol., Paris 1898-1999.

51. Lambert Th., *Nouveaux éléments d'architecture, 3ᵉ série. Villas et petites constructions*, Paris s.d. (1900).

52. Lambert Th., *Nouveaux éléments d'architecture. Maisons de campagne et villas*, Paris s.d. (1902).

53. Lahor J., *Les habitations à bon marché et un art nouveau pour le peuple*, Paris 1903.

54. Rivoalen E., *Petites maisons modernes de ville et de campagne récemment construites...*, Paris s.d. (1903).

55. *L'architecture au XXᵉ siècle. Choix des meilleures constructions nouvelles. Hôtels, maisons de rapport, villas, etc., etc. 1ᵉʳ volume*, directed by André Guédy, Paris s.d. (1904 ca.).

56. *L'architecture au XXᵉ siècle. .. 2ᵉ série*, Paris s.d. (1907 ca.).

57. Rivoalen E., *La Brique moderne. Recueil de documents pratiques sur les bâtiments les plus récemment construits en brique et le décor en briquetage*, Dourdan s.d. (1908).

58. *L'architecture au XXᵉ siècle. .. 3ᵉ série*, 2 volumes., Paris s.d. (1908, 1911 ca.).

59. Baudot A. de, *L'architecture et le ciment armé*, Paris 1909.

60. Lambert Th., *Répertoire de l'Habitation. Maisons de ville et de campagne, chalets, cottages, habitations à bon marché, mairies, hôpitaux, écoles, communs, garages, etc.*, Paris s.d. (1909).

61. Lucas C. - Darville W., *Les habitations à bon marché en France et à l'étranger*, Paris s.d. (1913 ca.).

62. Baudot A. de, *L'architecture, le passé, le présent*, Paris s.d. (1920).

63. *L'architecture au XXᵉ siècle. .. 4ᵉ série*, Paris s.d. (1920).

64. Magne H.M., *L'art français depuis 20 ans. L'architecture*, Paris 1922.

65. Gromort G., *Histoire abrégée de l'architecture en France au 19ᵉ siècle*, Paris 1924.

66. Guerrand R.H., *Les origines du logement social en France*, Paris 1960.

67. Emery M., *Un siècle d'architecture moderne, 1850-1950*, Paris 1971.

68. Roisecco G., *L'architettura del ferro: la Francia (1715- 1914)*, Roma 1973.

69. Marrey B., *Les grands magasins des origines à 1939*, Paris 1979.

70. Jullian R., *Histoire de l'architecture en France de 1880 à nos jours. Un siècle de modernité*, Paris 1984.

71. Lambert Th., *Nouveaux éléments d'architecture. 7ᵉ série. Habitations à bon marché*, Paris s.d.

72. Raguenet A., *Documents et matériaux d'architecture et de sculpture, classés par ordre alphabétique*, 4 vol., Paris s.d.

Essays and articles:

73. Larroumet G., "L'emploi de la céramique dans l'architecture", in *Revue des Arts Décoratifs*, XVIII (1897), pp. 33-45, 73-81.

74. Vogt G., "De l'emploi de la Céramique dans la construction", in *Art et Décoration*, VII

(3, 1904), pp. 93-100.

75. Saunier Ch., "Nouvelles applications du grès flammé au revêtement des façades", in *L'Architecte*, III (11 and 12), pp. 83-87, 91-94.

76. Segard A., "French Architecture and Decoration", in *The Studio Year Book of Decorative Art 1908*, pp. 37-42.

76.1. Riotor L., "L'Art à l'Ecole", in *L'Art Décoratif*, XI (I semester, 1909), pp. 92-99.

77. Forthuny P., "Dix années d'architecture", in *Gazette des Beaux-Arts*, LI (633 and 635, 1910), pp. 191-210, 426-440.

78. Taylor F.A., "French Architecture and Decoration", in *The Studio Year Book of Decorative Arts 1914*, pp. 143-172.

79. Gloton J.-J., "L'architecture en France autour de 1900", in *L'Information d'Histoire de l'Art*, III (1958), pp. 128-141.

80. Choay F., "Techniciens et architectes autour de 1900", in *Art de France*, III (1966), p. 311.

81. Jeanneau G., "L'Ecole rationaliste de 1900", in *Meubles et Décors*, LII (813, 1966), pp. 94-103.

82. Loyer F., "Art Nouveau Architecture in France", in *Art Nouveau Belgium - France*, exhibition cat., Houston Rice Museum and Chicago Art Institute, 1976, pp. 379-403.

83. Loyer F., *France. Viollet-le-Duc to Tony Garnier: The Passion for Rationalism*, in *Art Nouveau Architecture*, edited by par F. Russel, London 1979.

84. Marrey B., "L'Age d'or de la céramique", in *Architecture intérieure Cree*, 175, 1980, pp. 64-68.

PARIS 1900

Books:

85. Lambert Th., *Nouveaux éléments d'architecture. Escalier et ascenseurs*, Paris s.d. (1898 ca.).

86. Lambert Th., *Nouveaux éléments d'architecture. 2e série. Nouvelles constructions avec bow-window-loggias-tourelles-avant-corps*, Paris s.d. (1900 ca.).

87. Lambert TH., *Nouveaux éléments d'architecture. 4e série. Nouvelles constructions. Maisons de rapport*, Paris s.d. (1901 ca.).

88. Doniol A., *Histoire du XVIe arrondissement de Paris*, Paris 1902.

89. Lambert Th., *Nouveaux éléments d'architecture. 6e série. Hôtels privés*, Paris s.d. (1903).

90. Passard G., *Nouveau dictionnaire historique de Paris*, Paris 1904.

91. Lambert Th., *Nouvelles constructions. Maisons à loyers*, Paris s.d. (1905).

92. Lambert Th., *Nouveaux éléments d'architecture. 7e série. Habitations à bon marché*, Paris s.d. (1905 ca.).

93. Rivoalen E., *Maisons modernes de rapport et de commerce (ensemble et détail) publiées d'après les plans, devis et réglements communi-

qués par les architectes*, Paris s.d. (1907).

94. Lambert Th., *Nouveaux éléments d'architecture. 9e série. Décoration et ameublements intérieurs*, Paris s.d. (1910).

95. Lambert Th., *Nouveaux éléments d'architecture. 10e série. Nouvelles constructions en matériaux variés. Grès-faïence- briques-bronze. Plans-façades-coupes-détails*, Paris s.d. (1910).

96. Rochegude Marquis de, *Promenades dans toutes les rues de Paris, 1er arrondissement - XVIe arrondissement*, Paris 1910.

97. *Les Concours de façades de la Ville de Paris*, 2. vol., Paris s.d. (1910 ca.).

98. Escholier R., *Le Nouveau Paris. La vie artistique de la cité moderne*, Paris s.d. (1912).

99. Cheronnet L., *A Paris vers 1900*, Paris 1932.

100. Burnand R., *Paris 1900*, Paris 1951.

101. Roman J., *Paris fin de siècle*, Paris 1958.

102. Hillairet J., *Dictionnaire historique des rues de Paris*, 2 vol., Paris 1963.

103. Bastie J., *La croissance de la banlieue parisienne*, Paris 1964.

104. Braibant Ch. - Mirot A. - Le Moël M., *Guide historique des rues de Paris*, Paris 1965.

105. Marrey B., *Guide de l'art dans la rue du 20e siècle. Paris et sa banlieue*, Paris 1974.

106. Chemetov P. - Marrey B., *Familièrement inconnues . .. architectures Paris 1848-1914*, Paris 1976 and *Architectures à Paris 1848-1914*, Paris 1984.

107. Thézy M. de, *Paris, la rue (le mobilier urbain du Second Empire à nos jours*, Paris 1976.

108. Tharicat J. - Villars M., *Le logement à bon marché. Chronique. Paris 1850-1930*, Boulogne 1982.

109. Vigne G. - Andia B. de, *Le XVIe arrondissement Mécène de l'Art Nouveau 1895-1914*, exhibition cat., Paris, Beauvais, Bruxelles 1984.

110. Henning-Schefold M. - Schaefer I., *Architekturtendenzen in Paris und Brüssel im späten 19. Jahrhundert. Struktur und Dekoration*, s.l., s.d.

Articles:

111. Gardelle C., "Moderne Kunst in der französischen Architektur. Das pariser Haus", in *Dekorative Kunst*, bd. I (1898), pp. 177-184.

112. Forthuny P., "La rue pittoresque. Devantures et boutiques", in *Revue des Arts Décoratifs*, XIX (1899), pp. 237-252.

113. Mar L., "Les belles façades du XVIe arrondissement", dans *Bulletin de la Société Historique d'Auteuil et de Passy*, 1902, IV trimester, pp. 211 sqq.

114. Streiff R., "Moderne pariser Bauten", in *Schweizerische Bauzeitung*, bd. XLVI (1903, 20 and 22).

115. Mallet-Stevens R. - Rœderer J., "Notes from Paris", in *The Architectural Review*, vol.XXI (1907); vol. XXII (1907), pp. 18-20, 198-199, 310-312; vol. XXIII (1908),

pp. 254-259, 305- 310; vol. XXIV (1908), pp. 136-138, 186-191.

116. Christ Y., "Paris ou la Belle Epoque classée monument historique", in *Connaissance des Arts*, 54, 1956, pp. 64-67.

117. Desbruères M., "Maisons de 1900 de Paris", in *Bizarre*, 37, 1963, pp. 2-35.

118. Christ Y., "Paris fin-de-siècle disparaît", in *Sites et Monuments*, July-September 1965, pp. 3-5.

ARCHITECTURE AND FURNITURE AT THE WORLD EXHIBITION OF 1900

Books :

119. *Concours pour l'Exposition universelle de 1900: Projets exposés au Palais de l'Industrie*, Paris 1895.

120. *Catalogue général officiel*, Paris 1900.

121. *Les palais des Beaux-Arts*, Paris s.d. (1900).

122. *L'Exposition de Paris (1900) pub. avec la collaboration d'écrivains spéciaux et des meilleurs artistes*, Paris 1900.

123. *Mobilier et décoration: Rapport de la commission d'installation*, Saint-Cloud 1900.

124. Champier V., *Les industries d'art à l'Exposition Universelle de 1900*, Paris 1900.

125. Raguenet A., *Les principaux palais de l'Exposition*, s.l. 1900.

126. Gucrinct E., *La décoration et l'ameublement à l'exposition de 1900*, Paris 1901.

127. Lambert Th., *L'Art Décoratif moderne. Exposition universelle de 1900. Sections françaises et étrangères*, Paris s.d. (1901).

128. Quantin J., *L'exposition du siècle*, Paris 1901.

129. Geoffroy G., *Les industries artistiques françaises et étrangères à l'Exposition universelle de 1900*, Paris s.d. (1902).

130. *L'architecture à l'Exposition universelle de 1900*, Paris 1902.

131. *Rapport du Jury International - Groupe XII - Décoration et Mobilier des édifices publics et des habitations - Première partie - CLasses 66 à 71*, Paris 1902.

132. Picard A., *Exposition Universelle Internationale de 1900*, 7 vol., Paris 1902-03.

133. *Exposition universelle internationale de 1900. Direction Générale de l'exploitation. Section française. Comités d'installation*, Paris 1909.

134. Mandell R.D., *Paris 1900 - The great world's fair*, Toronto 1967.

135. Jullian P., *The Triumph of Art Nouveau Paris Exhibition 1900*, London 1974.

136. Lambert Th., *Meubles de style moderne. Exposition universelle 1900*, Paris s.d.

137. *L'architecture et la sculpture, Exposition de 1900*, Paris s.d.

138. Marx R., *La décoration et les industries à l'exposition universelle de 1900*, Paris s.d.

Articles:

139. "L'Exposition de 1900", in *La Construction Moderne*, VIII (1892-93), pp. 264, 313-315, 384, 601-603.

140. "L'Exposition universelle de 1900: Principes généraux de la composition du plan", in *La Construction Moderne*, X (1894- 1895), pp. 419-420, 430-432.

141. Calonne-Count A. de, "The French Universal Exposition of 1900", in *Architectural Record*, V (Jan.-March, 1896), pp. 217-226.

142. Planat P., "Les nouveaux palais des Champs-Elysées", in *La Construction Moderne*, 2nd serie, II (1896-1897), pp. 265-267, 295.

143. "Les nouveaux palais des Champs-Elysées", in *Le Moniteur des architectes*, 2nd serie, XII (1898), pp. 73-78.

144. Lucas C.L.A., "Notes sur les palais de l'Exposition de Paris en 1900", in *Journal of the Royal Institute of British Architects*, 3d serie, VII (1899-1900), pp. 149-169.

145. Rivoalen E., "L'Architecture à l'Exposition de 1900", in *La Construction Moderne*, 2nd serie, V (1899-1900), pp. 273- 374, 388-389, 402, 428-429, 448-449, 461-462, 472-473, 497-499.

146. Balmont J., "Le Pavillon de l'Union Centrale des Arts Décoratifs à l'Exposition Universelle", in *Revue des Arts Décoratifs*, XX (1900), pp. 169-172.

146.1. Barthélémy, "L'Architecture nouvelle à l'Exposition", in *Art et Décoration*, vol. VIII (7, 1900), pp. 12-20.

147. Boileau L.-C., "Causerie", in *L'Architecture*, XIII (1900), pp. 429-435., pl. 70-71.

148. Champier V., "L'Exposition Universelle de 1900 - Coup d'œil d'ensemble - Une orgie de staff salade de Paris le Château d'eau", in *Revue des Arts Décoratifs*, XX (1900), pp. 129-135.

149. Gallé E., "Le Pavillon de l'Union Centrale des Arts Décoratifs à l'Exposition Universelle", in *Revue des Arts Décoratifs*, XX (1900), pp. 217-224.

150. Genuys Ch., "L'Exposition Universelle de 1900 - Le Palais des Champs-Elysées", in *Revue des Arts Décoratifs*, XX (1900), pp. 161-168.

151. Genuys Ch., "Exposition Universelle de 1900 - Les Essais d'Art Moderne dans la décoration intérieure", in *Revue des Arts Décoratifs*, XX (1900), pp. 285-290.

152. Geoffroy G., "Promenade à l'Exposition", in *Gazette des Beaux-Arts*, 3d serie, XXIV (1900), pp. 5-24.

153. Guadet J., "L'Exposition Universelle. I. Avant l'ouverture 1855-1900", in *Revue de l'Art ancien et moderne*, 1900, 3, pp. 241-254.

154. Harvard H., "Le papier peint à l'Exposition de 1900", in *Revue des Arts Décoratifs*, XX (1900), pp. 301-314.

155. Jacques G.M., "Exposition Universelle. L'Art Nouveau Bing", in *L'Art Décoratif*, II (21, 1900), pp. 88-97.

156. Jacques G.M., "Le meuble français à l'Exposition", in *L'Art Décoratif*, II (22, 1900), pp. 142-149.

157. Jacques G.M., "Le meuble à l'Exposition", in *L'Art Décoratif*, III (25, 1900), pp. 16-20.

158. Jourdain F., "L'architecture à l'Exposition Universelle - Promenade à bâtons rompus", in *Revue des Arts Décoratifs*, pp. 245-251, 326-332, 342-350.

159. Magne L., "Les arts à l'Exposition Universelle de 1900: l'architecture", in *Gazette des Beaux-Arts*, XXIII (1900), pp. 267-277, 383-396; XXIV (1900), pp. 39-51.

160. Marx R., "Les arts à l'Exposition universelle de 1900", in *Gazette des Beaux-Arts*, XXIV (1900), pp. 397-421, 563- 576; XXV (1901), pp. 53-83, 136-168.

161. Mourey G., "L'Art Nouveau de M. Bing à l'Exposition Universelle", in *Revue des Arts Décoratifs*, XX (1900), pp. 550-569, 595.

162. Osborn M., "S. Bing's 'Art Nouveau' auf der Welt- Ausstellung", in *Deutsche Kunst und Dekoration*, VI (Aug. 1900), pp. 550-569, 595.

163. Saunier Ch., "Les petites constructions de l'Exposition", in *L'Art Décoratif*, III (26, 1900), pp. 55-70.

164. Soulier G., "L'ameublement à l'Exposition", in *Art et Décoration*, VIII (July 1900), pp. 33-45, 137-150.

165. "Pavillon de Restaurants", in *La Construction Moderne*, 2nd serie, VI (1900-01), pp. 6-7.

166. Gerdeil O., "Le meuble", in *L'Art Décoratif*, III (28, 1901), pp. 170-175.

167. *Gerdeil O., "Le meuble moderne", in L'Art Décoratif, III (36, 1901), pp. 214-216.*

168. Jourdain F., "L'art du décor à l'Exposition universelle de 1900", in *L'Architecture*, XIV (1901), pp. 1-3, 10-12, 17-19, 27-30, 34-36.

169. Magne L., "Le mobilier moderne à l'Exposition universelle de 1900", in *Revue des Arts Décoratifs*, XXI (1901), pp. 6- 16, 41-50.

169.1. S.(oulier) G., "Les Installations Générales de l'Exposition", in *Art et Décoration*, vol. IX, (5, 1901), pp. 156-165.

ARCHITECTURE AND FURNITURE AT THE SALONS

1898

170. Fourcaud L., "Les Arts décoratifs aux Salons de 1898", in *Revue des Arts Décoratifs*, XVIII (1898), pp. 129-143, 161-171, 197-203, 232-249.

171. Rivoalen E., "L'architecture au Salon des Machines - L'Architecture Décorative", in *La Construction Moderne*, 2nd serie, III (1897-98), pp. 397-398.

172. Soulier G., "Les Arts de l'ameublement aux Salons", in *Art et Décoration*, VI (1898), pp. 10-21.

1899

173. Jacques G.M., "L'art appliqué et l'archi-tecture aux Salons", in *L'Art Décoratif*, I (9, 1899), pp. 99-103.

173.1. R. G. de, "Les Salons de 1899. L'Art Décoratif", in *Le Moniteur des Arts*, XLIV (2398, 1899), pp. 1451-1453.

173.2. Dulong R., "Les Arts d'Ameublement aux Salons", in *Art et Décoration*, vol. VI (8, 1899), pp. 41-47.

1900

174. Forthuny P., "Les Arts Décoratifs au Salons de 1900", in *Revue des Arts Décoratifs*, XX (1900), pp. 145-148.

1901

175. Boileau L.-C., "Art décoratif et Objets d'art aux Salons de 1901", in *L'Architecture*, XIV (1901), pp. 157-164, 174- 179, 183-186, 190-194.

175.1. S.(oulier) G., "L'Ameublement aux Salons", in *Art et Décoration*, vol. IX (6, 1901), pp. 193-199; vol. X (8, 1901), pp. 33-40.

176. Gerdeil O., "L'Intérieur", in *L'Art Décoratif*, III (33, 1901), pp. 125-128.

177. Jacques G. M., "Les Arts Décoratifs", in *L'Art Décoratif*, III (33, 1901), pp. 91-93.

178. Jourdain F., "Les meubles et les tentures murales aux Salons de 1901", in *Revue des Arts Décoratifs*, XXI (1901), pp. 201-212.

179. Pascal J. L., "Les Salons de 1901. L'Architecture", in *Revue de l'Art ancien et moderne*, IX (50, 1901), pp. 341-353.

1902

180. Havard H., "Les Salons de 1902 - Les arts décoratifs", in *Revue de l'Art ancien et moderne*, XI (63, 1902), pp. 411-423.

181. Jacques G. M., "Le Salon des Industries et du Mobilier", in *L'Art Décoratif*, IV (49, 1902), pp. 298-304.

181.1. Jourdain F., "L'Architecture aux Salons de 1902", in *Art et Décoration*, I semester, 1902, pp. 188-196.

182. Pascal J. L., "Les Salons de 1902. L'Architecture", in *Revue de l'Art ancien et moderne*, XI (62, 1902), pp. 344-358.

183. Soulier G., "Le mobilier aux Salons", in *L'Art Décoratif*, IV (46, 1902), pp. 166-172.

Soc. Nationale des Beaux-Arts:

184. Sedeyn E., "Les Arts Décoratifs aux Salons de 1902. I. Société Nationale des Beaux-Arts", in *L'Art Décoratif*, IV (45, 1902), pp. 105-117.

1903

184.1. "L'Art Décoratif à la Société Nationale", in *Art et Décoration*, vol. XIII (I semester, 1903), pp. 173-194.

185. Hamel M.,- Alexandre A., *Salon de 1903*, Paris 1903.

186. Pascal J. L., "Les Salons de 1903. L'Architecture", in *Revue de l'Art ancien et moderne*, XIII (74, 1903), pp. 341-350.

187. Jourdain F., "Le mobilier au Salon National des Beaux- Arts", in *L'Art Décoratif*, V (56, 1903), pp. 209-218.

188. Jourdain F., "Le mobilier au Salon des Artistes Français", in *L'Art Décoratif*, V (57, 1903), pp. 60-66.

Salon d'Automne:

189. Felice R., "L'Art appliqué au Salon d'automne", in *L'Art Décoratif*, V (2nd semester, 1903), pp. 233-240.

Exposition de l'Habitation:

190. Havard H., "L'Exposition de l'Habitation", in *Revue de l'Art ancien et moderne*, XIV (79, 1903), pp. 265-284.

19O.1. Riat G., "Salon d'Automne", in *Art et Décoration*, vol. XIV (II semester, 1903), pp. 383-391.

1904

191 *L'architecture aux Salons. 1904. Société des Artistes Français - Société Nationale des Beaux-Arts*, Paris s.d.

192. Verneuil M.P., "Les Arts appliqués aux Salons", in *Art et Décoration*, VIII (6, 1904), pp. 165-196.

Soc. Nationale des Beaux-Arts:

193. Felice R. de, "L'ameublement au Salon (Société Nationale)", in *L'Art Décoratif*, VI (I semester, 1904), pp. 210-216.

194. Mourey G., "Les Salons de 1904 - Société Nationale des Beaux-Arts", in *Les Arts de la Vie*, vol. I, 5, 1904), pp. 281-305.

Soc. des Artistes Français:

195. Felice R. de, "l'Ameublement au Salon (Société des Artistes Français)", in *L'Art Décoratif*, VI (II semester, 1904), pp. 11-14.

196. Faure E., "Le Salon d'Automne", in *Les Arts de la Vie*, vol.II (11, 1904), pp. 289-299.
197. Pascal J. L., *Le Salon d'Automne en 1904*, Paris 1904.

Soc. des Artistes Décorateurs:

198. Felice R. de, "L'ameublement au Salon des Artistes Décorateurs", in *L'Art Décoratif*, VI (I semester, 1904), pp. 91-98.

199. Genuys Ch., "L'Exposition de la Société des Artistes Décorateurs", in *Art et Décoration*, VIII (3, 1904), pp. 78-92.

1905

200. *"L'architecture aux Salons de 1905 - Société des Artistes Français - Société Nationale des Beaux-Arts*, Paris s.d.

201. Pascal J. L., "Les Salons de 1905. L'Architecture", in *Revue de l'Art ancien et moderne*, XVII (98, 1905), pp. 321-326.

202. Sedeyn E., "Les meubles aux Salons", in *L'Art Décoratif*, VII (I semester, 1905), pp. 255-264.

203. Verneuil M. P., "L'Architecture et l'Art Décoratif aux Salons de 1905", in *Art et Décoration*, IX (7, 1905), pp. 1-13.

Salon d'Automne:

204. Felice R. de, "Les arts appliqués au Salon d'Automne", in *L'Art Décoratif*, VII (II semester, 1905), pp. 209-219.

205. Morice Ch., "Le Salon d'Automne de 1905", in *Mercure de France*, 1905, pp. 376-393.

1906

206. Pascal J. L., "Les Salons de 1906. L'Architecture", in *Revue de l'Art ancien et moderne*, XIX (111, 1906), pp. 433-440.

207. Sedeyn E., "Le Mobilier aux Salons", in *L'Art Décoratif*, VIII (II semester, 1906), pp. 23-32.

208. Vauxcelles L., *Salons de 1906*, Paris 1906.

209. Verneuil M. P., "Les Arts Décoratifs aux Salons de 1906", in *Art et Décoration*, X (6, 1906), pp. 177-208.

210. Plumet Ch., "Le Salon d'architecture à la Société Nationale des Beaux-Arts", in *L'Architecte*, I (15.5.1906), pp. 35-37.

Soc. des Artistes Français:

211. Yvon M.-A., "Société des Artistes Français - Salon d'Architecture 1906", in *L'Architecte*, I (1906), pp. 43-48, 51-54, 57-58.

Salon d'Automne:

212. Felice R. de, "L'art appliqué au Salon d'Automne", in *L'Art Décoratif*, VIII (II semester, 1906), pp. 177-184.

213. Holl J.C., *Le Salon d'Automne*, Paris 1906.

214. Felice R. de, "La Société des Artistes Décorateurs. Deuxième Exposition", in *L'Art Décoratif*, VIII (II semester, 1906), pp. 201-212.

215. Saunier Ch., "L'Exposition des Artistes Décorateurs au Pavillon de Marsan", in *Art et Décoration*, X (12, 1906), pp. 187-212.

1907

216. *Les Salons d'Architecture. Société des Artistes Français. Société Nationale des Beaux-Arts 1907*, Paris s.d. (1907).

217. Felice R. de, "L'art appliqué aux Salons", in *L'Art Décoratif*, IX (I semester, 1907), pp. 161-186.

218. Roy L., "Salon de la Société Nationale de 1907 - Section d'architecture", dans *L'Architecte*, II (May 1907), pp. 38-40.

219. Verneuil M.P., "L'Art décoratif au Salon de la Société Nationale", in *Art et Décoration*, XI (5, 1907), pp. 157-176.

Soc. des Artistes Français:

22O. Dauphin Th., "Salon de la Société des Artistes Français en 1907. Section architecture", in *L'Architecte*, II (May and June 1907), pp. 40-43, 45-50.

221. Verneuil M.P., "L'Art Décoratif au Salon des Artistes Français", in *Art et Décoration*, XI (6, 1907), pp. 209-224.

Salon d'Automne:

222. Mauclair C., "Le Salon d'Automne", in *L'Art Décoratif*, IX (vol. XVII, 1907), pp. 161-170.

223. Sedeyn E., "L'Art appliqué au Salon d'Automne", in *Art et Décoration*, XI (11, 1907), pp. 149-161.

Soc. des Artistes Décorateurs:

224. Cornu P., "L'Exposition des Artistes décorateurs au Pavillon de Marsan", in *Art et Décoration*, XI (12, 1907), pp. 197-208.

1908

225. *"Les Salons d'Architecture. Société des Artistes Français. Société Nationale des Beaux-Arts, 1908*, Paris s.d. (1908).

226. Belville E., "Les Arts appliqués et les Salons", in *L'Art Décoratif*, X (II semester, 1908), pp. 11-20.

227. Verneuil M.P., "L'Art décoratif aux Salons", in *Art et Décoration*, XII (6, 1908), pp. 183-205.

Soc. Nationale des Beaux-Arts:

228. Gelbert A., "L'architecture au Salon de la Société Nationale des Beaux-Arts", in *La Construction Moderne*, 3d serie, III (1907-08), pp. 351-352, 363.

229. Prudent H., "Les Salons d'architecture en 1908 - Société Nationale des Beaux-Arts", in *L'Architecte*, III (May 1908), pp. 33-35.

230. Yvon M.A., "Société Nationale des Beaux-Arts de 1908 (architecture)", in *L'Architecture*, XXI (1908), pp. 259- 261, 270-271.

Soc. des Artistes Français:

231. Prudent H., "Les Salons d'architecture en 1908 - Société des Artistes Français", in *L'Architecte*, III (1908), pp. 44-48, 49-51.

Salon d'Automne:

232. Mauclair C., "Le Salon d'Automne", in *L'Art Décoratif*, X (II semester, 1908), pp. 193-211.

233. Vaudoyer J.-L., "Le Salon d'automne", in *Art et Décoration*, XII (11, 1908), pp. 147-148.

Soc. des Artistes Décorateurs:

234. Belville E., "La Société des Artistes Décorateurs au Pavillon de Marsan", in *L'Art Décoratif*, X (I semester, 1908), pp. 1-16.

Exposition Franco-Britannique:

235. Monod F., "L'Art décoratif français à

l'Exposition Franco- Britannique", in *Art et Décoration*, XII (9, supplement, 1908), pp. 1-2.

1909

236. *"Les Salons d'architecture. Société des Artistes Français. Société Nationale des Beaux-Arts*, Paris s.d. (1909).

Soc. Nationale des Beaux-Arts:

237. P.(rudent) H., "Société Nationale des Beaux-Arts", in *L'Architecte*, IV (June 1909), pp. 43-44.

Soc. des Artistes Français:

238. André P. "Société des Artistes Français - Salon de 1909 (architecture)", in *L'Architecture*, XXII (26, 1909), pp. 205-208.

239. Chifflot L., "Les Salons d'architecture en 1909 - Société des Artistes Français", in *L'Architecte*, IV (June and July 1909), pp. 41-43, 49-53.

240. Rambosson Y., "Le Salon d'Automne", in *L'Art Décoratif*, XI (II semester, 1909), pp. 97-114.

1910

241. *Les Salons d'Architecture. Société des Artistes Français. Société Nationale des Beaux-Arts, 1910*, Paris s.d. (1910).

242. Bidou H., "Les Salons de 1910", in *Gazette des Beaux- Arts*, LII (May 1910), pp. 470-498.

243. Ossent E., "A propos des Salons d'architecture, in *L'Art Décoratif*, XII (II semester, 1910), pp. 251-258.

244. Verneuil M.P., "L'architecture aux Salons", in *Art et Décoration*, XIV (8, 1910), pp. 53-56.

Soc. Nationale des Beaux-Arts:

245. P.(rudent) H., "L'architecture au Salon de la Société Nationale des Beaux-Arts", in *L'Architecte*, V (June 1910), pp. 44-45.

246. Vauxcelles L., "Société Nationale des Beaux-Arts. Salon de 1910", in *L'Art Décoratif*, XII (I semester, 1910), pp. 10-31.

Soc. des Artistes Français:

247. Louvet A., "L'architecture au Salon des Artistes Français", in *L'Architecte*, V (June and July 1910), pp. 41-45, 49-53.

Salon d'Automne:

248. Vauxcelles L., "Le Salon d'automne de 1910", in *L'Art Décoratif*, XII (II semester, 1910), pp. 113-176.

249. Verneuil M.P., "Le Salon d'automne", in *Art et Décoration*, XIV (11, 1910), pp. 129-160.

Soc. des Artistes Décorateurs:

250. Saunier Ch., "Le 5e Salon de la Société des Artistes Décorateurs", in *Art et Décoration*, XIV (4, 1910), pp. 109-140.

251. Testard M., "Le Ve Salon de la Société des

Artistes Décorateurs", in *L'Art Décoratif*, XII (vol. XXIII, 1910), pp. 81-96.

1911

252. *Les Salons d'Architecture. Société des Artistes Français. Société Nationale des Beaux-Arts, 1911*, Paris s.d. (1911).

253. Ossent E., "A propos des Salons d'architecture 1911", in *L'Art Décoratif*, XIII (II semester, 1911), pp. 147-158.

254. Guadet P., "Le Salon d'architecture en 1911", in *L'Architecte*, VI (June, July and August 1911), pp. 41-42, 54- 56, 60-63.

255. Vauxcelles L. "Au Salon d'automne", in *L'Art Décoratif*, XIII (II semester, 1911), pp. 241-295.

Soc. des Artistes Décorateurs:

256. Clouzot H., "Le Mobilier moderne au 6e Salon des Artistes Décorateurs", in *Bulletin de l'Art ancien et moderne*, vol. XXIX (1911), pp. 261-274.

257. Maignan M., "A propos du Salon des Artistes Décorateurs", in *L'Art Décoratif*, XIII (vol. XXV, 1911), pp. 189-204.

258. Vauxcelles L., "Le 6e Salon des Artistes Décorateurs", in *Art et Industrie*, April 1911.

1912

259. *Les Salons d'Architecture. Société des Artistes Français. Société Nationale des Beaux-Arts*, Paris s.d. (1912).

260. Godefroy J., "Le Salon d'architecture en 1912", in *L'Architecte*, VII (May June and July 1912), pp. 33-44, 41- 47, 49.

261. Forthuny P., "Le Salon des artistes Décorateurs", in *L'Art Décoratif*, XIV (I semester, 1912), pp. 261-278.

1913

262. *Les Salons d'Architecture. Société des Artistes Français. Société Nationale des Beaux-Arts, 1912*, Paris s.d. (1913).

Soc. Nationale des Beaux-Arts:

263. Forthuny P., "Le Salon de la Société Nationale des Beaux- Arts", in *Les Cahiers de l'Art moderne*, 1913, 1, pp. 8-25.

Salon des Artistes Décorateurs:

264. Jeanneau G., "Le 8e Salon des Artistes Décorateurs", in *Art et Industrie*, November 1913.

265. Maignan M., "A propos du 8e Salon de la Société des Artistes Décorateurs", in *L'Art Décoratif*, XV (5, 1913), pp. 221-236.

266. Verneuil M.P., "Le Salon de la Société des Artistes Décorateurs", in *Art et Décoration*, XVII (March 1913), pp. 88-100.

1914

267. *Les Salons d'Architecture. Société des

Artistes Français. Société Nationale des Beaux-Arts, 1914*, Paris s.d. (1914).

Salon d'Automne:

268. Ohmann H., "A propos du Salon d'Automne", in *L'Art Décoratif*, XVI (January 1914), pp. 3-64.

Société des Artistes Décorateurs:

269. Roches F., "La question de l'art décoratif et notre temps. A propos du Salon des Artistes Décorateurs de 1914", in *L'Art Décoratif*, XVI (June 1914), pp. 161-176.

270. Verneuil M.P., "Le Salon des Artistes Décorateurs", in *Art et Décoration*, XVII (vol. I, 1914), pp. 97-108.

ARCHITECTS:

André Arfvidson:

271. Gauthier Ch.-A., "Causerie - Immeuble pour ateliers d'artistes", in *L'Architecture*, XXV (3, 1912), pp. 20-22, pl. 4-5.

272. "Planches VII et VIII - Maison d'artistes, 31, rue Campagne-Première, à Paris - A. Arfvidson, architecte (S.A.D.G.)", in *L'Architecte*, VII (February, 1913), pp. 12- 13; pl. VII-VIII.

Paul Auscher:

273. "Maison Potin, rue de Rennes, à Paris", in *La Construction Moderne*, 2nd serie, IX (1904-05), pp. 149, 162- 164; pl. 26-29.

Edouard Autant:

274. "Maison, rue d'Abbeville, à Paris", in *La Construction Moderne*, 2nd serie, VII (1901-02), p. 55; pl. 9-10.

Barbaud & Bauhain:

275. "Hôtel du Syndicat de l'Epicerie Française", in *La Construction Moderne*, 2nd serie, VII (1901-02), pp. 497-498, 513; pl. 86-89.

276. "Chapelle funéraire à Clamart", in *La Construction Moderne*, 2nd serie, VII (1901-02), pp. 438-439; pl. 81-82.

277. Uhry E., "La Décoration d'une Brasserie à Paris", in *L'Art Décoratif*, VII (II semester, 1905), pp. 137-142.

Léon Benouville:

278. Jacques G.M., "Quelques meubles", in *L'Art Décoratif*, III (27, 1900), pp. 116-117.

279. Jacques G.M., "Petits appartements", in *L'Art Décoratif*, III (35, 1901), pp. 195-201.

280. "Léon Benouville", in *L'Architecture*, XVI (43, 1903), pp. 405-406.

281. Lucas Ch., "Nécrologie", *La Construction Moderne*, 2nd serie, IX (1903-04), p. 48.

282. Dupuy Ch., "L'Exposition des œuvres de Léon Benouville au Musée Galliera", in *L'Architecture*, XVII (2, 1904), pp. 13-14.

283. Knight Ch., "Notice sur la vie et l'œuvre de Léon Benouville", in *L'Architecture*, XVII (11, 1904), pp. 97-101; pl. 18-21.

René Binet:

284. Binet R., *Esquisses décoratives*, préface de G. Geoffroy, Paris s.d. (1900);

284.1. Geoffroy G., "Esquisses Décoratives de René Binet", in *Art et Décoration*, vol. XIII (1903), pp. 33-37.

285. "Maisons de retraite des artistes dramatiques à Pont-aux- Dames", in *La Construction Moderne*, 2nd serie, X (1904- 05), pp. 258-259, 268-272; pl. 43-46.

286. "Transformation du Printemps", in *La Construction Moderne*, 2nd serie, XII (1906-07), pp. 6-8, 29-30.

287. Uhry E., "Croquis de René Binet", in *L'Art Décoratif*, IX (II semester, 1907), pp. 130-136.

288. D.(riart) A., "Les Bureaux des Téléphones à Paris", in *La Construction Moderne*, XXIII (1907-08), pp. 388-390; pl. 82- 83.

289. Driart A., "Le Bureau de poste de la Maison Dorée", in *La Construction Moderne*, XXIV (1908-09), pp. 473-476, 485-488; pl. 99-103.

290. D.(riart) A., "Les Nouveaux Magasins du Printemps", in *La Construction Moderne*, XXV (1909-10), pp. 353-355, 365-366; pl. 74-78.

291. Le Guen J., "Le nouveau Printemps", in *L'Architecte*, VI (1911), pp. 12-16; pl. X-XIII.

292. "M. René Binet 1866-1911", in *L'Architecture*, XXIV (3, 1911), pp. 249-250.

Maurice Du Bois d'Auberville:

293. Plantagenet R., "Une maison de rapport à Paris", in *L'Art Décoratif*, XI (I semester, 1909), pp. 1-10.

294. Dubuis J., "Un nouvel immeuble parisien", in *L'Art Décoratif*, XIII (II semester, 1911), pp. 21-26.

Louis Bonnier:

295. Gardelle C., "Moderne Kunst in der Französischen Architektur: II Der Architekt Louis Bonnier", in *Dekorative Kunst*, vol. I (1898), pp. 215-221.

296. Plumet Ch., "L'architecture et le paysage", in *L'Art et les Artistes*, III (28, 1907), pp. 208-212.

297. Saunier Ch., "Deux cottages de Louis Bonnier", in *Art et Décoration*, (I semester, 1907), pp. 187-192.

298. Bonnier L., "A propos d'un groupe scolaire", in *L'Architecte*, VII (1912), pp. 81-86, 89-96; pl. LXIV-LXXII.

299. Bonnier L., *A propos d'un groupe scolaire*, Paris 1913.

Georges Chedanne:

300. Balmont J., "Champs-Elysées Palace", in *Revue des Arts Décoratifs*, XIX (2, 1899), pp. 33-38.

301. "Palace Hotel des Champs-Elysées", in *La Construction Moderne*, 2nd serie, V (1899-1900), pp. 293-294, 303-304.

302. Champier V., "L'art moderne dans les habitations parisiennes. L'Hôtel de M. Dehaynin", in *Revue des Arts Décoratifs*, 1901, pp. 377-386.

303. Marx R., "A propos d'une construction récente de M. Chedanne", in *Art et Décoration*, XVI (II semester, 1904), pp. 155-164.

304. "Hôtel Mercédes, à Paris", in *La Construction Moderne*, 2nd serie, X (1904-05), pp. 87-88, 100-103, 113-115; pl. 16-19.

André Jules Collin:

305. "Habitation particulière", in *La Construction Moderne*, XXIII (1907-08), p. 174; pl. 38.

Louis and Alfred Feine:

306. Destève T., "La Maison de René Lalique", in *Art et Décoration*, VI (vol. XII, 1902), pp. 161-166.

307. "Maison. Cours La Reine, à Paris", in *La Construction Moderne*, XXVII (1911-12), pp. 65-69; pl. 14.

308. Darvillé W., "Immeubles pour familles nombreuses, Maison boulevard Bessières, à Paris", in *La Construction Moderne*, XXVII (1911-12), p. 65-69, pl.14.

Hector Guimard:

Books and articles by Hector Guimard:

309. *L'Art dans l'Habitation Moderne. Le Castel Béranger (1894- 1898)...*, Introduction by G. d'Hostingue, Paris 1898.

310. "La Renaissance de l'art dans l'architecture moderne", in *Le Moniteur des Arts*, 2nd serie, XIII (1899), pp. 1465-1471.

311. "An architect's opinion of 'L'Art Nouveau'", in *Architectural Record*, XII (1902), pp. 126-133.

312. "Correspondance", in *L'Architecture*, XV (1902), p. 82.

313. "Architecte d'art", in *L'Art Décoratif*, VI (I semester, 1904), no page number.

314. "Correspondance", in *La Construction Moderne*, 3d serie, II (1906-07), p. 184.

315. "Les immeubles de la rue Agar et l'Art Moderne", in *La Construction Moderne*, 3d serie, VIII (1912-13), pp. 235-237.

316. *La question des loyers pendant la guerre -*

Projet présenté aux commissions officielles le 5 mars 1915 par Hector Guimard, Paris 1915.

317. *Fontes artistiques pour Constructions, Fumisterie, Articles du Jardin et Sépultures, Style Guimard*. Société des Fonderies de Bayard et St.-Dizier, Commercial catalogue, s.d.

Publications on Hector Guimard:
Catalogues and biographies:

318. Lanier Graham F., *Hector Guimard*, New York 1970.

319. Blondel A. - Plantin Y., *Hector Guimard. Fontes artistiques*, Paris 1971.

320. Brunhammer Y., *Hector Guimard 1867-1942*, in *Pionniers du XXe siècle. Guimard - Horta - Van de Velde*, Paris 1971.

321. Culpepper R. *Bibliographie d'Hector Guimard*, Paris 1971 (2nd edition, Paris 1975).

322. Brunhammer Y. - Bussmann K. - Kock R., *Hector Guimard. Architektur in Paris um 1900*, exhibition cat., München 1975.

323. Naylor G. - Brunhammer Y., *Hector Guimard*, London 1978; French transl., Paris 1978.

324. Rheims M., *Hector Guimard architecte d'art*, Paris 1985.

Articles:

324.1. Boileau L.-C., "Causerie", in *Architecture*, 15.4.1899, pp. 126-133.

324.2. "Exposition de M. H. Guimard", in *L'Art Décoratif*, I (7, 1899), pp. 41-42.

325. Poinsot M.-C., "Beaux-Arts. Un bel exemple pour les jeunes. Hector Guimard", in *Les Pages Modernes*, May 1913, pp. 185- 187.

326. Jarlot G., "Guimard et l'Art Nouveau", in *Art de France*, IV (1964), pp. 378-383.

327. Colombo E. - Kœnig G.K., "Hector Guimard 1867-1942", in *Casabella*, 329, 1968, pp. 36-56.

328. Grady J., ""Hector Guimard an overlooked master of Art Nouveau", in *Apollo*, April 1969, pp. 284-295.

329. Cantacuzino S., "Guimard", in *The Architectural Review*, June 1970, pp. 393-395.

330. Culpepper R., "Hector Guimard (1867-1942)", in *Association pour la sauvegarde et la mise en valeur du Paris historique. Bulletin d'information*, 14, 1970, p.16.

331. Dali S., "The cylindrical monarchy of Guimard", in *Arts Magazine*, March 1970, pp. 42-43.

332. Peignot J., "Guimard 'Son graphisme est du grand art'", in *Connaissance des Arts*, 217, 1970, pp. 72-79.

333. Poupée H., "Actualité de Guimard", in *La Construction Moderne*, 4, 1970, pp. 41-57.

334. Blondel A. - Plantin Y., "Le monde plastique de Guimard", in *Plaisir de France*, XXXVIII (387, 1971), pp. 18-23.

335. Cornu M., "Guimard à Auteuil: le printemps de l'Art Nouveau", in *Les Lettres Françaises*, 10.3.1971, pp. 20-21.

336. Culpepper R., "Les premières œuvres d'Hector Guimard", in *L'Architecture d'aujourd'hui*, 154, 1971, pp. VIII- IX.

337. Guerrand R.-H., "Hector Guimard (1867-1942)", in *Bulletin de la Société des Amis de la Bibliothèque Forney*, Jan.-March 1971, pp. 5-8.

338. Haber F., "H. Guimard surviving works", in *Architectural Design*, XLI (1971), pp. 36-40

339. Mannoni E., "Hector Guimard", in *Gazette des Beaux- Arts*, CXIII (1226, 1971), pp. 159-176.

340. Rey J.D., "Hector Guimard", in *Le Jardin des Arts*, March 1971, pp. 22-25.

341. Talanti A.M., "Schede di architettura, pioneri del XX secolo. Hector Guimard", in*Edilizia Moderna*, XVII (12, 1971), pp. 8-11.

342. Kearney B., "The principle of active resistance. An investigation into the influence of Viollet-le-Duc on the work of Guimard", in *De Arte* (Afrique du Sud), XII (1972), pp. 42- 50.

343. Gantz Th.A. - Zangheri L., "La stagione felice di Hector Guimard", in *Necropoli*, 17-19, 1973.

344. Micchiardi G., "Hector Guimard et l'Art Nouveau", in *30 jours à l'Alliance française*, 14, 1973, pp. 10-15.

345. Blondel A. - Plantin Y., "Ornemental Cast Iron in Guimard's Architecturè", in *Art Nouveau Belgium-France*, exhibition cat., Houston Rice Museum et Chicago Art Institute, 1976, pp. 405-406.

346. Borsi F., "Lo'Stile Guimard'", in *Palladio*, XXVII (1, 1978), pp. 68-82.

347. Brunhammer Y., "Hector Guimard or the Obsession with Line", in *Arts in, Virginia*, XX (1, 1979), pp. 38-47.

348. Frontisi C., "Hector Guimard retrouvé", in *Revue de l'Art*, 51, 1981, pp. 86-91.

349. Thiébaut P., "Acquisitions. Musée d'Orsay. Un ensemble de fontes artistiques de Guimard", in *La Revue du Louvre et des Musées de France*, XXXIII (3, 1983), pp. 212-221.

Le Castel Béranger, Paris:

350. Boileau L.-C., "Les maisons de M. Guimard, rue La Fontaine", in *L'Architecture*, IX (10.12.1896), pp. 385-388.
351. Planat P., "Actualités", in *La Construction Moderne*, 2nd serie, IV (1898-99), pp. 133-135.

352. Boileau L.-C., "Causerie - Le temps passe vite - Le Castel Béranger", in *L'Architecture*, XII (1899), pp. 120-122.

353. Champier V., "Le Castel Béranger et M. Hector Guimard", in *Revue des Arts Décoratifs*, XIX (Jan. 1899), pp. 1-10.

354. Mery M;, "Le Castel Béranger", in *Le Moniteur des Arts*, XLIV (2376, 1899).

355. Molinier E., "Le Castel Béranger", in *Art et Décoration*, VII (Jan. 1899), pp. 76-81.

356. Planat P., "Actualités", in *La Construction Moderne*, 2nd serie, IV (1898-99), pp. 337-339.

357. R. - M.L., "Salon du Figaro - Le Castel Béranger", in *Le Figaro*, 12.4.1899, p. 2.

358. Soulier G., *Etudes sur le Castel Béranger d'Hector Guimard architecte professeur à l'Ecole Nationale des Arts Décoratifs*, Paris 1899.

359. "Exposition du Castel Béranger", in *La Construction Moderne*, 2nd serie, IV (1898-99), p. 336.

360. "Exposition du castel Béranger", in *la Construction Moderne*, 2nd serie, IV (1898-99), p. 384.

361. "Le Castel Béranger", in *La Construction Moderne*, 2nd serie, (1898-99), p. 324.

362. Frantz H., "The Art Movement, Castel Béranger, the new art in architectural decoration", in *The Magazine of Art*, vol. XXV (1901), pp. 85-87.

363. Blondel A. - Plantin Y., "L'Expressionnisme naturaliste de Guimard au Castel Béranger", in *L'Oeil*, 194, 1971, pp. 2-7, 60.

Humbert de Romans Concert Hall:

364. D.A. "La salle Humbert de Romans", in *Le Monde Musical*, 15.2.1901.

365. Mangeot A., La Salle de concerts Humbert de Romans", in *Le Monde musical*, 15.12.1901.

366. "La Salle Humbert de Romans", in *La Construction Moderne*, 2nd serie, VII (1901-02), p. 81.

367. Mazade F., "An'Art Nouveau'edifice in Paris. The Humbert de Romans building. Hector Guimard architect", in *The Architectural Record*, 2, 1902, pp. 50-66.

368. Blondel A. - Plantin Y., "Hector Guimard: la salle Humbert de Romans", in *L'architecture d'aujourd'hui*, XLIII (155, 1971), pp. XVII-XVII.

369. Miotto - Muret L.- Pallucchini - Pelzel V., "Une maison de Guimard", in *Revue de l'Art*, 3, 1969, pp. 75-79.

Castel Henriette, Sèvres:

370. Miotto - Muret L., "On détruit un Guimard de plus : le Castel Henriette à Sèvres", in *Le Monde*, 3.4.1969, p. 17.

Structures for the Metro:
Books:

371. Hervieu J., *Le Chemin de fer Métropolitain Municipal de Paris*, vol.I, Paris 1903; vol. II, Paris 1908.

372. Troske L., *Die pariser Stadtbahn, ihre Geschichte, Linienführung. Bau-, Betriebs - und Verkehrsverhältnmisse*, Berlin 1905.

373. Guerrand R.H., *Mémoires du Métro*, Paris 1961.

374. Guerrand R.H., *Le Métro*, Paris 1962.

375. Robert J., *Notre Métro*, Neuilly-sur-Seine 1967.

376. Dansel M., *Paris-Métro*, Nevers 1975.

Articles:

377. Bans G., "Les gares du Métropolitain de Paris", in *L'Art Décoratif*, III (25, October 1900), pp. 38-40.

378. Boileau L.-C., "Critique de l'un des édicules composés pour les stations souterraines par notre confrère M. Guimard", in *L'Architecture*, XIII (17.11.1900), p. 415.

379. Cerbelaud G., "L'ouverture du Métropolitain", in *L'Illustration*, 14.7.1900, pp. 22-23.

380. D.E., "Des Gares", in *Le Bulletin de l'Art ancien et moderne*, supplément 28.7.1900, p. 201.

381. Dumaus A., "Chemins de Fer - Le Métropolitain de Paris - Description générale du réseau projeté - Description détaillée de la partie exécutée", in *Le Génie Civil*, 21.7.1900, p. 205.

382. "La gare de l'Opéra", in *La Construction Moderne*, 2nde serie, IX (1904-05), p. 21.

383. Planat P., "L'Art Nouveau appliqué aux chemins de fer", in *La Construction Moderne*, 2nd serie, IX (1904-05), pp. 1-3.

Le "Chalet Blanc" à Sceaux:

384. "Nostalgie: Le Chalet Blanc d'Hector Guimard à Sceaux", in *Architecture mouvement continuité*, 33, 1974, pp. 75-84.

385. Rey J.D., "Le Chalet Blanc d'Hector Guimard", in *Jardin des Arts*, 196, 1971, pp. 22-26.

Groupe d'immeubles de la Rue Agar, Paris:

386. Couturaud P., "L'inauguration de la rue Agar", in *La Construction Moderne*, 3d serie, VIII (1912-13), pp. 62-63.

387. "Un groupe d'immeubles rue Agar, à Paris", in *La Construction Moderne*, 3d serie, VIII (1912-13), pp. 224-225; pl. 46-48.

Synagogue, Rue Pavée, Paris:

388. "Krinsky C.H., "Hector Guimard's'Art Nouveau'synagogue in rue Pavée", in *J. Jewish Art* (U.S.A.), XLIX (1979), pp. 105-111.

Le mobilier:

389. Blondel A. - Plantin Y., "Guimard architecte de meubles", in *L'Estampille*, 10, 1970, pp. 32-40.

390. Duvillards P., "H. Guimard", in *Revue de l'ameublement*, 7, 1970, pp. 105-109.
391. Mosteau P. "Guimard", in *Revue de l'ameublement*, 2, 1973, pp. 97-102.

Henri Gutton:

392. A.-L.-R., "Bazar de la rue de Rennes", in *La Construction Moderne*, 3d serie, II (1906-07), pp. 281-283; pl. 59-60.

393. "Planche XV - Grand Bazar de la rue de Rennes, à Paris - Henri Gutton, architecte", in *L'Architecte*, II (March 1970), pp. 27-28; pl. 15.

Georges Guyon:

394. "Groupe Municipal à Saint-Maurice (Seine)", in *La Construction Moderne*, 2nd serie, V (1899-1900), pl. 38-39.

395. "Exposition Universelle - Les habitations à bon marché", in *La Construction Moderne*, 2nd serie, VI (1900-1901), pp. 99-100.

396. Lucas Ch., "Habitations à bon marché", in *La Construction Moderne*, 2nd serie, VII (1901-02), pp. 292-293, 306-307.

397. "Oeuvre de la Chaussée du Maine", in *La Construction Moderne*, XXI (1905-06), p. 560; pl. 116-117.

Jacques Hermant:

398. Uhry E., "Une Taverne à Paris", in *L'Art Décoratif*, VIII (I semester, 1906), pp. 33-40.

Ernest Herscher:

99. "Ernest Herscher, architecte décorateur et graveur", in *Revue de l'Art ancien et moderne*, 1912, pp. 48-49.

Frantz Jourdain:

Works by Frantz Jourdain:

Books:

400. *Constructions élevées au Champ de Mars par M. Ch. Garnier... pour servir à l'histoire de l'habitation humaine*, Paris - New York - Bruxelles s.d. (1889).

401. *L'atelier Chantorel*, Paris 1893.

402. *Les Décorés, ceux qui ne le sont pas*, Paris 1895.

403. *Le Gage, comédie en un acte. ..*, Paris 1898.

404. *De choses et d'autres*, Paris 1902.

405. *Propos d'un isolé en faveur de son temps*, Paris s.d. (1914).

406. *Au pays du souvenir*, Paris 1922.

407. *Le Salon d'Automne*, Paris 1928.

408. *Feuilles mortes et fleurs fanées*, Paris 1931.

Articles:

409. "Art et progrès", in *La Construction Moderne*, III (1887), pp. 37-38.

410. "La décoration et le rationalisme architectural à l'Exposition universelle", in *Revue des Arts Décoratifs*, 1889, p. 37.

411. "Ouvriers du bâtiment", in *La Construction Moderne*, II (19.1.1889), pp. 169-171.

412. "Une révolution dans le papier peint", in *La Construction Moderne*, VII (24.10.1891), pp. 29-30.

413. "A propos du Salon de la Rose-Croix", in *La Construction Moderne*, VIII (26.3.1892), pp. 291-292.

414. "L'architecture au Salon du Champ de Mars", in *La Construction Moderne*, VIII (7.5.1892), pp. 361-362.

415. "Les architectes élèves de l'Ecole des Beaux-Arts", in *L'Architecture*, VII (44, 1894), pp. 361-362.

416. "L'Art du décor", in *L'Architecture*, VII (24, 1894), pp. 185-187.

417. "Encore un " "", in *L'Architecture*, VII (7, 1894), p. 53.

418. "Vieille rengaine, ancienne chanson", in *L'Architecture*, VII (43, 1894), p. 353.

419. "Le bal de bienfaisance", in *L'Architecture*, IX (5, 1896), pp. 37-38.

420. "Le Siam ancien par Louis Fournereau", in *L'Architecture*, IX (1, 1896), pp. 5-6.

421. "Communication au Congrès de 1896 au sujet de la 'Société d'assistance confraternelle des architectes français'", in *L'Architecture*, IX (44, 1896), pp. 326-327.

422. "Les objets d'art au Salon de 1896", in *La Grande Dame*, IV (1896), p. 222.

423. "Lettre aux éditeurs", in *Revue Populaire des Beaux-Arts*, 20.10.1898, pp. 350-351.

424. "La Classe 71 à l'Exposition universelle de 1900", in *Revue des Arts Décoratifs*, XVIII (1898), pp. 329-334.

425. "En vue de l'Exposition de 1900 - Le deuxième concours ouvert par l'Union Centrale des Arts Décoratifs", in *Revue des Arts Décoratifs*, XIX (1899), pp. 114-121.

426. "Le Concours de l'Union Centrale des Arts Décoratifs", in *Revue d'Art*, 6, 9.12.1899, pp. 88-91.

427. "Les meubles modernes", in *Revue d'Art*, 1, 4.11.1899.

428. "L'architecture au XIXᵉ siècle", in *Revue Bleue*, 4th serie, XIII (21.4.1900), p. 484.

429. "Hôtel et Café modernes", in *Revue des Arts Décoratifs*, XX (1900), pp. 33-40.

430. "Les conquêtes de la science", in *L'Architecture*, XIII (42, 1900), pp. 378-379.

431. "Roger Marx", in *Revue des Arts Décoratifs*, XXII (1902), pp. 219-221.

432. "La mise en scène", in *Les Arts de la Vie*, 2, 1904, pp. 98-102.

433. "Un divorce nécessaire", in *Les Arts de la Vie*, vol. IV, 21, 1905, pp. 150-154.

434. "Le Salon d'Automne", in *La Grande Revue*, 15.10.1907, pp. 352-356.

435. "Balcons fleuris", in *L'Assistance éducative*, V (7, 1907), p. 105; reprinted in *L'Architecture*, XXI (1908), pp. 263-264.

435.1. "La Maison d'Ecole et le Mobilier scolaire" in AA.VV., *L'Art à l'Ecole*, Paris s.d. (1907), pp. 43-54.

436. "L'architecture au XIXᵉ siècle", in *Revue Bleue*, 4th serie, XIII (21.4.1900), p. 484.

437. "Paris! Beau Paris", in *Touche à tout*, 15.3.1910.

438. "Le snobisme dans l'art", in *La Revue*, 15.10.1911, pp. 457-465.

439. "La maladie du passé", in *La Revue*, XCIX (November 1912), pp. 168-178.

440. "Viollet-le-Duc", in *Art et Bâtiment*, October 1929.

Books and articles on F. Jourdain:

441. Calvo G., "M. Frantz Jourdain et l'Art Nouveau", in *La Petite Illustration*, II (August 1902), p. 7.

442. Gothe M. (Gauthier M.), "Frantz Jourdain", in *Le Siècle*, 12.10.1912.

443. Vauxcelles L., "Frantz Jourdain", in *L'Amour de l'Art*, III (11, 1922), pp. 366-367.

444. Rey R., *Frantz Jourdain*, Paris 1923.

445. Dervaux A., "Frantz Jourdain", in *L'Architecture d'aujourd'hui*, 6, 1931, pp. 11-14.

446. Thubert E. de, "A propos de Frantz Jourdain", in *La Construction Moderne*, XLVII (1931), p. 50.

Villa at Chelles:

447. "Villa à Chelles", in *la Construction Moderne*, 2nd serie, III (1887-88), p. 307.

Outbuildings of a town house, Avenue du Bois de Boulogne, Paris:

448. "Communs d'un hôtel avenue du Bois de Boulogne", in *La Construction Moderne*, III (1887-88), pp. 51-52, 306-307.

Moët et Chandon Pavilion at the International Exhibition of 1900:

449. Boileau L.-C., "Causerie", in *L'Architecture*, XIII (28, 1900), pp. 249-254; pl. 37-38.

La Samaritaine:

450. "Marquise de magasin", in *La Construction Moderne*, IX (29.9.1894), p. 615.

451. Plumet Ch., "L'Architecture et la Décoration Moderne", *Supplément illustré de l'art et les artistes*, II (20, 1906), pp. I-IV.

452. Ford G.B., "The Samaritaine department store in Paris", in *The American Architect*, vol. XCII (1907), p. 123.

453. Uhry E., "Agrandissements des Magasins de La Samaritaine", in *L'Architecte*, II (Feb. 1907), pp. 13-14; pl. X-XII.

454. D.A., "Magasins de La Samaritaine à Paris - Nouvelle façade sur la rue de Rivoli", in *La Construction Moderne*, 3d serie, VII (1911-12), pp. 315-317.

455. "Du sacré au profane", in *L'Illustration*, CXLI (29.3.1913), p. 316.

456. "L'Annexe de la Samaritaine", in *Le Monde Illustré*, 28.10.1916, p. 260.

457. Staphati, "Annexe de la Samaritaine, 27, boulevard des Capucines", in *La Construction Moderne*, 49, 1917, pp. 2-3.

458. Cogniat R., "La Samaritaine par MM. Frantz Jourdain et Henri Sauvage", in *L'Architecture*, XLIII (1930), pp. 1-10.

459. Escande L., "Les grands travaux de la Samaritaine, in *La Technique des Travaux*, December 1933, pp. 1-17.

460. Laudet F., *La Samaritaine*, Paris 1933.

461. Clausen M.L., "La Samaritaine", in *Revue de l'Art*, 32, 1976, pp. 67-76.

Charles Klein:

462. "Maison, rue Claude-Chahu, à Paris", in *La Construction Moderne*, 2nd serie, VIII (1902-03), pp. 365-366; pl. 63-66.

463. Boileau L.-C., "Causerie", in *L'Architecture*, XVI (32, 1903), pp. 313-314; pl. 33.

464. Boileau L.-C., "Causerie", in *L'Architecture*, XVI (34, 1903), pp. 331-334.

465. Saunier Ch., "Une nouvelle construction en grès", in *L'Art Décoratif*, V (55, 1903), pp. 169-175.

A. Labussière:

466. "Groupe de maisons ouvrières. Rue Ernest-Lefèvre", in *La Construction Moderne*, 2nd serie, X (1904-05), pp. 543- 546, 555-557; pl. 91-92.

467. "Immeuble rue de l'Amiral Roussier", in *La Construction Moderne*, XXIII (1907-08), pp. 339-345, 353-356; pl. 71-73.

Jules Lavirotte:

468. Uhry E., "Constructions récentes de M. Lavirotte", in *L'Art Décoratif*, VII (II semester, 1905), pp. 24-32.

Apartment block, Square Rapp, Paris:

469. Boileau L.-C., "Causerie", in *L'Architecture*, XIV (17, 1901), pp. 141-147; pl. 29-30.

470. Sergent R., "Une maison de rapport", in *Art et Décoration*, vol. X (1901), pp. 140-146.

Apartment block, Avenue Rapp, Paris:

471. "Le Concours de façades à Paris en 1901 - Rapport sur les opérations du jury", in *L'Architecture*, XV (15, 1902), pp. 453-455; pl. 45.

472. "Maison Avenue Rapp, à Paris", in *La Construction Moderne*, 2nd serie, VI (1901-02), pp. 342-344; pl. 58-59.

Ceramic Hôtel, Avenue de Wagram, Paris:

473. "Concours de façades", in *La Construction Moderne*, 3^d serie, I (1906-07), pp. 524-525; pl. 110.

Low-cost dwellings, Boulevard Lefebvre:

474. "Maisons à petits loyers, à Paris", in *La Construction Moderne*, 2nd serie X (1905-06), pp. 449-450; pl. 95.

Town house and apartment block, Avenue and Rue de Messine, Paris:

475 "Planche XLV - Hôtel particulier, avenue et rue de Messine, à Paris - J. Lavirotte" A.D.P.G., in *L'Architecte*, III (August 1908), pp. 63-64; pl. XLV.

476. D.A., "Maison de rapport, rue de Messine, à Paris", in *La Construction Moderne*, 3^d serie, III(1908-09), pp. 341- 344.

477. "Hôtel privé, avenue de Messine, à Paris", in *La Construction Moderne*, 3^d série, III (1908-09), pp. 389-393; pl. 81-84.

478. "Hôtel privé à Paris. Détail de la façade", in *La Construction Moderne*, 3de serie, III (1908-09), p. 399.

479. Brincourt M., "Causerie - Hôtel et maison de rapport avenue et rue de Messine", in *L'Architecture*, XXIV (1, 1911), pp. 2-5; pl. 1-2.

Villa in the Parc Beauséjour:

480. "Villa au parc Beauséjour", in *La Construction Moderne*, 2nd serie, VIII (1903-04), p. 522; pl. 91-92.

Etablissement des eaux minérales:

481. "Etablissement des Eaux minérales du Châtelet", in *La Construction Moderne*, 3^d serie, VII (1911-12), pp. 101-104; pl. 21-23.

Pavillon des Balances pour une Société de Courses à Compiègne:

482. "Salon 1913: Artistes Français - Projet de Pavillon des Balances pour la Société des Courses dc Compiègnè", in *La Construction Moderne*, 3^d serie, VIII (1912-13), pp. 581-582; pl. 121-122.

Charles Letrosne:

483. Dupuy Ch., "Hôtel particulier avenue Malakoff, 59", in *L'Architecture*, XXV (51, 1912), pp. 446-447, pl. 94-95;

484. "Planche XXVIII - Hôtel particulier, 59 avenue Malakoff, à Paris - Ch. Letrosne, architecte (S.A.D.G.)", in *L'Architecte*, VIII (May 1913), pp. 37-38; pl. 28.

Louis-Pierre Marquet:

485. "Maison avenue des Gobelins", in *La Construction Moderne*, 2nd serie, IX (1903-04), pp. 123-124; pl. 21-22.

486. Uhry E., "Maison de rapport de L.P. Marquet à Paris", in *L'Art Décoratif*, VI (I semester, 1904), pp. 171-184.

Edouard Niermans:

487. "Concert Parisiana", in *La Construction Moderne*, 2nd serie, IV (1898-99), pp. 87-88; pl. 17.

488. "La Taverne Pousset", in *La Construction Moderne*, 2nd serie, IV (1898-99), p. 282; pl. 21-22.

489. Jourdain F., "La Décoration d'une Brasserie", in *Art et Décoration*, IV (1898), pp. 154-160.

Charles Plumet:

Articles by Charles Plumet:

490. "Le meuble et la maison", in *Mercure de France*, February 1898, pp. 627-631.

491. "Le Mensonge de l'Architecture Contemporaine", in *Les Arts de la Vie*, Vol. I (1, 1904), pp. 36-41.

492. "La reconstruction du Musée du Luxembourg", in *Les Arts de la Vie*, Vol. I (3, 1904), pp. 160-163.

493. "L'Architecture et la Décoration moderne", *Supplément illustré de l'Art et les Artistes*, II (20 and 21, 1906), pp. I-III, I-V.

494. "La Décoration moderne. Robert, ferronnier, Ch. Rivaud, joaillier", in *L'Art et les Artistes*, III (25, 1907), pp. 27-32.

495. "L'Art décoratif au Salon", in *L'Art et les Artistes*, III (26 and 27, 1907), pp. 92-97, 173-174.

496. "L'architecture et le paysage", in *L'Art et les Artistes*,, III (29, 1907), pp. 263-267.

497. "L'Architecture et la Décoration moderne - A propos du Salon de l'Automobile", *Supplément illustré de l'Art et les Artistes*, II (22, 1907), pp. I-IV.

498. "L'Architecture et la Décoration moderne - Les villes nouvelles - Le Caire", *Supplément illustré de l'Art et les Artistes*, II (23, 1907), pp. I-V.

499. "Les arts réunis", in *L'Art et les Artistes*, III (36, 1908), pp. 586-587.

Books and articles on Charles Plumet:

500. Forthuny P., "Un maître d'œuvre: Charles Plumet", in *Revue des Arts Décoratifs*, XIX (6, 1899), pp. 179-191.

501. Gardelle C., "Charles Plumet, architecte", in *L'Art Décoratif*, I (5, 1899), pp. 201-203.

502. Boileau L.-C., "Causerie", in *L'Architecture*, XIV (3, 1901), pp. 19-24.

503. Boileau L.-C., "Causerie", in *L'Architecture*, XVI (35, 1903), pp. 342-343.

504. Soulier G., "Maison de ville et maisons de champs", in *L'Art Décoratif*, V (52, 1903), pp. 60-69.

505. Boileau L.-C., "Causerie", in *L'Architecture*, XX (3, 1907), pp. 18-22; pl. 4-9.

506. Badovici J., *Maisons de rapport de Charles Plumet*, Paris 1923.

Apartment block, Avenue Poincaré, Paris:

507. Boileau L.-C., "Causerie", in *L'Architecture*, IX (52, 1896), pp. 396-399.

Town house, Avenue du Bois de Boulogne and Avenue Malakoff, Paris:

508. *L'Architecture*, XIV (2, 1901), pl. 4.

509. Saunier Ch., "Une nouvelle construction de Ch. Plumet", in *L'Art Décoratif*, III (28, 1901), pp. 154-164.

510. "Planches XXII et XXIII - Maison de rapport, avenue Victor Hugo, à Paris - Charles

Plumet, architecte", in *L'Architecte*, II
(April 1907), pp. 35-36; pl. XXII-XXIII.

510.1. Jourdain F., "Une maison, un mobilier
moderne", in *Art et Décoration*, vol. XIII (I
semester, 1903), pp. 149-161.

Town house, 50, Avenue Victor-Hugo, Paris:

511. "Planche X - Hall intérieur, 49, avenue
Victor Hugo, à Paris - Plumet, architecte", in
L'Architecte, I (15.2.1906), p. 16; pl. X.

Town house, Rue Marbeau, Paris:

512. D.A., "Hôtel privé, rue Marbeau, à
Paris", in *La Construction Moderne*, 3ᵈ serie, II
(1907-08), pp. 508-509; pl. 106-107.

Villa, Boulevard Richard Wallace, Neuilly-sur-
Seine:

513. Mourey G., "Une villa de Charles
Plumet", in *Art et Décoration*, vol. XXX
(September 1911), pp. 277-288.

514. "Planches XLIX à LI - Hôtel particulier,
boulevard Richard Wallace à Neuilly-sur-Seine -
Charles Plumet, architecte", in *L'Architecte*, VI
(September 1911), p. 70; pl. XLIX-LI.

Pavillon de l'Art Décoratif français at Turin
Exhibition:

515. Alfassa P., "Le Pavillon de l'Art Décoratif
français à l'Exposition de Turin", in *Art et
Décoration*, vol. XXX (October 1911),
pp. 317-322.

516. Kœchlin R., "L'Art décoratif à
l'Exposition de Turin", in *L'Art décoratif*, XIII
(October 1911), pp. 129-136.

517. "Planche IV - Hall circulaire - Ch. Plumet,
architecte", in *L'Architecte*, VIII (January
1913), p. 7; pl. IV.

Town house, 81, Boulevard Montmorency:

518. "Couturaud P., "Hôtel privé, boulevard
Montmorency, à Paris", in *La Construction
Moderne*, 3ᵈ serie, VIII (1912-13), pp. 508-512;
pl. 106-108.

519. "Planche II et III - Villa, 81, boulevard
Montmorency, à Paris - Ch. Plumet, architecte",
in L'Architecte, VII (January 1913), pp. 6-7;
pl. II-III.

Works in collaboration with Tony Selmersheim:

520. Forthuny P., "La Rue pittoresque -
Devantures et boutiques", in *Revue des Arts
Décoratifs, XIX (11, 1899), pp.* 237-252.

521. *Jacques G.M., "Du compliqué au simple",
in L'Art Décoratif*, II (14, 1899), pp. 53-57.

522. J., "Nos Illustrations", in *L'Art Décoratif*,
II (14, 1899), pp. 89-90.

523. Soulier G., "Charles Plumet et Tony
Selmersheim", in *Art et Décoration*, vol. VII
(1, 1900), pp. 11-21.

524. Soulier G;, "Les aménagements de
magasins", in *Art et Décoration*, Vol. VII
(2, 1900), pp. 33-38.

525. Gerdeil O., "Croquis d'intérieur", in
L'Art Décoratif, IV (39, 1901), pp. 104-110.

526. Jacques G.M., "Rues et boutiques", in
L'Art Décoratif, IV (37, 1901), pp. 104-110.

527. Soulier G., "Croquis d'intérieur", in *L'Art
Décoratif*, IV (41, 1902), pp. 190-196.

528. Felice R. de, "Le sentiment architectural
dans l'ameublement", in *L'Art Décoratif*,
VI (II semester, 1904), pp. 191-200.

Joachim Richard:

529. D.(riart) A., "Maison de rapport, avenue
Perrichont", in *La Construction Moderne*,
XXIII (1907-08), pp. 449-452.

530. D.(riart) A., "Hôtel particulier, rue
Boileau à Paris", in *La Construction Moderne*,
XXIV (1910-11), pp. 74-75.

Lucien Roy:

531. Félice R. de, "Un hôtel particulier à
Paris", in *L'Art Décoratif*, VII (I semester,
1905), pp. 136-144.

Henri Sauvage:

532. Soulier G., "Henri Sauvage", in *Art et
Décoration*, vol. V (1899), pp. 65-75.

533. Uhry E., "Logements hygiéniques à bon
marché et maison de rapport", in *L'Art Décoratif*, VI (II semester, 1904), pp. 128-135.

534. "Un artiste: l'œuvre de l'architecte Henri
Sauvage", in *L'Organe National*, 2, 1925,
pp. 41-47.

535. Mourey G., *Henri Sauvage*, Paris s.d.
(1928).

536. Zahar M., "L'architecture vivante: Henri
Sauvage", in *L'Art Vivant*, IV (1928),
pp. 628-631.

537. Rambosson Y., "Un grand architecte
d'aujourd'hui: Henri Sauvage", in *Le Journal
des Arts*, 28.11.1931, p. 1.

538. *Henri Sauvage. Travaux d'architecture
1907-1930*, Strasbourg 1932.

539. Dervaux A., "Henri Sauvage", in
L'Architecture d'aujourd'hui, III (March 1932),
pp. 55-56.

540. Duijer J., "Henri Sauvage", in *De 8 en
Opbouw*, 1932, pp. 132-133.

541. H., "Henri Sauvage", in *La Cité*, X
(9, 1932), pp. 133-138.

542. Dumerle D. - Hasson E. et R., "Henri
Sauvage", in *Architecture-Mouvement-
Continuité*, 37, 1975, pp. 38-47.

543. Grumbach A., "Le Pur et l'Impur", in
Architecture- Mouvement-Continuité, 37,
1975, pp. 47-48.

544. Miotto-Muret L., "Henri Sauvage (1873-
1932)", in *Architecture*, 395, 1975, pp. 27-29.

545. *Henri Sauvage 1873-1932*, Exhibition cat.
edited by M. Culot et L. Grenier, Bruxelles 1976.

546. Jullian R., "Sauvage et Sant'Elia: le
problème des maisons à gradins", in *Bulletin de
la Société de l'Art Français*, 1978, pp. 291-298.

Two salons at the Café de Paris:

547. "Henri Sauvage", in *Dekorative Kunst*, III
(6, 1900), pp. 232-235; ill. pp. 236-237.

548. Jacques G.M., "Deux Salons de
Restaurant par M. H. Sauvage", in *L'Art
Décoratif*, II (18, 1900), pp. 244-249.

Villa Majorelle, Nancy:

549. Boileau L.-C., "Villa rue Palisot à Nancy",
in *L'Architecture*, 40, 1901, pp. 343-347.

550. Mourey G., "Une Villa Moderne", in
L'Illustration, 12.4.1902, pp. 254-255.

551. Jourdain F., "La Villa Majorelle à Nancy",
in *L'Art Décoratif*, IV (47, 1902), pp. 202-208.

Installation of Jansen's shop in Paris:

552. "Intérieurs", in *L'Art Décoratif*, V
(55, 1903), pp. 148-152.

Apartment block, Rue Trétaigne, Paris:

553. Taylor B.B., "Sauvage and hygienic
housing or the Cleanliness Revolution in Paris",
in *Archithèse*, 12, 1974, pp. 13-16, 55.

Villa in Bretagne:

554. Mourey G., "Une Villa en Bretagne par
MM. Sauvage et Sarazin", in *Art et Décoration*,
VIII (2, 1904), pp. 63-68.

Villa in Compiègne:

555. D.A., "Villa à Compiègne", in
La Construction Moderne, 3ⁿᵈ serie, III
(1907-08), pp. 520-521.

Country house in Biarritz:

556. Blum R., "Une maison de campagne par
MM. Sauvage et Sarazin", in *Art et Décoration*,
XII (11, 1908), pp. 163-172.

Gabled house, Rue Vavin, Paris:

557. "Maison à gradins, rue Vavin, à Paris", in
La Construction Moderne, 3ᵈ serie, IX (1913-
14), pp. 577-578.

558. "Maison rue Vavin, à Paris", in
L'Architecte, 1924, pp. 82-84;
pl. LXVIII-LXIX.

Xavier Schœllkopf:

Town house, Avenue d'Iéna, Paris:

559. J., "Le modernisme dans l'architecture",
in *L'Art Décoratif*, I (8, 1899), pp. 45-48, 55-60.

560. J., "Neues in der Architektur", in
Dekorative Kunst, II (8, 1899), pp. 41-43,
49-57.

561. "Hôtel, avenue d'Iéna 4", in
La Construction Moderne, 2ⁿᵈ serie, V (1899-
1900), pp. 172-173, 185-186, 198; pl. 33- 35.

Apartment block, Avenue de la République,
Paris:

562. Rivoalen E., "Détails en façade de maison
de rapport", in *La Construction Moderne*, 2ⁿᵈ
serie, VI (1900-01), pp. 282-283.

Town house of Yvette Guilbert, Paris:

563. "Hôtel de Madame Yvette G., à Paris", dans *La Construction Moderne*, 2nd série, VLI (1901-02), pp. 379, 390- 391; pl. 71-73.

564. Saunier Ch., "L'hôtel de Mme Yvette Guilbert", in *L'Art Décoratif*, III (29, 1901), pp. 190-197.

565. Lévèque J.J., "Trois intérieurs du début de la troisième République (ceux de Sarah Bernhardt, de Mme Valtesse de la Bigne et d'Yvette Guilbert)", in *Gazette des Beaux-Arts*, LXXXVII (1286, 1976), pp. 89-99.

Apartment block, Boulevard de Courcelles, Paris:

566. Soulier G;, "Une maison de rapport", in *L'Art Décoratif*, IV (50, 1902), pp. 319-326.

Pierre Selmersheim:

567. Jourdain F., "Concours du Louvre pour 1897 - Voiture Automobile -Rapport du jury", in *L'Architecture*, 1897, pp. 213-216.

568. Soulier G., "Un intérieur", in *L'Art Décoratif*, IV (51, 1902), pp. 381-390.

569. Belville E., "Un hôtel particulier à Paris", in *L'Art Décoratif*, X (II semester, 1908), pp. 41-58.

570. "Cottage à Bethysy-Saint-Pierre", in *La Construction Moderne*, 27.11.1909, pp. 102-103; pl. 22.

571. "Un bureau-fumoir exécuté pour M. B. à Paris", in *La Construction Moderne*, 27.11.1909, pp. 101-102; pl. 21.

572. "Projets de Salon des Arts Décoratifs pour l'Exposition de Bruxelles", in *La Construction Moderne*, 22.10.1910, pp. 45; pl. 10.

573. Selmersheim P., *Exposition Internationale de Milan. 1906. Section française*, Paris 1910.

Tony Selmersheim:

574. Thiébault-Sisson , "A propos d'une Décoration d'intérieur", in *Art et Décoration*, vol. I (1897), pp. 25-29.

575. J., ""M. Tony Selmersheim", in *L'Art Décoratif*, I (5, 1899), pp. 203-204.

576. Soulier G;, "Le Mobilier", in *Art et Décoration*, vol. X (1901), pp. 113-124.

576.1. Soulier G., "Les Sièges", in *Art et Décoration*, Vol. X (1901), pp. 155-161.

577. Jourdain F., "Tony Selmersheim", in *Art et Décoration*, vol. XVI (12, 1904), pp. 182-198.

578. Riotor L., "Un intérieur moderne", in *L'Art Décoratif*, VI (I semester, 1904), pp. 194-200.

579. "Salon de l'Automobile-Club. Chambres d'Hôtels", dans *L'Art Décoratif*, VI (I semester, 1905), pp. 78-80.

580. Prudent H;, "La décoration et le mobilier d'une Villa moderne", in *Art et Décoration*, 10, 1910), pp. 121-128.

581. Saunier Ch., "Concours pour un Cabinet du Président du Conseil Municipal de Paris", in *Art et Décoration*, I[st] semester, 1912, pp. 89-96.

Louis-Pierre Sézille:

582. Genuys Ch., "Deux villas au bord de la mer", in *Art et Décoration*, XIX (I semester, 1906), pp. 38-40.

583. Verneuil M.P., "Maisons de campagne", in *Art et Décoration*, XXI (I semester, 1907), pp. 91-96.

584. Verneuil M.P., "Une villa au Vésinet. 'La Douce Vie", in *Art et Décoration*, (II semester, 1906), pp. 121-126.

585. Verneuil M.P., "Ma Maison", in *Art et Décoration*, (II semester), 1910, pp. 65-74.

René Simonet:

586. "Maison rue Boursault, à Paris", in *La Construction Moderne*, 2d série, VII (1901-02), pp. 407-408; pl. 76.

587. Jourdain F., "Une petite Maison à Loyer", in *Art et Décoration*, VI (vol.. XI, 1902), pp. 124-127.

Louis Sorel:

588. Prudent H., "La décoration et le mobilier d'une villa moderne", in *Art et Décoration*, (II semester, 1910), pp. 121-128.

Lucien Woog:

589. Uhry E., "Un théâtre-concert à Paris (La Cigale)", in *L'Art Décoratif*, VIII (I semester, 1906), pp. 129-135.

FRENCH FURNITURE

General

Books:

590. Nocq H., *Tendances nouvelles, enquête sur l'évolution des industries d'art*, Paris 1896.

591. Champier V., *Documents d'atelier, art décoratif moderne*, Paris 1898.

592. Lambert T., *Meubles et ameublements de style moderne depuis 1900*, Paris 1904.

593. Mourey G., *Essai sur l'art décoratif français moderne*, Paris 1921.

594. Sedeyn E., *Le mobilier*, Paris 1921.

595. Moussinac L., *Le meuble français moderne*, Paris 1925.

596. Olmer P., *La renaissance du mobilier français (1890- 1910)*, Paris-Bruxelles 1927.

597. Mannoni E., *Style 1900, meubles et ensembles*, Paris 1968.

598. Bossaglia R., *Le mobilier Art Nouveau*, Paris 1972.

Articles:

599. Esquié P., "Les Essais du Mobilier et de Décoration Intérieure", in *L'Art Décoratif*, vol. I (1897), pp. 105-108.

600. "Französisches mobiliar", in *dekorative Kunst*, Vol. II (1898), pp. 89-109.

601. Fourcauld L. de, "Le bois", in *Revue de l'Art ancien et moderne*, 1900, 45, pp. 371-388.

602. Jacques G.M., "Intérieurs modernes", in *L'Art Décoratif*, III (26, November 1900), pp. 70-72.

603. Gerdeil O., "Le meuble", in *L'Art Décoratif*, III (28, Jan. 1901), pp. 170-175.

604. Gerdeil O., "L'intérieur et le meuble", in *L'Art Décoratif*, III (34, July 1901), pp. 158-163.

605. "Le meuble moderne", in *La Construction Moderne*, 2nd série, VI (1900-1901), pp. 199-200.

606. Jacques G.M., "Le meuble", in *L'Art Décoratif*, IV (43, April 1902), pp. 17-23.

607. Kœchlin R., "L'Art décoratif moderne", in *Les Arts*, 1916, 155, pp. 2-12.

608. Kœchlin R., "L'Art décoratif moderne", in, *Journal des Débats*, 22.5.1910.

609. Viaux J., "Les origines du mobilier français contemporain", in dans *Revue de l'ameublement*, 1961, 1-3, pp. 49-55.

610. Guillaume J., "L'industrie du meuble après 1900", in *Meubles et Décors*, 1966, pp. 33-39.

The Art Nouveau Bing:

Works by S. Bing:

611. *Artistic Japan: illustrations and essays*, London 1888- 1891 (French transl., Paris 1888-1891; German transl., Leipzig 1888-1891).

612. *Salon de l'Art Nouveau*, Paris 1896.

613. *La culture artistique en Amérique*, Paris 1896.

614. "Wohin teriben wir", in *Dekorative Kunst*, I (1898), p. 1.

615. "L'Art Nouveau", in *The Architecural Record*, XII (1902), pp. 279-285.

Articles on S. Bing:

616. Osborne M., "S. Bing's 'Art Nouveau' auf der Weltausstellung", in *Deutsche Kunst und Dekoration*, Vol. IV (1900), pp. 550-569.

617. Jacques G.M., "Un petit salon", in *L'Art Décoratif*, III (31, 1901), pp. 23-30.

618. Janneau G., "L'Art Nouveau Bing", in *Meubles et Décors*, 1966, 811, pp. 116-125.

619. Weisberg G.P., "Samuel Bing: Patron of Art Nouveau", in *Connoisseur*, 1969, Oct., pp. 119-125; 1969, pp. 294-299; 1970, Jan., pp. 61-68.

620. De Rudder J.L., "Il y a cent ans: Bing inventait l'art Nouveau", in *L'Estampille*, 1971, 17, pp. 33-37, 55.

621. Weisberg G.P., "Samuel Bing International Dealer of Art Nouveau", in *Connoisseur*, 1971, March, pp. 200-205; 1971, April, pp. 275-283; 1971, May p.49-55, 1971, July pp.211-219.

622. Weisberg G.P., "Bing Porcelain in America", in *Connoisseur*, 1971, Nov., pp. 200-203.

623. Brunhammer Y., "L'Art Nouveau Bing", in *Art Nouveau Belgium-France*, Exhibition cat., Houston Rice Museum and Chicago Art Institute, 1976, pp. 130-132.

On the s. Bing's shop, and L. Bonnier's project, see:

624. Boileau L.-C., "La maison de l'Art Nouveau'", in *L'Architecture*, IX (2, 1896), pp. 14-15.

625. Koch R., "Art Nouveau Bing", in *Gazette des Beaux-Arts*, CI (Vol. LIII, 1959), pp. 179-180.

Les Six

626. J., "Chronique", in *L'Art Décoratif*, I (4, 1899), pp. 197-198.

627. "Les Six", in *L'Art Décoratif*, I (6, 1899), p. 305.

628. "Exposition des Six", in *L'Art Décoratif*, I (9, 1899), p. 137.

L'Art dans Tout

629. "Les Petits Salons. 4ᵉ Exposition de l'Art dans Tout", in *Le Moniteur des Arts*, XLIV (2392, 19.5.1899), p. 1360.

630. "La Société de l'Art dans Tout", in *Art et Décoration*, Vol. V (1899), pp. 82-89.

631. Jacques G.M., "L'Art dans Tout", in *L'Art Décoratif*, I (10, 1899).

632. "Un Architecte. L'Art dans Tout", in *La Construction Moderne*, 2ⁿᵈ serie, V (1899-1900), pp. 148-149.

633. Jourdain F., "L'Exposition de la rue Caumartin", in *Revue des Arts Décoratifs*, XX (1, 1900), pp. 1-8.

634. Vignaud J., "L'Art dans Tout", in *Art et Décoration*, Vol. VII (4, 1900), pp. 47-50.

635. Forthuny P., "L'Art dans Tout", in *Revue des Arts Décoratifs*, III (1901), pp. 97-112.

636. Jacques G.M., "L'Art dans Tout", in *L'Art Décoratif*, III (32, 1901), pp. 45-68.

637. Soulier G., "L'Art dans Tout", in *Art et Décoration*, Vol. IX (4, 1901), pp. 129-140.

Félix Aubert:

638. "M. Félix Aubert", in *L'Art Décoratif*, I (4, 1899), pp. 157-161.

639. Souza R. de, "Un intérieur de Bellery-Desfontaines", in *L'Art Décoratif*, VII (II semester, 1905), pp. 168-172.

640. Clément-Janin, "Bellery-Desfontaines", in *L'Art Décoratif*, XI (vol.. XXI, 1909), pp. 169-184.

Rupert Carabin:

641. Coquiot C., "Les figurines de Carabin", in *L'Art Décoratif*, XI (I semester, 1906), pp. 25-30.

Alexandre Charpentier:

642. Mourey G., "A decorative Modeller: Alexandre Charpentier", in *The Studio*, XII (1898), pp. 95-102.

643. Jacques G.M., "Les limites du décor", in *L'Art Décoratif*, II (16, 1900), pp. 141-144, 168-169.

644. Mourey G., "Interview on Art Nouveau with Alexandre Charpentier", in *The Architectural Record*, XII (June 1902), pp. 121-125.

645. Mourey G., "Alexandre Charpentier", in *L'Art et les Artistes*, Vol. VI (October 1907 - March 1908), pp. 337-344.

Jean Dampt:

646. "Jean Dampt and his atelier", in *The Artist*, 1897, pp. 205-207.

647. Moreau-Vauthier Ch., "Une Salle de l'Hôtel de la Comtesse de Béarn par Jean Dampt", in *Art et Décoration*, X (Vol. XIX, 4, 1906), pp. 109-118.

Georges De Feure:

648. Mourey G., "Georges de Feure", in *The Studio*, XII (1898), pp. 95-102.

649. Jacques G.M., "L'intérieur rénové", in *L'Art Décoratif*, II (4, 1900), pp. 217-228.

650. Jacques G.M., "Un petit salon", in *L'Art Décoratif*, III (31, 1901), pp. 23-30.

651. Torquet Ch., "La vitrine de G. de Feure", in *L'Art Décoratif*, III (33, 1901), pp. 116-125.

652. Uzanne O., "G. de Feure", in *Art et Décoration*, V (1901), pp. 77-88.

653. Gerdeil O., "Un atelier d'artiste", in *L'Art Décoratif*, IV (40, 1902), pp. 144-148.

654. Laran J., "Quelques meubles de G. de Feure", in *Art et Décoration*, XII (Vol. XXIV, 10), 1908), pp. 115-132.

Auguste Delaherche:

655. Félice R. de, "Auguste Delaherche", in *L'Art Décoratif*, IX (Vol..XVII, 1907), pp. 155-158. 656. Lecomte G., *A. Delaherche*, Paris 1922.

657. Tisserand E., "Auguste Delaherche", in *L'Art Vivant*, IV (15.6.1928), pp. 473-475.

658. Demoriane H., "A la recherche de Delaherche", in *Connaissance des Arts*, 1970, 221, pp. 74-79, 100.

Maurice Dufrène:

659. Musey-Grévin, "Un jeune", in *L'Art Décoratif*, II (24, 1900), pp. 237-241.

660. Verneuil M.P., "Maurice Dufrène Décorateur", in *Art et Décoration*, X (Vol. XIX, 3, 1906), pp. 73-84.

661. Martinie A.H., "Maurice Dufrène", in *L'Art Vivant*, 1931, 146, pp. 93-97.

Paul Follot:

662. Saunier Ch., "Paul Follot", in *Art et Décoration*, XIII (Vol. XXV, 1, 1909), pp. 31-36.

663. Testard M., "Paul Follot, décorateur", in *L'Art Décoratif*, XI (Vol.. XXI, 1909), pp. 47-54.
Riotor L., *Paul Follot*, Paris 1923.

665. Rutherford J., "Paul Follot", in *Connoisseur*, CCIV (820, 1980), pp. 86-91.

Eugène Gaillard:

666. Soulier G., "Quelques meubles d'Eugène Gaillard", in *Art et Décoration*, VI (1902), pp. 21-27.

667. Gaillard E., *A propos du mobilier*, Paris 1908.

Léon Jallot:

668. Verneuil M.P., "Les meubles de Jallot", in *Art et Décoration*, XIII (Vol. XXV, 4, 1909), pp. 127-136.

Abel Landry:

669. Sedeyn E., "Intérieurs", in *L'Art Décoratif*, V (52, 1903), pp. 13-20.

670. Leclère T., "Abel Landry. Architecte et Décorateur", in *L'Art Décoratif*, IX (Vol. XVII, 1907), pp. 49-60.

Typesetting: Genius Brussels
Engraving: B.B.N. Brussels
Printing: Grafos S.A. Barcelona